MARIJUANA
LAW

Second Edition

by Richard Glen Boire
Attorney at Law

Ronin Publishing, Inc.   Box 1035   Berkeley CA 94701

Marijuana Law
(Second Edition)
ISBN: 0-914171-860
Copyright © 1992 by Richard Glen Boire

Published by
Ronin Publishing, Inc.
Post Office Box 1035
Berkeley, California 94701

Printed in the United States of America
First Edition 1993
Second Edition 1996

9 8 7 6 5 4 3 2 1

Project Editors: Sebastian Orfali, Beverly Potter
Manuscript Editors: Aiden Kelly, Sebastian Orfali, Dan Joy
Layout and Design: William Capps III, Anthony Doe
Cover: Brian Groppe

U.S. Library of Congress Cataloging in Publication Data
Boire, Richard Glen, 1964 –
          Marijuana law / by Richard Glen Boire.
                    p.   cm.
          Includes index.
          ISBN 0-914171-62-3 : $14.95
          1. Marijuana—Law and legislation—United States—Popular works.
2. Criminal procedure—United States—Popular works. I. Title.
KF3891.M2B65   1993
345.73 ' 0277—dc20   93–192
[347.305277]   CIP

DEDICATION

For all my relations

FOREWORD

by J. Tony Serra, Attorney at Law

WE MARIJUANA SMOKERS in the United States are an oppressed category of citizen. We are tracked down like animals, mostly by secret police, treated brutally, ripped off by lawyers, and ultimately physically broken by unfair law and bad judges. We are being savaged by the legal system. Basic constitutional rights are denied to us. Harsh and inequitable jail sentences make martyrs of us all. Law and law enforcement have targeted us for extinction.

We are also victims of false law-enforcement propaganda about marijuana. We know the truth: that all of the evidence shows that marijuana is good for people, first as medicine and more meaningfully as a consciousness enhancer. Why should we be sacrificed to governmental falsity alleging negative attributes of marijuana use?

A government that knowingly issues false dogmas concerning marijuana and then through its laws ruthlessly crushes marijuana users, must be resisted and defied at the same level that it threatens us. That level is the legal-judicial realm. We must be armed in that realm in order to preserve ourselves. We must be armed with the "law."

Richard Boire's *Marijuana Law* gives us the legal armaments with which to resist unfair police methods. His book contains the most important things about marijuana law that a user must know. It is like our self-defense manual to guide us to freedom through the maze of onerous anti-marijuana laws.

The author lays out all the marijuana law in the field for us: arrest, search and seizure, court procedures, sentencing, fourth-amendment rights, drug testing, etc. His work is articulate and complete. If we are to survive we all must read and learn these principles. They connect directly with our freedom and ultimate ability to overthrow these unfair laws.

I urge every marijuana smoker to turn Richard Boire's book *Marijuana Law* into usable knowledge. We must know the law to fight the law. We must fight fire with fire. We must know the law to resist and defy injustice.

Table of Contents 7

Foreword by J. Tony Serra 5

Preface to 2nd Edition 11

Prologue 13

Introduction 15

1. Crimes & Punishment 17
"Marijuana" Defined 17
Separating Seeds And Stems 18
"Marijuana" vs. "Hashish" vs. "Hashish Oil" 19
November 1, 1995 Guideline's Revision: Terms Defined 20
Synthetic Equivalents 21
The Crime of Possessing Marijuana 21
The "Usable Amount" Controversy 24
Challenges to the Constitutionality of Possession Laws 25
The "Momentary Possession" Defense .. 25
Sale or Distribution of Marijuana 26
Selling Bogus Marijuana 28
The Crime of Offering To Sell Marijuana 29
Marijuana Paraphernalia Crimes 29
Pipes As Paraphernalia 31
Growing Marijuana 31
"Attempted" Manufacture 32
Transportation of Marijuana 33
Driving Under the Influence of Marijuana 33
Aiding and Abetting a Marijuana Crime 33
Boobytrapped Gardens on Federal Property 33
Penalties for Possessing Marijuana 34
Smoke A Joint, Lose Your License 34
State Taxes On Marijuana—Double Jeopardy 36
Punishment for Possessing Marijuana with Intent to Distribute 37
Punishment for Selling or Manufacturing Marijuana Within 1000 feet of a School . 37
Federal Marijuana Crimes— Schedule I 38
State and Federal Prosecution for the Same Crime 38
Mandatory Minimums Under Federal Law 39
Mandatory Minimum Safety Valve 39
Federal Punishment for Simple Possession 40
Federal Punishment for Growing, Distributing, Importing, Exporting or Trafficking Marijuana 40
November 1, 1995 Guideline's Revision: All Cannabis plants equated to 100 g. 42

Defining A Cannabis Plant Under Federal Law 44
1995 Guideline's Revision: "Plant" Defined 45
Multiple Stemmed Plants 45
Sex of the Plants 45
1995 Guideline's Revisions: Wet vs. Dry Marijuana 46
Seizure and Loss of Assets 46
Forfeiture of Currency Found Near Marijuana 51

2. Constitutional Law Basics 53
The Exclusionary Rule 54
The "Good Faith Exception" to the Exclusionary Rule 55
Outrageous Police Conduct Can Invalidate a Search 56
Rights Depend on Who Conducts the Search 57
The Hotel-Maid Example 57
Sending Marijuana Through Private Mail Carriers 58
State Constitutions vs. The Federal Constitution 59
Double Jeopardy 60
The Burden of Proof 61
The Jury's Power to Judge the Law 62

3. Gathering Information: Big Brother Is Watching You 65
The Citizen Informer 65
The Anonymous Citizen Informer 66
The Confidential Informant 67
Paid Confidential Informants and Conduct by the Government 68
Controlled Buys 70
Undercover Cops and the Doctrine of "Misplaced Trust" 70
Direct Sales—Undercover Drug Agents— Entrapment 73
Children as Informers 73
Mail Orders as Evidence 74
Garbage as Evidence 77
Electric Bill as Evidence 79
Thermal Imaging Devices & Forward Looking Infrared Devices 80
The DEA's NADDIS Database 84

4. Encounters with Police 87
Contact 87
Detention 88
Detaining Your Belongings 91

Demanding to See Your Identification 92
Frisks or Pat-Searches 93
Legal Detentions Without Reasonable
Suspicion 95
The Drug-Courier Profile 95
Juvenile Truants and Curfew Violators .. 98
Arrest 98

**5. Searches: With & Without
Warrants 101**
When a Police Officer's Search or Seizure
Is Legal Even Though He Doesn't Have a
Warrant 102
Consenting to a Search 102
How Mr. Puff Asserted His Constitutional
Rights 104
The Plain-View Rule 104
How Wayne Learned about the Plain-View
Rule 106
Plain-View Paraphernalia 106
Distinct Drug-Carrying Devices 106
Abandoning Marijuana 109
The Marijuana Aroma 111
The Marijuana Aroma and Dog Sniffs .. 112
Canvassing Dog Sniffs 113
Border Searches 114
Border Strip Searches And Body Cavity
Searches 114
Exigent Circumstances 115
Swallowing Incriminating Evidence 116
Searches at School If You Are a Student 118
Marijuana and Your Telephone 118
Pen Registers and Trap & Trace
Devices 120
Clone Pagers 121
Marijuana and the U.S. Mail 121
Mail Covers 122
The "Drug Package Profile" 123
The "No Knowledge" Defense for
Marijuana Received In The Mail 123

6. Marijuana & Your Car 125
When Can a Police Officer Stop
Your Car? 125
Roadblocks 125
Ordering You Out of Your Car 126
When Can a Police Officer Search Your
Car Without a Warrant? 126
Vehicle Search for Officer Safety 126
Vehicle Searches Based on Probable
Cause 127
Air Fresheners 127
Aroma, Hand-Rolled Cigarettes, Seeds &
Roach Clips 128

Trucks vs. Passenger Cars 131
Opening Your Trunk 132
Vehicle Searches-Incident to Arrest 133
Throwing Marijuana from a Moving
Vehicle 134
Automobile Inventory Searches 135
Containers in Cars 136
Your Car and the Plain-View Rule 137
Furtive Movements 137
Consenting to a Search of Your Car and
Withdrawing Consent 138
Whose Pot Is It? 139
Driving Under the Influence of
Marijuana 139

7. Marijuana & Your Home 143
A Home Is Entitled to Maximum
Protection 143
A Home's Outdoor Private Areas Also
Receive Maximum Protection 144
The Front Door is Usually Not Part Of
Curtilage 144
Human Sniff At Garage Door 145
Search Warrants 145
If It's Nighttime You're Probably Safe .. 147
The Knock-Notice Rule 148
Warrants and the Plain-View Rule 149
People on the Scene 149
If It's Your Home, It's Presumed to Be Your
Marijuana 151
The Plain-View Rule and Your Home ... 152
Police Use Of Binoculars 152
Consenting to a Search of Your Home .. 154
Officers Who Threaten to Obtain
a Warrant 157
Who Can Consent to a Search of Your
Home? 158
Landlords and Hotel Employees 158
Roommates and Spouses 158
Children 159
Your Home and "Exigent
Circumstances" 159

8. Gardens 163
Marijuana Gardens in the Home 163
Marijuana Gardens Inside the Curtilage of a
Home 163
Creating a Curtilage in the Eyes of a Court
165
Successfully Constructed Curtilages 166
Gardens Situated Outside a Home's
Curtilage 168
An Unsuccessful Curtilage 170

Searching Your Home Based on Seeing
Your Backyard Garden 172
Linking Remote Gardens To
The Gardener 173
Evidence of an Indoor Garden Is
Insufficient For A Search Warrant 174
Police Fly-overs 175
The DEA's Domestic Marijuana
Eradication Program 179
Marijuana Gardens on Public Property 180
High-Tech Surveillance of Government
Land 181

9. Medicinal Marijuana and
the Law 183
Attempts To Reschedule Marijuana Under
Federal Law 184
Compassionate Use 185
The Marinol Hypocrisy 186
The Medical Necessity Defense 186
Denial of the Medical Necessity Defense 187
The Medical Necessity Defense
Succeeds 189

10. Marijuana, Religion, and
the Law 193
The Religious Freedom Restoration Act 196

11. If You're Arrested 199
Arrest Warrants 199
If Arrested Outside, Don't Go Inside! ... 199
No Expectation Of Privacy While In
Backseat Of Police Car 201
Searches After Arrest 201
Booking Searches 202
Miranda Rights 202
When the Police Must Read You Your
Rights 203
Don't Waive Your Miranda Rights 203
Police Interrogation Techniques 205
The Right to Counsel 209
Public Defenders and Court Appointed
Attorneys 210
Choosing a Private Attorney 211
Attorney Fees 212
Private Investigators 213
Working With Your Attorney 213
Plea Bargains vs. Going To Trial 214
Should You Testify? 215
Tips On Testifying 216
Monitoring Jail-House Conversations .. 216
Release Pending Trial 217
How Bail Is Paid 218

Tips On Going To Court 219
Cleaning Up a Marijuana Conviction
Record 220

12. Drug Testing 223
Urine Tests 223
Creating False Negatives 224
False Positives 225
Blood Testing 225
Hair Testing 225
"Possession" Of Marijuana Based On A
Positive Drug Test 226
Drug Tests While on Probation Or
Parole 227
Employment Drug Testing 227
Government Employees 227
Drug Testing of Private Employees 228
The Drug-Free Workplace Act of 1988 . 229
What to Expect If You're Urine-Tested at
Work 229

Epilogue 231
Appendix A: Bill of Rights 233
Appendix B: Wallet Cards 235
Appendix C. State-By-State
Punishment for Marijuana Crimes 237
Appendix D: The 13 Federal
Circuits 257
Index 259

PREFACE TO 2ND EDITION

THE SECOND EDITION of this book contains almost twice as much information than the first edition. While much can be gained by reading this book in a straight line from cover to cover, I have purposely written it so that it can also be read in a modular fashion. As a result, while most information on any given topic will be found under a single heading, some will also be found under associated topics. The index is the best map to the contents, and should be consulted to make sure that you have found all the information on a given topic.

This edition captures the range of legal happenings currently composing the edifice of law facing marijuana smokers. I've tried to include cases from across the country not only to make the book helpful to more people, but also to give every reader a feel for how the rules seem to be trending. As you read this book, you will come across some cases discussed with reference to the federal circuit court deciding the case. It turns out that while referring to the circuit court by name adds some unwanted legalese to the book, it's a lot simpler than listing all the states in which the court's decision is binding. Therefore, unless you already know which judicial circuit you live in, I encourage you to quickly flip to Appendix D and determine your federal judicial circuit. Then, when you read about a particular federal case you will know whether the case is binding on the federal courts for your jurisdiction. Remember, however, that even if a particular federal case was not decided by your circuit court, the decision in that case will signal how a federal court in your jurisdiction is likely to rule if presented with a factually similar case for the first time.

PROLOGUE

AT THE OUTSET, I should express my intentions in conveying the information herein. A review of recent decisions by the United States Supreme Court makes painfully clear that the constitutional rights guaranteeing some of our most cherished freedoms are being drastically narrowed. Moreover, in many cases the Court has justified its decision, in part, with the "War on Drugs." This book is intended to document some of the rights we are losing under the guise of fighting the "War on Drugs." Primarily, however, this book is written in the hopes that people will begin to stridently exercise and protect what constitutional protections remain.

Our country was founded on the principle of individual liberty and freedom. Does this principle not presuppose the right of each individual, at the very least, to retain control over his body and his mind? Is not the primary right in a free society the right of each individual to do with his body and his mind as he thinks best — provided no injury comes to others? What freedom remains when one loses the right to be the sole controller of his mind and body?

It is my belief that the current laws making criminal the possession and personal use of natural plants such as *Cannabis*, are unjust and contrary to the most fundamental of human freedoms. I perceive the government's banning of *Cannabis* as not one whit different than the government's banning of a particular book. I will read the books I choose regardless of the government's proscriptions. I will hold the thoughts I believe are just and true, regardless of the government's attempts to limit them. Likewise, I alone, shall decide how to manage my consciousness. My mind is my own.

INTRODUCTION

*If a nation expects to be ignorant and free, it expects what
never was and never will be . . . . The people cannot be safe
without information. Where the press is free, and every man
able to read, all is safe.*

—Thomas Jefferson

CURRENTLY, over 30 million people in the United States regularly smoke marijuana. Many smoke to unwind after a busy day, to relieve stress, or simply for fun. Some smoke for spiritual reasons such as to assist in meditation, to be more conscious of the present moment, or to enhance their awareness at all levels. Others, suffering from AIDS, cancer, chronic pain, glaucoma, and stomach ailments, smoke marijuana because they find it to be an effective, safe, and inexpensive treatment for their condition.

Despite the fact that the vast majority of marijuana smokers are otherwise law-abiding and productive citizens, the federal government, as well as every state, has chosen to make even the possession of marijuana a crime, and has vowed to fight the "War on Drugs." As a result, in the average year, 400,000 people are arrested on some type of marijuana charge.

Perhaps recognizing the impact of this war on individual liberties, the War's leader has officially been labeled the "Drug Czar." The Czar's field commanders in the War are agents of the Drug Enforcement Administration and various state law-enforcement agencies. Indicative of the commanders' vilification of marijuana and those who smoke it is a statement made by outgoing Los Angeles Chief of Police, Daryl Gates, who in testimony before the Senate Judiciary Committee stated that he favored the death penalty even for casual users of marijuana.

Fortunately, because our nation's founders rebelled against a government they perceived as tyrannical, they had the foresight to create the Bill of Rights. Those first ten amendments to the Constitution (especially the Fourth, Fifth, and Sixth Amendments) protect citizens in the United States from overzealous government officials such as Mr. Gates. Unfortunately, caught up in the fervor of their misguided attempt to win the war on drugs, police and drug agents consistently trample the Bill of Rights. This blatant disregard often goes unresisted because citizens are ignorant of their rights and therefore fail to assert them.

As the quotation by Thomas Jefferson above so eloquently states, citizens must be informed of their rights in order to preserve them and remain free. The purpose of this book is to inform marijuana users of their rights and how to protect and assert them.

This book is based on both federal and state law. The federal law is applicable to all people in the U.S. regardless of their state of residence. The state law discussed will likewise be applicable to just about every reader, regardless of his or her state of residence. Forty-eight states, as well as the District of Columbia, have adopted the same basic anti-drug laws known as the Uniform Controlled Substances Act or the Uniform Narcotic Drug Act. In these states, the laws are generally identical except with respect to sentencing. The only two states that have not adopted the U.C.S.A. or U.N.D.A. are New Hampshire and Vermont; however, the law in those states is nearly identical to that in all the others.

After reading this book, you will be armed with a thorough understanding of your legal rights in general and specifically with regard to marijuana. An emphasis will be placed on protections under the United States Constitution. For example, you will learn when a police officer can legally stop you, when he can search you, when you have to be read your rights, what to do if an officer comes to your home with a search warrant, and how to counter many questionable police tactics simply by knowing and asserting your rights.

Many of the examples in this book are taken from actual court cases. Occasional factual changes have been made to help illustrate particular principles.

As a final comment, I should note that although this book was initially written in the early part of 1992 and completely updated and revised in late 1996, the law is always changing. Therefore, if you retain a lawyer to defend you on a marijuana charge you should follow his or her advice whenever it conflicts with this book.

Best of Luck.
R.G.B.

CHAPTER 1

CRIMES & PUNISHMENT

THE LAWS REGARDING MARIJUANA are like to the rules of the board game "Monopoly." As in Monopoly, the better you know the rules, the more likely you'll be able to use them to your advantage and win the game. Unlike Monopoly, however, the marijuana game is for real. If you lose, you pay real fines with real money and spend real days behind real jail bars.

Just about any activity involving the *Cannabis* plant is a criminal offense. In every state it is an offense to possess marijuana, transport marijuana, drive under the influence of marijuana, sell marijuana, and grow *Cannabis*. As an introduction to the laws concerning marijuana, this chapter will begin with several definitions and then move on to discuss the various marijuana crimes, their associated punishments, and the laws concerning seizure of assets.

"Marijuana" Defined

> *"When I use a word," Humpty Dumpty said, in rather a*
> *scornful tone, it means just what I choose it to mean—*
> *neither more nor less."*
> *"The question is," said Alice, "whether you can make*
> *words mean so many different things."*
> *"The question is," said Humpty Dumpty, "which is to be*
> *master—that's all."*
> —Lewis Carroll, *Through The Looking Glass*

Federal and state statutes commonly define "marijuana" as "all parts of the plant *Cannabis sativa L.*, whether growing or not." This includes viable seeds, resin, and any derivatives, mixtures, or preparations of the plant. The only noteworthy parts of the *Cannabis* plant excluded from the definition of marijuana are the mature stalks of the plant and the sterilized seeds.

The federal definition of "marijuana" reads as follows:

> The term "marijuana" means all parts of the plant *Cannabis*
> *sativa L.*, whether growing or not; the seeds thereof; the resin

extracted from any part of such plant; and every compound, manufacture, salt, derivative, mixture, or preparation of such plant, its seeds, or resin. Such term does not include the mature stalks of such plant, fiber produced from such stalks, oil or cake made from the seeds of such plant, any other compound, manufacture, salt, derivative, mixture, or preparation of such mature stalks (except the resin extracted therefrom), fiber, oil or cake, or the sterilized seed of such plant which is incapable of germination. (*21 USC sec. 802[16].*)

Marijuana users have often been more sophisticated than the legislators who wrote the statutory definition of "marijuana." In several court cases, users charged with possession of marijuana argued that they possessed the species *Cannabis indica*, not *Cannabis sativa*, and that the law, by its own terms, only outlawed the species *Cannabis sativa*.

Faced with such arguments, most federal and state courts broadly interpreted the definition of "marijuana" to include *all* species of *Cannabis*. Therefore, although many statutory definitions of marijuana only mention *Cannabis sativa*, all courts will find that all species of *Cannabis*, including *Cannabis indica* and *Cannabis ruderalis*, are outlawed. Some states, such as New York, have avoided the entire problem by crafting their legislation to broadly outlaw "all plants of the genus *Cannabis*."

Courts which have faced the issue have ruled that THC content is irrelevant in defining "marijuana." In one recent Virginia case, for example, a man was convicted and sentenced to twenty years in prison after harvesting wild *Cannabis* that he stumbled upon during a camping trip. In his appeal, he argued that the trial court unfairly barred him from introducing expert testimony showing that the "ditchweed" *Cannabis* was so low in THC content (about .12 percent, by his expert's calculations) that it was not capable of producing a high if smoked. The Virginia Court of Appeal rejected the man's argument with the explanation: "a substance is marijuana because it is a part of a *Cannabis* plant, not because of the amount of THC it contains." (*Howard v. Com. [Va.App. 1993] 437 S.E.2d 420; see also, McElroy v. State [Ala.Crim.App. 1992] 611 So.2d 431.*)

Separating Seeds And Stems

Some states define marijuana crimes based partially on the weight of the marijuana sold. For example, in Missouri it is a class B felony to sell more than 5 grams of marijuana, but only a class C felony to sell 5 grams or less. The maximum sentence for a class B felony is fifteen years, but only seven years for a class C felony.

In states where the crime is actually defined with reference to the weight of the marijuana when the government crime laboratory weighed the seized marijuana, it must first separate out any items — sterilized seeds, stalks, and stems, for example—which are not within the state's definition of "marijuana." As one court in Missouri explained in a case where the government failed to separate out sterilized seeds before determining the weight of the marijuana:

> It is not a crime to possess, sell, or otherwise transfer non-controlled substances. It is the state's burden to establish that defendant sold controlled substances and, if pertinent, the amount. Sterilized seed is not a controlled substance anymore than blue grass or wheat. If the controlled substance is mixed with a non-controlled substance and the weight of the controlled substance is important, the state must establish what that weight is." (*State v. Hyzer [Mo.App. 1991] 811 S.W.2d 475, quoting State v. Bethel [1978] 569 S.W.2d 270.*)

Although most statutes exclude sterilized seeds and mature stalks from the definition of "marijuana," some federal courts have held that for *the purposes of calculating a defendant's sentence* under the federal guidelines, the weight of a defendant's marijuana is determined without weeding out stems or seeds. The courts base this conclusion on the fact that the guidelines specifically advise that when calculating a defendant's federal sentence, the weight of a controlled substance "refers to the entire weight of any mixture or substance containing a detectable amount of the controlled substance."

Although the guidelines where amended in 1993 to state that "mixture or substance does *not* include materials that must be separated from the controlled substance before the controlled substance can be used" at least the Sixth Circuit has continued to hold that because it is not *absolutely necessary* to remove seeds or stalks before smoking marijuana, those objects should be *included* in the weight for sentencing purposes.

Given the possibility that a court will calculate weight, and hence punishment, based on the total weight of the marijuana found, the cases teach that a highly risk averse marijuana smoker who desires to minimize potential punishment in the event of arrest, would be wise to immediately remove any unsmokeable stems and seeds from his marijuana immediately upon obtaining it. (*US v. Vincent [6th Cir. 1994] 20 F.3d 229.*)

"Marijuana" vs. "Hashish" vs. "Hashish Oil"

Although the federal statutory definition of "marijuana" appears to make no distinctions, the federal sentencing guidelines subdivide *Cannabis* preparations into three categories for the purpose of calculating the punishment for a federal

Cannabis crime. The federal sentencing guidelines distinguish: (1) marijuana; (2) hashish; and (3) hashish oil. Until they were revised in 1995, the guidelines failed to define these terms. As a result, the federal courts were left with the job of characterizing *Cannabis* preparations on a case-by-case basis. This does not always prove easy.

For example, in one case in 1993, a federal court in Florida was faced with a classifying a substance that was a "dark greenish, almost black, tarry, gummy paste which does not flow. The substance has the odor of marijuana." The court was able to determine that the substance had an average THC content ranging somewhere between 16% and 23%, and that it was "made from the left-over portions of marijuana plants, after the useful parts (such as the flowers) have been removed." Under the federal sentencing guidelines the severity of the defendant's punishment depended on whether the court classified the paste as marijuana, hashish or hashish oil.

The court accepted the DEA's definition of "hash oil," stating: "the name hash oil is used by illicit drug users and dealers but is a misnomer in suggesting any resemblance to hashish other than its objective of further concentration. Hashish oil is produced by a process of repeated extraction of *Cannabis* plant materials to yield a dark viscous liquid, current samples of which average about 20% THC. In terms of its psychoactive effect a drop or two of this liquid on a cigarette is equal to a single "joint" of marijuana." The court then defined hashish as "the purified extract obtained mainly from marijuana flowers."

Using these definitions, the court determined that the substance in question was not a viscous liquid, but was instead a paste that did not flow, and hence, the substance did not fit the definition of "hash oil." The court also found that because the substance was made from *Cannabis* plant left-overs rather than the flowers, the substance was not "hashish." By a process of elimination, therefore, the court concluded that the substance was best characterized as simple "marijuana." As a result of this classification, the defendant was subject to the lowest offense level (and hence the least severe punishment) under the federal guidelines. (*U.S. v. Gravelle [S.D. Fla. 1993] 819 F.Supp. 1076*; *See also United States v. Schults [S.D. Ohio 1992] 810 F.Supp. 230*.)

November 1, 1995 Guideline's Revision: Terms Defined

Effective November 1, 1995, the federal guidelines were amended to include definitions of "hashish" and "hashish oil." The definitions rely on a checklist scheme examining which discrete psychoactive constituents are found in the substance under examination and whether it contains "plant material"

> As defined under the new provisions, "hashish means:
> a resinous substance of *Cannabis* that includes (i) one or more

of the tetrahydrocannabinols . . ., (ii) at least two of the following: cannabinol, cannabidiol, or cannabichromene, and (iii) fragments of plant material (such as cystolith fibers.) *(Sec. 2D1[c], as revised.)*

"Hashish oil," is defined as:
A preparation of the soluble cannabinoids derived from *Cannabis* that includes (i) one or more of the tetrahydrocannabinols . . . and (ii) at least two of the following: cannabinol, cannabidiol, or cannabichromene, and (iii) is essentially free of plant material (e.g., plant fragments.) Typically, hashish oil is viscous, dark colored oil, but it can vary from a dry resin to a colorless liquid. *(Sec. 2D1[c], as revised.)*

In short, all other things being equal, the guidelines view hashish oil as a liquid version of hashish, the difference between the two being the absence of plant material in hashish oil.

Synthetic Equivalents

In addition to the *Cannabis* plant, and its natural by-products, federal and state laws have criminalized the possession of all synthetic equivalents of the active substances contained in the *Cannabis* plant. These human-made substances are usually referred to by the legal term "tetrahydrocannabinols."

The Crime of Possessing Marijuana

Under federal law and the laws of every state, it is a crime to possess marijuana. In order to convict a person of possession, most states require that the prosecution prove three things (known as "elements" of the crime): 1. The act of possession: that the person had physical possession of the marijuana or dominion and control over it; 2. Knowledge: that the person had knowledge of the marijuana's presence; 3. Useable amount: that there was a sufficient amount of marijuana to use as a controlled substance. If the prosecution fails to prove even one of these elements, the correct verdict is *not guilty* of possessing marijuana.

A jury deciding a marijuana case is informed of the above elements and told that it can only convict the defendant of possessing marijuana if it finds that each element was proved beyond a reasonable doubt. After all the evidence in the case has been presented, the jury is informed of the three elements by the judge who instructs them on the law. A typical jury instruction read to a jury in a marijuana-possession case states:

The defendant is accused of having committed the crime of illegal possession of a controlled substance, in violation of the Health and Safety Code.

Every person who possesses a controlled substance, namely, marijuana, is guilty of the crime of illegal possession of a controlled substance. In order to prove such crime, each of the following elements must be proved:

(1) The defendant exercised control or the right to control marijuana,
(2) The defendant had knowledge of its presence,
(3) The defendant had knowledge of its nature as a controlled substance, and
(4) The substance was in an amount sufficient to be used as a controlled substance.

The prosecution must prove the element of possession. The prosecution can prove this element two different ways. The prosecutor can try to show that the defendant had *actual physical possession* of the marijuana; for example, holding a joint in his hands, lips, or pocket. However, if the prosecutor is unable to prove that the person actually held the marijuana, he will try to prove the possession element by showing that the marijuana was within the person's "dominion and control." This is known as *constructive possession* and is often established by showing that the marijuana was found in an area or container that was under the defendant's control, for example, in the person's house, car, or backpack. The California jury instruction regarding these two types of "possession" states:

Actual possession requires that a person knowingly exercise direct physical control over a thing.

Constructive possession does not require actual possession but does require that a person knowingly exercise control or the right to control a thing, either directly or through another person or persons.

In one case in Texas, police discovered marijuana in two locked chests inside a vehicle's trunk. A man who neither owned the vehicle nor had ever driven it was convicted of possessing the marijuana! The court held that the man was guilty of possessing the marijuana because he was found with keys that unlocked the vehicle's trunk and the two chests containing the marijuana. According to the court, these keys gave him "dominion and control" over the marijuana in question.

The theory of constructive possession is often used in cases where marijuana is found in a public place. These cases are very difficult for the prosecution to win. The courts of all states have ruled that a person's mere proximity to marijuana found in public is insufficient to convict the person of possessing the marijuana. The following scenario illustrates this rule in operation.

Two officers were assigned to handle drug detail at a local concert. Both officers were in uniform and simply walked among the concert-goers looking for people smoking pot, and hoping that their uniformed presence would deter people from smoking. As the officers walked down an aisle, the first officer observed a baggie of "green vegetable matter" on the ground near the feet of Marley, an eighteen-year-old concert-goer, wearing a Grateful Dead shirt. The officer grabbed the baggie and by its aroma tentatively identified it as containing marijuana. The officers arrested Marley, who was seated directly above the baggie.

Marley's lawyer argued that there was insufficient evidence to convict Marley of possessing the marijuana since, other than the fact that Marley was the person closest to the marijuana, there was no evidence that Marley had "dominion and control" over it. Marley denied that the marijuana was his.

The court that heard Marley's case agreed that Marley could not be convicted without more evidence linking him to the marijuana. The court explained that the crucial fact was that the marijuana was found on public property and could have been dropped by any one of the 6,000 concert fans. Because the officers didn't see Marley smoking marijuana, actually holding the baggie, or tossing it to the ground, there was no proof that he had dominion and control over the marijuana. Consequently, the evidence was insufficient to convict him of possessing the marijuana.

In addition to proving that the defendant possessed the marijuana (actually or constructively), the prosecutor must prove that the person had knowledge that the item he or she possessed was marijuana or some other unlawful substance. Since the government has not yet figured out a way to tap into people's thoughts, it is often unable to prove *actual kowledge*. Therefore, the knowledge element is generally proved circumstantially. This means the prosecutor will try to prove, based on the person's behavior before or after arrest, that the person knew the substance was marijuana. Often, for example, the prosecutor will show that the defendant tried to hide the marijuana, or gave evasive answers when questioned by the police officer. Almost anything indicating that the person knew he or she possessed marijuana as opposed to an innocuous substance can be used to prove the knowledge element. Moreover, most juries require very little proof of knowledge. The reality is that when police officers catch a person in possession of marijuana, most jurors find it very hard to believe that the person didn't know what the substance was.

The "Usable Amount" Controversy

Because the state laws defining the crime of possession all use slightly differing language, the courts of the various states have reached different conclusions as to whether or not the government must prove that the defendant possessed a "usable amount" of marijuana. In some states, the crime of possession is only committed if the person has a "usable amount" of marijuana. Other states outlaw possession of *any* marijuana. A final group of states altogether fails to address the question of quantity. As of this writing courts in Arizona, the District of Columbia, Oregon, and Texas, have interpreted their laws as outlawing possession of a "usable quantity" of marijuana. These courts theorize that when the legislature outlawed marijuana possession, it must have intended to target those people who "pose a danger to society." A person possessing an unusable amount of marijuana poses no danger and hence should not be labeled a criminal. These courts also reason that it is not cost effective to prosecute people who possess unusable or minute amounts of marijuana.

In states requiring a usable amount of marijuana, how much is considered "usable?" The general trend is that a usable amount requires a sufficient quantity to smoke in a pipe. A case in Arizona held that .3 gram of marijuana was a usable amount. A case in Oregon held that six roaches was a usable amount, and a case in Texas held that a single .1 gram roach was a usable amount. Also, several courts hold that if the police actually see the defendant smoking marijuana, a possession conviction is valid even though the amount of marijuana recovered is less than a usable amount. Lastly, even in states that require a usable amount, the prosecution does not need to prove that the amount was actually sufficient to produce a "narcotic effect," nor need it prove the purity or potency of the marijuana.

The rule is different in California, Colorado, Connecticut, Florida, Georgia, Illinois, Maryland, Minnesota, New Jersey, New Mexico, New York, Nevada, Ohio, and Wisconsin. In these states, the courts have held that possession of *any* amount of marijuana (so long as there is enough for a laboratory to positively identify the substance as marijuana) is sufficient for a possession conviction. There are cases in several of these states where "a few minute particles" of marijuana lint in a person's pocket was sufficient for conviction!

California has recently changed its rule. Prior to 1993, a possession conviction in California required proof of a usable amount. However, in 1993, the California Supreme Court, for all practical purposes, did away with California's usable amount requirement. In this case, the California Supreme Court redefined "usable amount" as anything beyond a "blackened trace or a useless trace." In other words, *any* amount of marijuana, beyond a residue such as might be found on a pipe screen, now qualifies as a "usable amount" in California. (*People v. Rubacalba [1993] 6 Cal.4th 62.*)

Challenges to the Constitutionality of Possession Laws

Shortly after possession of marijuana was made a crime, many people arrested for simple possession argued that the anti-marijuana possession laws violated the federal constitution. Almost every approach was tried and rejected. For example, it was argued that the laws violated federal constitutional guarantees to due process and equal protection; that the laws impermissibly intruded on the fundamental rights of liberty and the pursuit of happiness; that the laws interfered with the right to possess and use private property; that the laws were irrational since other, more harmful, substances are not outlawed; that it was unconstitutional to make the degree of punishment depend on the quantity of the marijuana possessed; that the laws violated the First Amendment right to freely exercise religion; that any penalty for possession of marijuana was cruel and unusual punishment; and that the laws violated the right to privacy.

The only success occurred in the free-minded state of Alaska, where in 1975 the State Supreme Court held that the right to privacy guaranteed by the Alaska constitution protected the right of adults to smoke marijuana in their own homes. (*People v. Ravin [1975] 537 P.2d 494.*) Freedom reigned for almost fifteen years. Things changed, however, in 1990 when a group of anti-marijuana crusaders succeeded in a getting a referendum on the Alaska ballot that would recriminalize possession of marijuana. To the dismay of the state's marijuana smokers and many other people concerned with the erosion of their right to privacy, the referendum passed in 1990, implementing a punishment of up to 90 days in jail and a $1,000 fine for possession of even personal use amounts of marijuana.

As of this writing, the legal effect of the Alaska referendum is unclear. In fact, in 1993, Ketchikan Superior Court Judge, Michael Thompson, declared the referendum unconstitutional and refused to punish Patrick McNeil, a logger caught with a single marijuana roach. The Alaska Supreme Court has yet to decide the issue.

The "Momentary Possession" Defense

In some states, including California, there is one clearly defined situation in which it is actually legal to possess marijuana. In California it is legal to possess marijuana if it is possessed "solely for the purpose of abandonment, disposal, or destruction," *and* the marijuana was obtained in order to terminate or prevent illegal possession by another person.

Clearly, such scenarios seldom form the basis for legal defenses against marijuana possession. The law was enacted to immunize parents who confiscate marijuana from their kids, as well as anti-marijuana crusaders who take another person's marijuana but are arrested before they have had an opportunity to destroy the confiscated marijuana or turn it over to the police.

Sale or Distribution of Marijuana

Under the laws of every state, it is a crime to knowingly possess marijuana with the intent to sell or distribute it. This crime is often referred to as "possession for sale." However, it is important to note that many states don't require an actual sale or even an intent to sell *(i.e., exchange for money.)* In these states, as under federal law, the prosecution must prove an intent to *distribute* marijuana and not necessarily an intent to *sell* it.

In order to convict a person of possessing marijuana with intent to sell or distribute, the prosecution in most states must prove two things: (1) actual or constructive possession, and (2) the intention to sell or distribute the marijuana. Unlike the crime of possession, most states do not require the prosecutor to prove that the person possessed a usable amount of marijuana.

The first element (actual or constructive possession) is the same as that discussed in the previous section regarding the crime of possession. The only additional element is the intent to sell or distribute. Prosecutors often prove intent by demonstrating that an actual sale has occurred. If the police were not able to catch the defendant actually selling or distributing marijuana, they will attempt to prove the defendant's intent with circumstantial evidence. This is often accomplished by showing that when the police arrested the person they also seized such items as scales, cash, pay-owe sheets, or numerous baggies filled with small accurately weighed quantities of marijuana.

The case of Roger Davis, decided by a Virginia court, is representative of how marijuana-distribution cases are often proven. Roger was at home when he heard a knock at his front door. The next moment, police officers with a search warrant were in his home. The officers immediately searched Roger. Inside his jacket pocket, they found $800 cash but no marijuana. Feeling scared and intimidated, Roger told the officers that all the marijuana was downstairs in the basement. The officers searched the basement and found a white plastic bag containing a little over 6 ounces of marijuana. They also found a stem from a *Cannabis* plant, scissors, numerous *Cannabis* seeds, two boxes of sandwich baggies, and a box of twist ties. One of the boxes was found on top of a scale. Near the scale, were some gram weights and a conversion chart from grams to ounces.

At Roger's trial, a police officer with "extensive training and experience" in marijuana crimes testified that marijuana is often sold in plastic sandwich baggies secured by twist ties. In addition, the officer testified that the typical marijuana cigarette contains approximately .4 gram of marijuana and that most people who smoke marijuana (but don't sell it) ordinarily keep less than an ounce of the drug on hand. Therefore, the officer testified, an amount of 6 ounces was not consistent with personal use and could only indicate that Roger intended to distribute some of the marijuana.

The court held that the totality of the evidence, although circumstantial, was sufficient to support Roger's conviction for possession with intent to distribute marijuana.

The United States Supreme Court has held that possession of a large amount of a controlled substance may, in and of itself, establish the element of intent to sell or distribute. The case which established this precedent concerned heroin rather than marijuana, so presently it is unclear what quantity of marijuana the Supreme Court considers large enough to demonstrate intent to distribute.

Under one Federal provision, possession of one ounce or less of marijuana is presumed to be for personal use, unless other evidence suggests otherwise. Evidence which can show an intent to sell includes:

(1) Evidence, such as drug scales, drug distribution paraphernalia, drug records, drug packaging material, method of drug packaging, drug "cutting" agents and other equipment, that indicates an intent to process, package or distribute;

(2) Information from reliable sources indicating possession of a controlled substance with intent to distribute;

(3) The arrest and/or conviction record of the person or persons in actual or constructive possession of the controlled substance for offenses under Federal, Sate or local law that indicates an intent to distribute a controlled substance;

(4) The controlled substance is related to large amounts of cash or any amount of prerecorded government funds;

(5) The controlled substance is possessed under circumstances that indicate such a controlled substance is a sample intended for distribution in anticipation of a transaction involving large quantities, or is part of a larger delivery; or

(6) Statements by the possessor, or otherwise attributable to the possessor, including statements of conspirators, that indicate possession with intent to distribute. *(21 CFR 1316.91.)*

State courts differ widely as to how much marijuana must be possessed to circumstantially indicate a person's intent to sell or distribute. In one case, for example, a court found that possession of 70 marijuana plants reasonably indicated an intent to distribute. In another case however, a court found that a defendant's possession of a one-pound brick of marijuana was *insufficient* to uphold the defendant's conviction for possession with intent to distribute. Most cases make clear that even a small amount of marijuana can be sufficient to establish an intent to sell if the marijuana is packaged in individual small amounts. The marijuana need not be divided into baggies. For example, in one 1993 case in Louisiana, a man was convicted of possession with intent to distribute marijuana because police found 26 joints in his jacket pocket. *(State v. Tucker [1993] 626 SO.2d 707.)*

A Virginia court of appeal recently reversed a man's conviction for possession of marijuana with intent to distribute, because he was found in possession of slightly less than three quarters of an ounce of marijuana in a *single* bag, and because a drug test showed he was *positive* for THC. The court held that such evidence was consistent with the man's personal use of the marijuana rather than with an intent to sell. (The case was close, because the man was also found with almost $5,000 cash. He explained that the money was from the country store he operated and the court apparently believed him, explaining that although his possession of such a large amount of cash created suspicion, proof of intent to distribute may not be based on speculation alone.) *(Rice v. Com. [Va.App.1993] 429 S.E.2d 879.)*

Selling Bogus Marijuana

Almost every state has enacted laws making it illegal to sell a perfectly legal substance claiming that it is marijuana. The primary purpose of their laws is to protect undercover narcotics agents who get duped by sellers of bogus marijuana. As police began running more and more undercover operations in which they posed as interested buyers of marijuana, they occasionally were unknowingly sold fake marijuana. The seller was arrested and charged with distributing marijuana. When the laboratory report revealed that the substance was not marijuana, but rather some perfectly legal "green leafy substance," the government had no option but to dismiss the charges against the seller.

In order to prevent these dismissals, states began enacting laws making it a crime to agree to sell marijuana and then deliver another substance. The basic elements of this offense are: (1) agreeing to sell marijuana; and (2) delivering a legal substance that a reasonable person would think was marijuana. In most states, the punishment for selling bogus marijuana is identical to and sometimes greater than the punishment for selling the same amount of marijuana!

Charles Holliman was sentenced to five years probation and fined $500 for selling a third of an ounce of fake marijuana. Mr. Holliman unwittingly approached an undercover police officer in a bar and asked him if he wanted to buy some marijuana. The happy officer jumped at the offer and about an hour later Mr. Holliman returned with a small manila envelope which the officer later testified contained a "greenish brown leafy substance which contained seeds." The officer, believing he was purchasing marijuana, paid Mr. Holliman $30, received the envelope, and immediately arrested Mr. Holliman. When the police crime lab determined that the substance was not marijuana but rather an unidentified plant material, the government dropped the charges of selling marijuana and replaced them with charges of selling a "simulated controlled substance." Mr. Holliman was convicted. *(Holliman v. State [Tex.App. 1985] 692 S.W.2d 120.)*

A few courts have addressed the issue of whether or not laws against counterfeit substances might infringe on the First Amendment rights of pro-marijuana groups demonstrating for the legalization of marijuana by selling "joints" filled with tea leaves or some other non-drug substance. The courts that have considered this issue have stated that the counterfeit substance laws would not violate the First Amendment rights of such demonstrators because a reasonable person who purchased one of the "joints" at such a demonstration would not believe the substance was a controlled substance.

The Crime of Offering To Sell Marijuana

In many states, simply *offering* to sell marijuana is a crime. Here, the prosecutor need *not* prove that the person ever possessed marijuana. The prosecutor need only prove that the person offered to sell some marijuana. The crime is akin to soliciting a prostitute or soliciting someone to commit murder.

Marijuana Paraphernalia Crimes

Under federal law, and under some state and municipal statutes, it is a crime to possess, sell, offer to sell or send through the mail "marijuana paraphernalia." (*21 USC sec. 863*.) The federal law, which is based on a model law created by the DEA, sets the punishment for committing a paraphernalia offense at a maximum of three years in federal prison.

The federal law is quite explicit about what devices are outlawed as paraphernalia. The term "drug paraphernalia" means any equipment, product, or material of any kind which is primarily intended or designed for use in manufacturing, compounding, converting, concealing, producing, processing, preparing, injecting, ingesting, inhaling, or otherwise introducing into the human body a controlled substance, possession of which is unlawful under this subchapter. It includes items primarily intended or designed for use in ingesting, inhaling, or otherwise introducing marijuana, cocaine, hashish, hashish oil, PCP, or amphetamines into the human body, such as:

    (1) metal, wooden, acrylic, glass, stone, plastic, or ceramic pipes with or without screens, permanent screens, hashish heads, or punctured metal bowls;

    (2) water pipes;

    (3) carburetion tubes and devices;

    (4) smoking and carburetion masks;

    (5) roach clips: meaning objects used to hold burning material, such as a marijuana cigarette, that has become too small or too short to be held in the hand;

(6) miniature spoons with level capacities of one-tenth cubic
centimeter or less;
(7) chamber pipes;
(8) carburetor pipes;
(9) electric pipes;
(10) air-driven pipes;
(11) chillums;
(12) bongs;
(13) ice pipes or chillers;
(14) wired cigarette papers; or
(15) cocaine freebase kits.

Even if a particular item is not listed above, it can still be considered "paraphernalia" if other factors show that it is likely to be used with marijuana or if it was specifically designed for such use. When determining whether a particular unlisted product is "paraphernalia," courts are instructed to examine:

(1) instructions, oral or written, provided with the item concerning its use;
(2) descriptive materials accompanying the item which explain or depict its use;
(3) national and local advertising concerning its use;
(4) the manner in which the item is displayed for sale;
(5) whether the owner, or anyone in control of the item, is a
legitimate supplier of like or related items to the community, such as a licensed distributor or dealer of tobacco
products;
(6) direct or circumstantial evidence of the ratio of sales of the
item(s) to the total sales of the business enterprise;
(7) the existence and scope of legitimate uses of the item in the
community; and
(8) expert testimony concerning its use.

For awhile, the only noteworthy exemption to the paraphernalia ban per-
tained to "any item that, in the normal lawful course of business, is imported, exported, transported, or sold through the mail or by any other means, and traditionally intended for use with tobacco products, including any pipe, paper, or accessory." Such items are not considered "paraphernalia." Knowing this, many paraphernalia sellers adopted the tactic of placing a disclaimer in the store window or on advertisements, stating something along the lines of: "These products are designed and intended for use only with tobacco products."

In 1994, however, a decision by the United States Supreme Court put an end to this tactic, and made it practically impossible to legally sell many of the traditional marijuana tools. The Court explained the meaning of the phrases "designed for use" and "primarily intended for use" in the statutory definition of paraphernalia. (See the first paragraph of the Federal paraphernalia statute.) According to the rule set down by the Court, an item is "designed for use," as drug paraphernalia "if it is principally used with illegal drugs by virtue of its objective features, i.e., features designed by the manufacturer." Items that meet the "designed for use" standard therefore constitute drug paraphernalia irrespective of the knowledge or intent of one who sells or transports them.

The Court went on to examine the phrase "primarily intended for use with controlled substances," and specifically addressed the question of *whose* intent is relevant, the seller's or the buyer's. The Court held that the phrase "primarily intended for use with a controlled substance" refers to a product's *likely* use by the *buyer* rather than to the seller's state of mind. The Court reasoned that the purpose of a seller of drug paraphernalia is to sell his product; the seller is indifferent as to whether that product ultimately is to be used in connection with illegal drugs or otherwise. The Court noted that the knowledge standard in this context simply requires an awareness on the seller's part that *customers* in general are *likely* to use the merchandise to ingest illegal drugs.

In short then, this 1994 case did away with the tactic of selling marijuana paraphernalia with a tobacco-use disclaimer. Under the Court's interpretation of the federal law, it doesn't matter what disclaimer a seller makes. The seller violates the federal law by selling any device which a reasonable person would know is likely be used to ingest marijuana or some other illegal drug. *(Posters N Things, Ltd. v. US [1994] 114 S.Ct. 1747.)*

Pipes As Paraphernalia

How have courts distinguished pipes used to smoke marijuana from pipes used to smoke tobacco? Suffice it to say that even judges can tell the difference. In one case in Washington, D.C., for example, a man was convicted of possessing an illegal pipe largely because it was "equipped with an air vent," and because the bowl contained marijuana residue. In an Indiana case, a man was convicted of possessing drug paraphernalia because he was caught with a small green and silver pipe "similar to pipes in which marijuana is commonly smoked, given its size and the presence of a screen to filter seeds and stems."

Growing Marijuana

In every state it is a crime to cultivate *Cannabis*. Under federal law the same crime is referred to as "manufacturing" marijuana.

Under federal law, "manufacturing" is defined as "planting, cultivation, growing or harvesting of a controlled substance." It is a violation of federal law, therefore, not only to grow *Cannabis*, but also to harvest wild *Cannabis* plants. It is also considered manufacturing or cultivating to extract, process or cook marijuana to create hashish, or any other concentrated *Cannabis* product. (*State v. Horsely [1979] 596 P.2d 661.*)

In every state, if a person is convicted of cultivating, manufacturing, drying, or processing marijuana, he or she can be sent to prison. The crime does not require a full-scale *Cannabis* grow operation. Numerous convictions have resulted from people simply harvesting wild marijuana.

In a 1993 case in Arkansas the court reported that David Craig grew a single, large *Cannabis* plant outside his place of business and in plain view. The plant was approximately seven feet tall and six feet wide. Prior to his arrest, Craig had taken some leaves from the plant and was drying them inside his office.

The Arkansas Supreme court wasted no time in finding that watering, pruning and generally tending a marijuana plant constitutes "manufacturing." The court went further, however, and explained that even if Craig had done nothing more than pinched leaves from the plant his actions would still constitute "manufacturing" of marijuana since in Arkansas (like most states) "manufacturing" is defined to include processing or harvesting marijuana. (*Craig v. State [Ark. 1993] 863 S.W.2d 825.*)

A manufacturing conviction can be sustained prior to even planting *Cannabis* seeds. Danny LaMaster, for example, was convicted of manufacturing marijuana in violation of Missouri law and sentenced to three years in prison, after "the sheriff found a plate with [*Cannabis*] seeds lying in it between two wet paper towels." In another room, the officers found a fully outfitted growroom, complete with plastic covered windows, fluorescent lights, a thermometer, plant fertilizer and potting soil. This was sufficient evidence, said the Missouri court, that Mr. LaMaster was manufacturing marijuana, although he was obviously in only the early stages of the project. (*State v. LaMaster [Mo.App. 1991] 811 S.W.2d 837.*)

"Attempted" Manufacture

Under federal law and state law it is illegal to *attempt* to grow *Cannabis*. A conviction for attempted manufacture or cultivation requires proof that the defendant: (1) intended to grow *Cannabis*; and (2) intentionally carried out some act that was a "substantial step" toward that goal.

In one case, a conviction for attempted manufacture was upheld after police found a nearly completed hydroponics growing system with 198 growing chambers, grow lights, fertilizer, starter pots, water pumps, filters, and an electrical timer. This alone would not have been sufficient evidence since the builder of the system could well have intended to grow an innocuous crop such as tomatoes. Unfortunately however, the police also found a container of viable *Cannabis* seeds. The combination of the seeds and the hydroponic system was held to satisfy the two elements required for a federal conviction of attempted manufacture of marijuana.

Transportation of Marijuana

Needless to say, in every state it is a crime to transport *any* amount of marijuana in a vehicle. In California, if you are convicted of transporting one ounce or less, the fine is $100. However, if you are convicted of transporting more than one ounce, you can be imprisoned for up to four years.

Driving Under the Influence of Marijuana

In every state, it is illegal to drive a motor vehicle while under the influence of marijuana. If you are caught driving under the influence of marijuana in California (and you have no prior convictions for driving under the influence of alcohol or a drug), you face a minimum fine of approximately $1,000, two days in county jail, and suspension of your driver's license for up to six months. The details of this crime are discussed in more detail in Chapter 5.

Aiding and Abetting a Marijuana Crime

Most states have laws that make anyone who knowingly aids in committing a crime guilty of that crime. In other words, if you aid in the commission of a crime, you can be convicted and *sentenced for the crime* itself. These laws have been applied in the context of marijuana crimes.

In one Washington case, an undercover police officer asked a man if he knew where he could get some marijuana. Not realizing he was talking to an undercover officer, the man replied that his brother had some marijuana and would sell it for $100 an ounce. The officer told the man that $100 was too high, whereupon the man replied that it was "good pot well worth the price." The court held that this statement proved that the man was aiding the sale. Consequently, he was punished just as if *he* had *sold* marijuana. Many courts have upheld convictions based on a person's arrangement of a meeting between a seller of marijuana and a buyer. *(State v. Wilson [Wash. 1981] 631 P.2d 362.)*

Boobytrapped Gardens on Federal Property

It is an explicit federal crime to boobytrap a *Cannabis* garden located on federal property. This law makes it a crime to assemble, maintain, place, or cause to be placed a boobytrap on federal property where a controlled substance is being manufactured, distributed or dispensed. The law defines a boobytrap to include:

> . . . Any concealed or camouflaged device designed to cause
> bodily injury when triggered by any action of any suspecting
> person making contact with the device. Such terms include
> guns, ammunition, or explosive devices attached to trip wires

or other triggering mechanisms, sharpened stakes, and lines or
wires with hooks attached. *(21 USC 841[e].)*

A person convicted of boobytrapping is punished by a well-deserved ten
years imprisonment and a maximum fine of $10,000.

Penalties for Possessing Marijuana

As Appendix C makes clear, the punishment for possessing marijuana varies
widely from state to state. Currently, the most lenient states are California, Maine,
New York, Ohio, and Oregon. In those states, conviction for possessing a small
amount of marijuana (usually less than an ounce) will result in a fine, but no jail
time. Regardless of which state you live in, the sentence for possessing marijuana
depends on several factors, including: how much marijuana was found, how old
you were when arrested, how many prior convictions you have, and the type of
property you were on or near when the crime was committed. Needless to say, all
these factors can make sentencing rather complex.

In California, for example, when determining the sentence for marijuana
possession, the magic number is 28.5 grams (roughly an ounce). Regardless of
your age, if you are convicted in California of possessing 28.5 grams or less of
marijuana and have no prior convictions, you will be issued a citation, fined
approximately $100, and (as discussed in greater detail below) lose your driver's
license for six months. You will not be arrested and will not spend any time in
jail so long as you have proof of your identity.

In almost all states, the punishment for possessing marijuana is considerably
harsher if your crime occurred on the grounds of an elementary, junior high, or
high school when a school activity was in session. In such a case in California, if
you possess an ounce or less, you will be fined a maximum of $500 and/or
sentenced to 10 days in county jail.

Smoke A Joint, Lose Your License

The federal government, through the Federal Highway Administration, gives
state governments billions of dollars every year to help build and maintain the
highway system. In 1990, at the height of George Bush's War on Drugs, the
federal government got the idea that highway funds could be used to coerce state
governments to increase the punishment for marijuana and other drug offenses.
The method decided upon was to withhold 10 percent of the federal highway
funds from any state that did not agree, by October 1, 1995, to implement a six-
month driver's license suspension for any person convicted of a drug offense.
State that fail to comply stand to lose millions of dollars worth of highway funds.
The only way a state can get the federal funds but not impose the license
suspension is for its legislature to pass an "opt-out" resolution stating its

opposition to the license suspension provision and for its governor to go on record in agreement with that resolution.

In states that have passed the law, a person convicted of a marijuana crime, *even if it has nothing to do with a motor vehicle*, will have their driver's license suspended for six months in addition to whatever other punishment is imposed under the state's criminal laws.

The following table compiled by the Marijuana Policy Project (POB 77492, Capital Hill, Washington, DC, 20013) indicates which states have adopted "smoke a joint, lose your license" or a similar license suspension provision.

Table 1. **State Driver's License Suspension Provisions**

STATE	SUSPENSION FOR MARIJUANA POSSESSION
AL	6 months
AR	6 months
CA	6 months [1]
CO	3 months [3]
DC	6 months - 2 years
DE	1 -2 years
FL	6 months - 2 years
GA	180 days
IA	180 days
IL	1 year [4]
IN	6 months - 2 years
KS	30 days
LA	90 days - 1 year
MA	up to 5 years
MI	6 months [5]
MN	30 days [4]
MS	6 months
MT	6 months [6,7]
NJ	6 months - 2 years
NH	60 days - 2 years
NY	6 months [2]
OH	6 months - 5 years
OK	180 days
PA	6 months
RI	6 months [8]
SC	6 months
SD	90 days [8]
TX	180 days
UT	6 months
VA	6 months
WI	6 months - 5 years

Notes:

[1] Law sunsets on December 1, 1995.

[2] Law sunsets on October 1, 1995.

[3] Applies to a felony offense, such as cultivating one or more marijuana plants, distributing more than one ounce of marijuana to another person for no consideration, or distributing less than one ounce of marijuana to another person for consideration.

[4] Applies to controlled substance violations while the individual is in actual control of motor vehicle, e.g., possessing a baggie of marijuana while driving.

[5] Waived if person is to serve more than 1 year in prison.

[6] Not required, but available as part of an alternative to prison for drug felony (not simple pot possession.)

[7] Most recent available data were from 1993.

[8] Only if controlled substance violation was in vehicle.

Compiled by the Marijuana Policy Project.

State Taxes On Marijuana—Double Jeopardy

Approximately 22 states have enacted laws that impose taxes on the possession of marijuana. The statutes imposing these taxes are usually included in the state's revenue code, but failure to pay the taxes can result in criminal penalties. The typical tax is $3.50 for each gram of marijuana possessed. Montana and New Mexico are slightly different. Montana, for example, taxes marijuana at 10 percent of its market value or $100 per ounce, whichever is greater. Anyone who possesses marijuana is supposed to pay the tax, though for obvious reasons no one does.

In June 1994, the United States Supreme Court struck down the Montana tax, ruling that states cannot exact a tax from a person who has previously been convicted and punished for possessing the drugs. *(Dept. Of Revenue of Montana v. Kurth Ranch et al, N0. 93-144, June 6, 1994, 94 DAR 7673.)* To exact such a tax after a person has already been criminally punished, held the Court, violates the Double Jeopardy Clause of the Fifth Amendment. The Double Jeopardy Clause, besides protecting against a second prosecution for the same offense after acquittal or conviction, also protects against multiple punishments for the same offense.

Prior to the *Kurth Ranch* decision, the Supreme Court had never found a tax to be in violation of the Double Jeopardy Clause. In the *Kurth Ranch* case, however, the Court examined the tax imposed on a Richard and Judith Kurth after police raided their Montana farm and seized 1,811 ounces of harvested marijuana. In a criminal proceeding, the Kurths were found guilty and sentenced to prison.

Montana then assessed a tax of $181,000 ($100 per ounce of marijuana) against the Kurths. The Kurths argued that the tax was actually a second punishment that violated the Fifth Amendment's guarantee against Double Jeopardy.

In a close 5-4 decision, the United States Supreme Court agreed with the Kurths. The Court found that Montana's tax had punitive characteristics because the tax was extremely high and had an obvious deterrent purpose. As the Court explained: "Taken as a whole, this drug tax is a concoction of anomalies too far-removed in crucial respects from a standard tax assessment to escape characterization as punishment for the purpose of Double Jeopardy analysis." The Court, however, left Montana (and the other 22 states with similar tax laws) a way out in future cases, explaining: "Montana no doubt could collect its tax on the possession of marijuana, for example, if it had not previously punished the taxpayer for the same offense, or indeed, if it had assessed the tax in the same proceeding that resulted in his conviction."

Punishment for Possessing Marijuana with Intent to Distribute

In every state, and under federal law, possession of marijuana with the intent to sell or distribute is a separate and more serious crime than simply possessing marijuana. In most states, selling to, or employing, a minor severely increases the punishment. (In fact, in some states it's a separate crime akin to, but more serious than, contributing to the delinquency of a minor.) As discussed next, the penalties are further increased if a sale occurred on school property or in a public park.

Punishment for Selling or Manufacturing Marijuana Within 1000 feet of a School

Under federal law (and in a rapidly increasing number of states) punishment for committing a marijuana related offense can be severely increased if the offense occurred within 1000 feet of a school. Under the federal law, any person who sells or manufactures over 5 grams of marijuana on or within 1000 feet of "the real property comprising a public or private elementary, vocational, or secondary school or a public or private college, junior college, or university, or a playground, or within 1000 feet of a public or private youth center, public swimming pool, or video arcade facility" is subject to twice the normal maximum term of punishment as well as twice the normal maximum fine. (*21 USC sec. 860.*)

The courts have routinely interpreted these laws very broadly, applying the increased punishment whenever possible. For example, the courts consider the parking-lots of the above enumerated facilities when calculating the 1000 foot distance. In one case the penalty was applied to increase the sentence of someone who sold heroin inside a bar that just happened to be within 1000 feet of a school. Likewise, there are numerous cases in which people have had their sentences doubled simply because their home or apartment, in which they grew or sold marijuana, happened to fall within 1000 feet of a school. The courts have made clear that the punishment will be increased even if the seller had no idea that he was within 1000 feet of a school. As one court explained, "Congress intended that dealers and their aiders and abettors bear the burden of ascertaining where schools are located and removing their operation from those areas or else face enhanced penalties."

Finally, the courts have refused to limit application of the statute to the hours while school is in session. "Nothing in the statute," explained one court "requires that school be in session or that children be near or around the school at the time of the offense . . . the language of the statute is unambiguous and does not require that a school be open at the time of the offense."

Federal Marijuana Crimes— Schedule I

Under the federal government's scheme for regulating and controlling drugs, a drug is placed into one of five "schedules." The drugs most tightly controlled, and for possession of which the severest penalties may be imposed, are placed in "Schedule I." There are three criteria for placing a drug into Schedule I. The drug must: (1) have a high potential for abuse, (2) have no currently accepted medical use, and (3) lack safety even under medical supervision.

Closing its eyes to the scientifically proven fact that marijuana is not physically addictive and has never directly caused a single death, and refusing to acknowledge that marijuana is helpful to many people suffering from illness and disease, the federal government has classified marijuana as a Schedule I drug, along with heroin. Numerous marijuana users have challenged the scheduling of marijuana, arguing that it does not meet the criteria for placement in Schedule I. In every case, however, the courts have rejected these arguments.

State and Federal Prosecution for the Same Crime

The federal laws on marijuana are very similar to the state laws. Therefore, if you are in violation of a state marijuana law, you are very likely *also* violating a federal marijuana law. As the Supreme Court has interpreted the Double Jeopardy clause of the Fifth Amendment, you can be prosecuted by *both* the state and the federal governments for the same act. The theory is that the state and federal governments are "separate sovereigns," and since your single act violates the laws of both, each sovereign can prosecute you for violating its law. At present, such multiple prosecutions rarely occur, though given the current antidrug hysteria, this may change.

Mandatory Minimums Under Federal Law

Federal law designates certain weights of marijuana and/or certain numbers of *Cannabis* plants as requiring a mandatory minimum sentence. Mandatory minimums mean exactly that; they are unavoidable sentences. Table 2, below, shows the triggering quantities for five and ten year minimum sentences.

Table 2. **Federal Mandatory Minimums**

YEARS	TRIGGER/ MANUFACURING OR DISTRIBUTING
5	100 kilograms (220 pounds) of marijuana
5	2 kilograms (4.4 pounds/70 ounces) of hashish oil
5	20 kilograms of hashish
5	100 *Cannabis* plants
10	1000 kilograms (2204 pounds) of marijuana
10	20 kilograms (44 pounds) of hashish oil
10	200 kilograms of hashish
10	1000 *Cannabis* plants

Derived from 21 USC sec. 841 (1994).

Mandatory Minimum Safety Valve

The harshness of the mandatory minimum sentence provisions was slightly lessened as part of the federal crime bill signed into law by President Clinton on September 13, 1994. Under a provision in the new crime bill, a marijuana offender who would ordinarily be sentenced to either a five- or ten-year mandatory minimum, can avoid that minimum sentence if he or she meets *all* of the following five criteria:

(1) Defendant has not been previously convicted of a crime requiring incarceration for more than 60 days; and

(2) Defendant did not use violence or a dangerous weapon or induce another to use violence or a dangerous weapon; and

(3) The offense did not result in death or serious bodily injury; and

(4) Defendant was not an organizer, leader, manager, or supervisor; and

(5) Defendant has provided the government all information concerning the offense prior to sentencing. (The fact that the defendant has no relevant or useful information shall

not preclude the court from deciding that he or she has met
this requirement.)

Unfortunately, the safety valve is not retroactive. It applies only to those
defendants who were convicted after September 13, 1994. Additionally, should
a republican crime bill come down the pike, it is quite possible that it would repeal
the safety valve provisions.

Federal Punishment for Simple Possession

A first offender convicted of the federal crime of simple possession of marijuana
(i.e., possession without intent to distribute) is punished by a sentence of from
zero to one year in federal prison and a mandatory fine of $1,000. There is no
federal mandatory minimum for a first time conviction for simple possession of
harvested marijuana regardless of the quantity possesses. As a practical matter,
however, possession of more than a relatively small quantity of marijuana will
result in conviction of possession *with intent to distribute* rather than simple
possession. (The crime of possession with intent to distribute is punished the
same as the crimes of distributing or cultivating marijuana.) *(21 USC sec. 844.)*
    A first offender convicted of simple possession of marijuana is eligible for
probation if: (1) he has never before been convicted of a federal or state drug
crime; and (2) he has not previously received probation for simple possession.
Assuming both prongs of that test are satisfied, a judge is permitted to forego
sentencing the defendant and instead place him on probation for up to one year.
If the person completes his probation term without violating any conditions of the
probation, the judge is required to dismiss the proceedings against the person and
discharge him from probation. *(18 USC 3607[a].)*
    A person with one prior conviction is sentenced to between 15 days and two
years imprisonment and a mandatory minimum fine of $2,500. A third time
offender is sentenced to between 90 days and three years imprisonment and a
mandatory minimum fine of $5,000. *(21 USC sec. 844.)*

Federal Punishment for Growing, Distributing, Importing, Exporting or Trafficking Marijuana

Assuming a mandatory minimum has not been triggered, a defendant convicted
of a federal marijuana crime (other than simple possession) committed on or after
November 1, 1987, will have his or her sentence calculated by reference to the
Drug Quantity Table contained in federal sentencing guidelines. The Drug
Quantity Table sets punishment based on the weight of the marijuana that the
defendant was convicted of growing, distributing, importing, exporting or
trafficking (or possessing with the intent to do any of these.) In the simplest case,
the sentencing court simply looks up the weight of the marijuana and imposes the

sentence indicated by the corresponding offense level. Table 3 shows a slightly simplified breakdown of punishments administered under federal sentencing guidelines for nonviolent first offenders caught with harvested marijuana.

The guidelines utilize a Drug Equivalency Table (DET) for persons convicted of crimes involving hashish oil, *Cannabis* resin, hashish, or tetrahydrocannabinol. The DET establishes the following equivalencies:

1 gram of Hashish Oil = 50 grams of marijuana
1 gram of *Cannabis* Resin or Hashish = 5 grams of marijuana
1 gram of Tetrahydrocannabinol (synthetic or organic) = 167 grams of marijuana.

The above equivalencies can be plugged into Table 3 to calculate federal punishment.

Table 3. Federal Punishment for Distributing, Importing, Exporting or Trafficking Harvested Marijuana

WEIGHT (kg)	PRISON (mo.)	FINE
less than 250	0-6	$500-$5,000
.250-.999	0-6	$1000-$10,000
1- 2.4	6-12	$2,000-$20,000
2.5 - 4.9	10-16	$3,000-$30,000
5 - 9.9	15-21	$4,000-$40,000
10-19	21-27	$5,000-$50,000
20-39	27-33	$6,000-$60,000
40-59	33-41	$7,500-$75,000
60-79	41-51	$7,500-$75,000
80-99	51-63	$10,000-$100,000
100-399	63-78	$12,500-$125,000
400-699	78-97	$12,500-$125,000
700-999	97-121	$15,000-$150,000
1000-2,999	121-151	$17,500-$175,000
3000-9,999	151-188	$17,500-$175,000
10,000-29,999	188-235	$20,000-$200,000
30,000-99,999	235-293	$25,000-$250,000
100,000-299,999	292-365	$25,000-$250,000
300,000 or more	30 yrs. to life	$25,000-$250,000

Derived from Sentencing Guidelines 2D1.1 (1994).

The sentence is determined differently if the defendant is caught with live, unharvested *Cannabis plants* rather than harvested marijuana. To deal with the situation where live plants are confiscated, Congress initially enacted an "equivalency provision," that employs the following system:

> In the case of an offense involving marihuana plants, if the offense involved (A) 50 or more marihuana plants, treat each plant as equivalent to 1 KG [kilogram] of marihuana; (B) fewer

than 50 marihuana plants, treat each plant as equivalent to 100
G [grams] of marijuana. *Provided,* however, that if the actual
weight of the marihuana is greater, use the actual weight of the
marihuana. *(Sec. 2D1.1[c] n.)*

In other words, under the federal law which was in effect until Nov. 1, 1995,
a person convicted of manufacturing 50 *Cannabis* plants was sentenced as if he
had been found with 50 kilos (50,000 grams) of marijuana. However, if the exact
same person was found with only *one* less plant, the equivalency provision treated
him as having been found with only 4.9 kilos (4,900 grams) or over *ten times less
marijuana than had he grown only one more plant!* Translated into punishment,
that meant that a person caught growing fifty plants was sentenced to between 33-
44 months and fined between $7,500 and $75,000, while a person caught growing
forty-nine plants was sentenced to between 10-16 months and fined between
$3,000 and $30,000.

November 1, 1995 Guideline's Revision: *All Cannabis* plants equated to 100 grams

As described above, the 49- versus 50-plant distinction built into the federal
sentencing guidelines resulted in a disproportionately harsher sentence for any
person who unwarily grew 50 (or more) *Cannabis* plants as opposed to 49 plants.
Because of the concerted efforts of advocates like the Marijuana Policy Project
and Families Against Mandatory Minimums (FAMM), the absurdity of the
distinction was impressed upon the commission charged with revising the
sentencing guidelines. In the most recent amendments to the guidelines, which
took effect November 1, 1995, the Sentencing Commission discarded the
distinction, replacing it with an across-the-board 100 gram equivalency regardless of the number of plants. Additionally, to the happiness of many imprisoned
marijuana growers, the new equivalency provision was made retroactive which
means that approximately 950 federal inmates "serving time" for marijuana
cultivation will have their sentences significantly reduced.

As revised, the new equivalency provision reads:

For marijuana the commission has adopted an equivalency of
100 grams per plant, or the actual weight of the usable marijuana whichever is greater. The decision to treat each plant as
equal to 100 grams is premised on the fact that the average yield
from a mature marijuana plant equals 100 grams of marijuana.
In controlled substance offenses, an attempt is assigned the
same offense level as the objet of the attempt . . . . Consequently, the Commission adopted the policy that each plant is
to be treated as the equivalent of an attempt to produce 100
grams of marijuana, except where the actual weight of usable

marijuana is greater. *(Sec. 2D1.1 Revised Background Commentary.)*

The Commission published its reasons for unifying the equivalency to 100 grams regardless of the number of plants, explaining:

> The one plant = 100 grams of marijuana equivalency used by the Commission for offenses involving fewer than 50 marijuana plants was selected as a reasonable approximation of the actual yield of marijuana plants taking into account (1) studies reporting the atual yield of marijuana plants (37.5 to 412 grams depending on growing conditions); (2) that all plants regardless of size are counted for guideline purposes while, in actuality, not all plants will produce usable marijuana (e.g., some plants may die of disease before maturity, and when plants are grown outdoors some plants may be consumed by animals); and (3) that male plants, which are counted for guideline purposes, are frequently culled because they do not produce the same quality of marijuana as do female plants. To enhance fairness and consistency, this amendment adopts the equivalency of 100 grams per marijuana plant for all guideline determinations.

Table 4 reflects the 1995 equivalency change and shows the punishment range for a first offender convicted of cultivating *Cannabis* plants. Recall, however, that if the prosecutor can show that the actual yield of the plants was greater than 100 grams, the actual weight is used rather than the equivalency.

Table 4. **Federal Punishment for Growing *Cannabis* Plants**

NO. OF PLANTS	PRISON (mos.)	FINE
1-2	0-6	$500-$5,000
3-9	0-6	$1000-$10,000
10-24	6-12	$2,000-$20,000
25-49	10-16	$3,000-$30,000
50-99	15-21	$4,000-$40,000
100-199	21-27	$5,000-$50,000
200-399	27-33	$6,000-$60,000
400-599	33-41	$7,500-$75,000
600-799	41-51	$7,500-$75,000
800-999	51-63	$10,000-$100,000
1,000-3,999	63-78	$12,500-$125,000
4,000-6,999	78-97	$12,500-$125,000

7,000-9,999	97-121	$15,000-$150,000
10,000-29,999	121-151	$17,500-$175,000
30,000-99,999	151-188	$17,500-$175,000
100,000-299,999	188-235	$20,000-$200,000
300,000-999,999	235-293	$25,000-$250,000
1,000,000-2,999,999	292-365	$25,000-$250,000
3,000,000 or more	360 to life	$25,000-$250,000

Derived from Sentencing Guidelines 2D1.1, as revised Nov. 1, 1995.

Defining A *Cannabis* Plant Under Federal Law

Given the growth progression of a *Cannabis* seed into a mature *Cannabis* plant, it is not always easy for courts to determine just when a "plant" comes into being. For example, John Burke was arrested in 1991 in Bangor, Maine, after police officers searched his home under a warrant and found a basement growing room containing 34 *Cannabis* plants ranging in size from one to three feet. Additionally, the officers found 16 one-to-three inch cuttings that were each growing in a separate pot. The District Court sentenced Mr. Burke under the pre-Nov. 1, 1995 federal guidelines by calculating his offense based on 50 plants (34 plants + 16 plant cuttings) which bumped the calculation up to the much harsher one-kilo-per-plant standard then in existence.

Mr. Burke contested the calculation by arguing that some of the 16 cuttings were so fresh that they could not yet be considered "plants." (If even one cutting could be disqualified, the sentence would have to be recalculated based on the more lenient 100-grams-per-plant standard.) Mr. Burke presented the testimony of a botany expert who stated that the root-like growth at the bottom of the cuttings was simply *primordia*, or the precursor of roots yet to form. The expert testified that this newly emerging growth at the base of the cuttings was not "roots" because it was not yet capable of absorbing water, and hence the cuttings were not really viable "plants" in their own right.

The First Circuit Court of Appeals rejected Mr. Burke's argument, holding that for purposes of the federal sentencing guidelines, "plant status is sufficiently established when there is some observable evidence of root formation. In other words, at the first sign of roots, a plant exists for sentencing purposes." (*US v. Burke [1st Cir. 1993] 999 F.2d 596*.)

The Sixth, Eighth and Ninth Circuits have all followed suit, ruling that a "plant" exists once it has developed root structures that can be seen with the naked eye. As the Ninth Circuit put it:

Marijuana plants have three characteristic structures, readily apparent to the unaided lay person's eye: roots, stems, and leaves. Until a cutting develops roots of its own, it is not a plant itself but a mere piece of some other plant. We therefore adopt the rule that cuttings are not "plants" unless there is readily observable evidence of root formation. *(U.S. v. Robinson [9th Cir.1994] 35 F.3d 442.)*

1995 Guideline's Revision: "Plant" Defined

As part of the 1995 revisions of the federal sentencing guidelines, the Sentencing Commission defined the word "plant." The Commission essentially adopted the Ninth Circuit's definition as stated above in the *Burke* case. Specifically, beginning November 1, 1995, for the purposes of the federal guidelines, a plant is defined as:

> . . . An organism having leaves and a readily observable root formation (e.g., a marijuana cutting having roots, a rootball, or root hairs is a marijuana plant.) *(Sec. 2D1.1 Application Note 22, as revised)*

Multiple Stemmed Plants

Because experts agree that *Cannabis* is a single stem plant (i.e., one seed, when germinated, will typically produce one stem), at least the Ninth Circuit has adopted the rebuttal presumption that "each stalk protruding from the ground and supported by its own root system should be considered one plant, no matter how close to the other plants it is and no matter how intertwined are their root systems." Rebuttable presumptions function as general rules. Therefore, a defendant with an unusual multi-stem plant has the burden of proving that the multiple stems emerge from a single root system and that there is thus only a single plant for sentencing purposes.

Sex of the Plants

The First, Second Third, Eighth, and Ninth Circuits have held that although most growers weed out and discard male *Cannabis* plants, *both male and female* plants are equally counted under the federal sentencing guidelines. *(US v. Gallant[1st Cir. 1994] 25 F.3d 36.)*

The November 1995 revisions make this explicit by stating that *Cannabis* plants *regardless of sex* are treated as the equivalent of 100 grams of marijuana.

Accordingly, all federal courts will now count both male and female plants when calculating a defendant's sentence.

1995 Guideline's Revisions: Wet vs. Dry Marijuana

The Seventh and Tenth Circuits have held that the water naturally contained in freshly harvested marijuana which has not yet had time to dry is part of the "mixture or substance" containing the controlled substance, and hence if a defendant was arrested with undried marijuana in those circuits, his sentence was calculated based on the *wet* weight of the marijuana, rather than its dry weight. (*US v. Garcia [C.A.7 Ind. 1991] 925 F.2d 170; US v. Pinedo-Montoya [C.A.10 N.M. 1992] 966 F.2d 591*.)

Effective November 1995, however, the guidelines were amended to include a brief "application note," concerning the moisture content of harvested marijuana. Since freshly harvested marijuana naturally contains a large percentage of water within its cells, it weighs much more than the same amount of marijuana which has been allowed to dry. Similarly, since marijuana grown outdoors is often harvested just as fall rains are beginning, rain soaked marijuana is occasionally confiscated.

Because wet marijuana is essentially "unusable," and must be dried in order to be smoked, the November 1995 revision instructs federal judges that they must determine the weight of marijuana based on its *dry* weight:

> . . . In the case of marijuana having a moisture content that renders the marijuana unsuitable for consumption without drying (this might occur, for example with a bale of rain-soaked marijuana or freshly harvested marijuana that had not been dried), an approximation of the weight of the marijuana without excess moisture content is to be used. *(Sec. 2D1.1, Application Note 1, as revised.)*

Seizure and Loss of Assets

If you are convicted, or in many cases merely arrested, for engaging in a marijuana crime, the government may try to take any and all property that has been used to "facilitate" your crime. This seizure is legal under various "forfeiture laws that have been enacted the last seven years. In California alone, more than $180,000,000 worth of assets have been seized under the state forfeiture law since it went into effect in 1989. In fact, you may have seen the advertisements for auctions at which drug dealers' cars, boats, and homes are sold.

There's no question that police officers are highly motivated to initiate forfeiture proceedings. In some states, law enforcement agencies are permitted to use seized assets and property to fund and implement future drug investigations. In fact, the federal government openly encourages forfeiture actions by pointing out to federal and state police agencies how seized property can benefit the agency. For example, one recent government manual on forfeiture published by the Department of Justice counseled:

> The seizure of a boat valued at six figures that was purchased as a result of illegal narcotics profiteering can certainly ease the strain of tight government budgets and increase the availability of "buy" or "flash" money . . . . Asset forfeiture can be a financial benefit to all levels of government if the illicit assets are converted to funds that benefit the law-enforcement community. *(US DOJ, Asset Forfeiture "Public Record and other information on Hidden Assets, 2nd in a series, p.1, reprinted January 1992.)*

In fact, in the fall of 1990, the Justice Department circulated a bulletin to federal prosecutors pleading with them to seize more property in order to meet budget projections. The memo urged, "Every effort must be made to increase forfeiture income during the remaining three months of 1990."

One of the most heinous abuses of the forfeiture laws occurred on October 2, 1992, when state and federal drug agents raided Donald Scott's 200 acre ranch in Malibu, California. Responding to his wife's screams when agents kicked in their front door, Mr. Scott grabbed his gun, ran to his wife's aid, and was shot twice in the chest by intruding agents. He died from his wounds.

The raiders, attempting to justify the raid, claimed it was based on an aerial observation of *Cannabis* plants growing on Mr. Scott's property. In fact, however, no plants were ever found, nor was any evidence seized suggesting that such plants ever existed. After a five month investigation, a 62 page report concluded that the raid "was motivated, at least in part, by a desire to seize and forfeit the ranch for the government." Or, as stated by the Ventura County District Attorney, the "primary purpose of the raid was a land grab by the Sheriff's department."

Usually the items that the government takes are sold at a public auction and the government keeps the money. In some states, if the police request it, the property (usually a car) is turned over to the law-enforcement agency that seized it and is used in undercover operations. Under both federal and state forfeiture laws, any items used to help grow, process, or transport marijuana are subject to forfeiture. In addition, any money furnished "in exchange for a controlled substance" or "traceable to such an exchange" is subject to forfeiture. Likewise, any property purchased with cash derived from marijuana sales is subject to seizure by the government.

In many states, *forfeiture proceedings can be initiated without any criminal conviction and even without any criminal charges being filed.* To make matters even worse, forfeiture proceedings are often considered civil rather than criminal.

Under the federal civil forfeiture laws, for example, the government takes legal action against your *property*, not you. Since you are not the defendant (your property is), your guilt or innocence on the criminal charge is often irrelevant. In fact, in approximately 80 percent of forfeiture cases, the property owners are never charged with any crime. Moreover, even if a person is found *not guilty* in a criminal case or if the charges are dropped, the government often still proceeds against his or her property under the civil forfeiture laws.

Additionally, because many forfeiture proceedings are labeled "civil" rather than "criminal," other constitutional protections that apply in criminal cases do not apply in forfeiture proceedings. For example, in most states, you have no right to legal counsel in forfeiture proceedings. (This means the government is not obligated to provide you with counsel if you are unable to afford one. You may, of course, hire your own attorney to represent you at such proceedings, and should do so if your finances allow.)

In the last few years there have been some big legal victories for citizens contesting federal forfeiture actions. Recently, the United States Supreme Court held that despite the federal government's machinations to the contrary, a seizure of a person's property under the federal civil forfeiture law can constitute "punishment," and hence a seizure that is greatly disproportionate to the crime can run afoul of the Eighth Amendment's bar against "excessive fines." *(Austin v. U.S. [1993] 113 S.Ct. 2801.)* In another recent case, the Ninth Circuit ruled that the Double Jeopardy Clause of the Fifth Amendment can bar a civil forfeiture of property if the defendant has already been prosecuted. In other words, if you are prosecuted for a marijuana crime, and then, later, *in an entirely separate proceeding*, the government seeks forfeiture of your property, you might be able to bar the forfeiture proceeding by arguing that it violates the Fifth Amendment's guarantee against being placed in double jeopardy. Unfortunately, the government can circumvent this ruling by bringing *both* the criminal action and the forfeiture action in the *same* proceeding. *(U.S. v. $405,089.23 U.S. Currency [9th Cir. 1994] 33 F.3d 1210.)*

The overall situation regarding forfeiture still heavily favors the government. With the exception of the victories just mentioned, both federal and the state courts regularly interpret forfeiture laws in favor of the government. For example, the courts in California have held that an illegal search and seizure (though it will cause the evidence seized to be excluded from *criminal* proceedings) will not protect the seized property from forfeiture.

Often, forfeiture proceedings move very fast, clearly to the detriment of the accused. In some states, once the prosecution gives notice that it is seeking to seize assets under the forfeiture laws, the property owner must file an answer within ten days. This is a very short amount of time in which to retain an attorney, especially if the property owner is in custody. The federal scheme is only slightly less lenient, allowing the owner twenty days to file a claim stating ownership of the seized property. Failure to file a timely response can result in the property's forfeiture by default.

In California, your car, boat, or plane is subject to forfeiture if it has been used to facilitate possession, sale, or cultivation of ten pounds or more of marijuana as measured by the marijuana's dry weight. California has a special exception for cars owned by married people. Under this exception, if one spouse uses the family vehicle to sell more than five pounds of marijuana, and the other spouse is innocent of any wrongdoing, the innocent spouse is permitted to keep the vehicle as long as it is not worth more than $10,000. If the vehicle is worth more than $10,000, the innocent spouse can still keep it, but must pay the state the amount in excess of $10,000.

As noted above, most states can also take any cash, checks, securities, or other things of value that were furnished or intended to be furnished by any person in exchange for marijuana. In other words, any money or property that the state can show was obtained by selling marijuana is subject to forfeiture. When determining whether cash should be forfeited, the courts will often employ a "net worth" analysis, where the government shows that the alleged marijuana dealer has substantial assets but no legitimate or declared source of income that could account for the his degree of wealth. The government's case is often supported by proof that the alleged dealer has not filed income tax returns in several years. With such a strategy, the government can often force the forfeiture of huge sums of money. Similarly, if the government can show (by a very low standard of proof) that drug money was used to purchase property such as cars or homes it can also seize such property.

In many states, the government need only show that the property was *linked* to a marijuana crime. To keep the property, the owner must prove that the property was not used or obtained in violation of the drug laws, or that it was so used or obtained without his or her knowledge or consent.

The government does not have to trace the proceeds to a particular marijuana transaction; it is enough if the proceeds can be linked to marijuana trafficking generally. Also, cars, homes, and other property acquired during or shortly after the period of the crime are presumed to be acquired with proceeds from the crime. The owner may rebut the presumption if he or she can prove that the property was acquired with legally obtained funds, rather than with "drug money."

Sometimes property is forfeited because of statements made by the defendant. For example in one recent Tennessee case, police officers discovered a well-tended crop of 52 *Cannabis* plants in John Hill's garden. In addition to punishing him under the criminal law, Tennessee also took his car because Mr. Hill allegedly made a statement to police admitting that he used the car to bring the *Cannabis* seeds to Nashville from California. In the court's words, "these seeds were turned into a thriving and potentially highly profitable marijuana crop." In other words, the car was used to facilitate the transportation of raw materials used to manufacture a controlled substance and hence subject to forfeiture. (*Hill v. Lawson [Tenn.App. 1992] 851 S.W.2d 822.*)

In some states, there are a few built-in exceptions that offer some protection against asset forfeiture. For example, in California, as mentioned above, a vehicle is subject to forfeiture only if it was used to facilitate a crime involving ten pounds or more of marijuana. In other words, at least under the California law, if a police officer finds a few joints in your car, you are not going to lose your car to the state. Federal law is much harsher. Under the federal scheme, the government can take your vehicle if *any* marijuana was found inside, or if the vehicle was used in any way to help commit a marijuana crime. For example, the government took Edna Salas' *1975 Mercedes 280S* after a DEA agent found four joints in the ashtray. The agent's affidavit stated:

> I personally searched said vehicle at said location on said date and in the ashtray, located in the area of a vehicle commonly referred to as the "dashboard," I found the partial remains of four (4) cigarette butts, which appeared, in my experience, to be Marihuana. I have been a Special Agent for the Drug Enforcement Administration for approximately eight (8) years (including its predecessor agencies) and I have spent one (1) year as a Criminal Investigator for the United States Bureau of Customs prior to that. I have seen and smelled Marihuana on hundreds of occasions and I am very familiar with its appearance and aroma.

The federal "zero tolerance" rule is abused by law enforcement. In July 1992 the police in Oakland, California, feeling too constrained by the state's ten-pound rule restricting automobile forfeitures, teamed up with federal DEA agents in a marijuana crackdown. In this sweep, the Oakland police cited 77 marijuana buyers and, using the DEA agent's authority under *federal law*, confiscated forty-three cars. At least one such seizure occurred after a ten-dollar marijuana deal! In a similar raid two months earlier, thirty-nine cars were seized. Eventually, all but three cars were returned after the owners paid an "assessment fee."

In addition to taking your cash and your car, the state and federal governments can take your home and real-estate. On a positive note, California revised its forfeiture laws in 1994 and, in doing so, removed all marijuana crimes as triggers for *real property* forfeiture. In other words, in California a person cannot lose his or her home to the government for growing *Cannabis* on the property. In contrast, the federal government can seize a home and real-estate if even a single *Cannabis* plant is found on the property. Under federal law even if the marijuana was solely for the person's own use and not for sale, it can form the basis for property forfeiture. The federal government took a man's vehicle after finding only "thirteen *grains* of marijuana" in the vehicle. Leonard Willis lost his Michigan home after officers found two *Cannabis* plants in an attic growroom.

If the federal government finds that you were growing *Cannabis* on your property, it can force you to give up the *entire* piece of property, not just the portion where the *Cannabis* was found growing. For example, in one federal case, a man was charged with possessing more than 700 *Cannabis* plants with intent to distribute them. The evidence was undisputed that all the plants were grown on a very small portion of land. Despite this fact however, a federal court ordered the forfeiture of the man's *entire 40-acre* parcel of land. In another case, the federal government successfully seized a man's condominium for selling $250 worth of cocaine on the premises.

Some people, after being arrested on a marijuana charge, try to shield their assets from possible forfeiture by transferring title to the property to a friendly innocent party. Suffice it to say that the government is not so easily tricked. To protect against such ploys most states have created "the doctrine of relation back." Under the relation-back doctrine, the title to property is judged at the time the property was used to commit the crime. Therefore, transferring title in property after an arrest does no good, because title has already vested in the government at the time the property was used to commit the crime.

In fact, many absolutely innocent people get caught up in this doctrine when they purchase a vehicle only to learn later, when the government takes it, that it was previously used in a drug deal. These people must then prove their own innocence, by showing that they had no knowledge that the vehicle was in any way related to illegal drugs. The attorney fees to handle such a matter often exceed the value of the car; so for practical reasons, many people do not contest the seizure, despite their innocence.

Forfeiture of Currency Found Near Marijuana

Under federal law and under many state laws, money that is found "in close proximity to forfeitable controlled substances" is itself forfeitable on the presumption that it was obtained from illegal drug transactions. This presumption places the burden on the money's owner to prove that money was legally acquired. It can be very difficult to rebut this presumption.

In one 1993 case in Missouri, Robert Meister forfeited $9,593.22 after police stopped his van for speeding and discovered a small amount of marijuana on Mr. Meister and his passenger. At the police station, Mr. Meister's van was inventoried, during which the police discovered a volleyball size bag of a substance resembling marijuana (but which was never proven to be marijuana); numerous books about marijuana growing; numerous patches depicting *Cannabis* leaves; a box containing 147 small wooden pipes, and several bags containing a substance labeled "herbal bliss."

Mr. Meister testified that he traveled the country selling marijuana novelty items. He testified that the nine thousand dollars was the legal proceeds from these sales, and was not related to the small amount of marijuana found in the van.

He produced invoices from some of his sales, but refused to provide tax information. The court held that Mr. Meister had not presented sufficient evidence to overcome the presumption that the money was actually drug proceeds. As a result, Mr. Meister lost over nine thousand dollars to the government. (*State v. Meister [Mo.App.W.D. 1993] 866 S.W.2d 485.*)

Likewise, in a recent Georgia case, police found a quarter ounce of marijuana in Butch Moore's pocket, along with $200 cash. The court upheld the forfeiture of the 200 dollars because of its close proximity to the marijuana. Additionally, because Mr. Moore was driving his 1987 Camero when he was arrested, the court ruled that the car was being used to facilitate what would have been a marijuana sale. As a result, Mr. Moore was forced to forfeit his Camero. All this for one-quarter ounce of marijuana! (*Moore v. State [Ga.App. 1993] 432 S.E.2d 597.*)

CHAPTER 2

CONSTITUTIONAL LAW BASICS

The right of the people to be secure in their persons, houses, papers, and effects, against unreasonable searches and seizures, shall not be violated. . . .

—Fourth Amendment

Y OUR RIGHT TO BE FREE from unreasonable governmental searches and seizures by government agents is guaranteed by the Fourth Amendment to the United States Constitution. There is no hard and fast definition of the word "search." However, generally speaking, a search occurs whenever a government agent (such as a police officer) accesses an area in which you have a reasonable expectation of privacy. In the words of the Supreme Court, a "search" occurs when an agent of the government "compromises the individual interest in privacy."

Most courts apply a two-part test to determine whether or not a police officer's action constituted a "search" under the Fourth Amendment. First, the court will examine whether the individual who claims he was "searched" has "exhibited an actual (subjective) expectation of privacy." The court will look to see what efforts the person took to preserve the privacy of an area or item. Second, the court will examine whether the person's expectation of privacy is "one that society is prepared to recognize as reasonable." In other words, even if a person has shown a subjective expectation of privacy, a court will *not* give Constitutional protection to the person's expectation if an average person would find the expectation unreasonable. More will be said about this in the chapters to come.

A "seizure" occurs when a government agent either takes something that you possess or in some way severely restrains your freedom or liberty. Using the words of the Supreme Court: a "seizure" occurs when an agent of the government "deprives the individual of dominion over his or her person or property." In other words, not only can an officer seize your property, but he can also seize you. As will be explained in the next chapter, the law calls an officer's seizure of a person either a "detention" or an "arrest."

The most important question to ask when analyzing the legality of a search or seizure is: "was it reasonable?" Reread the above clause from the Fourth Amendment, and you'll see that it protects you only against *unreasonable* searches and seizures. Therefore, only those searches that a court determines are *unreasonable* are unconstitutional.

The Exclusionary Rule

If a court decides that a police officer's search or seizure was illegal (i.e., unreasonable), then whatever the officer saw or seized will not be admissible in court as evidence. This is known as the "exclusionary rule," and its purpose is to deter police officers from making illegal searches and seizures. For example, if an officer illegally searches your car and finds 100 pounds of marijuana, the exclusionary rule will prevent the prosecutor from introducing the marijuana in court. Usually this will result in the dismissal of your case for lack of evidence, despite the fact that you were found with 100 pounds of marijuana. (Of course, you don't get the marijuana back!)

It may seem strange to let unquestionably guilty people go free, but this turns out to be the only effective way of forcing police officers to comply with the Fourth Amendment. In fact, even with the exclusionary rule, police officers are still motivated to conduct illegal searches and seizures because, although the evidence will be excluded from court, the police have confiscated the marijuana and forced the person to undergo the stress and embarrassment of being arrested and charged with a crime. Plus, the person will have to pay a high-priced lawyer to argue that the search and seizure was illegal and there's still no guarantee that the judge will agree.

One very important aspect of the exclusionary rule is that the rule applies only when a government agent's illegal search or seizure has violated *your* reasonable expectation of privacy. The United States Supreme Court has held that Fourth Amendment rights are of a personal nature. In other words, even if a police officer has made a clearly illegal search that turned up incriminating evidence against you, you will be unable to assert the exclusionary rule if the officer obtained the incriminating evidence against you by searching *another* person or *another* person's property in which you had no reasonable expectation of privacy. Simply put, *you* must have been the victim of the police officer's search in order for the exclusionary rule to apply. For example, police officers in Georgia caught Stephen Karlovich tending a *Cannabis* garden on some property owned by his friend Thomas. Stephen argued that the officers discovered the *Cannabis* garden, as well as his presence there, only by conducting an illegal search. However, the court refused to hear his argument, finding that the officers entered Thomas's property, not Stephen's. The court held that, even if the officers' search was illegal, *Stephen* had no Constitutional protection because *he* had no reasonable expectation of privacy on Thomas's land.

A counterpart to the exclusionary rule is what's known as the doctrine of the "fruit of the poisonous tree." Under this doctrine, not only is the evidence directly obtained by the illegal search or seizure excluded, but so is any evidence obtained indirectly as a result of such a search or seizure. For example, in one case the police illegally searched a man's home and found numerous *Cannabis* plants. After the search, the police arrested the man and took him to jail. At the jail, the man confessed that he had been growing and selling marijuana for the last three years, ever since losing his job.

The court that heard the man's case held that, because the *Cannabis* plants were obtained through an illegal search, they must be excluded from evidence. In addition, the court also excluded the man's subsequent confession, because it was obtained after the police made the illegal search and *as a result of the illegal search*. Consequently, although the police found *Cannabis* plants in the man's home and obtained the man's confession, after the exclusionary rule and the fruit-of-the-poisonous-tree doctrines were applied, no admissable evidence remained. Therefore, the man's case was dismissed for lack of evidence.

The "Good Faith Exception" to the Exclusionary Rule

As you are probably aware, anytime a court applies the exclusionary rule and suppresses illegally seized evidence, law enforcement agencies scream about how a guilty person was allowed to go free because of a "technicality." The popular press, probably for lack of understanding or perhaps to sensationalize a story, often reports on such cases by painting the officer's constitutional violation as a trivial technicality. Many people bristle at the idea of a guilty person going free because a police officer "made a mistake."

Perhaps motivated by such popular sentiment, judges have continually attempted to narrow the scope of the exclusionary rule, applying it to fewer and fewer violations by the police. The major limitation on the exclusionary rule was enunciated by the United States Supreme Court in 1984 when it created what is now known as "the good faith exception" to the exclusionary rule.

Under the good faith exception, the exclusionary rule will not be applied to an illegal search if the search was conducted under a valid warrant which is later determined to be invalid. In other words, if a police officer obtains a search warrant and conducts a search pursuant to that warrant, but the warrant is later judged to be invalid because it was not supported by probable cause, the exclusionary rule will not be applied and the seized evidence will be admitted despite the fact that it was seized under an unconstitutional warrant.

The good faith exception is arguably justifiable since the purpose of the exclusionary rule is to deter *police officers* from making unconstitutional searches. An officer who obtains a search warrant from a neutral judge and executes it within the bounds of the law was not doing anything wrong, even if the warrant is later determined to have been issued without sufficient probable cause. Consequently, judges reason that applying the exclusionary rule in such circumstances would be unfair to the police officer who conscientiously obtained a warrant he believed was valid.

The Supreme Court, made clear, however, that there are four instances in which a police officer's reliance on a valid search warrant does *not* support the good faith exception, and hence should still result in exclusion of the evidence:

(1) The judge that issued the warrant was biased in some way.
(2) The officer knowingly included false statements in the search warrant affidavit, or included statements with a reckless disregard for the truth.
(3) A reasonably well-trained officer would have known that the warrant was defective by its failure to specifically describe the place to be searched or the things to be seized.
(4) The warrant was based on an affidavit that was so defective that a reasonably well-trained officer would have known that it failed to state probable cause.

In any case involving one or more of the above four factors, the good faith exception should not apply since in those situations the officer is again at fault and should be punished in some way. As you can see, however, these four factors leave considerable leeway, which is often exploited by courts to uphold the validity of a questionable search. In all but the most extreme cases, therefore, courts will apply the good faith exception even if the warrant is later determined to be defective. In practice this means that if an officer obtains a search warrant, the exclusionary rule will seldom be applied, and hence, any evidence seized under the warrant will almost always make its way into court.

Outrageous Police Conduct Can Invalidate a Search

Occasionally, in their zeal to rid the world of *Cannabis* and incarcerate anyone favorably disposed to it, the police go too far. Outrageous police conduct can cause a court to invalidate an otherwise legal search and seizure.

In a recent New York case, for example, the DEA, as the result of a lawful wiretap, learned that Mr. Henry was about to make a drug delivery. They staked-out his house and saw him load a large cardboard box into the back of his vehicle and drive away. According to the court's opinion, the agents "followed him into the Bronx where they stopped him on the Henry Hudson parkway with machine guns and handguns drawn, despite no apparent reason to believe defendant was armed. Defendant was forcibly removed from his vehicle, handcuffed and told to lie face down on the ground. A search of the vehicle yielded a leather shoulder bag on the front seat, containing a small quantity of marijuana and $70,000 in cash in small denominations . . . . The cardboard box in the rear was found to contain ten plastic bags of marihuana, weighing approximately one pound each. All of these items were seized." Mr. Henry was subsequently convicted of possessing marijuana and sentenced to five years probation.

Mr. Henry's conviction was reversed on appeal. The court of appeal was appalled at the strong-arm methods used by the DEA, explaining that "the requirement that searches and seizures be reasonable limits the police use of unnecessarily frightening or offensive methods of investigation." Here, the DEA's use of machine guns unnecessarily and callously threatened Mr. Henry with the immediate use of deadly force. The court explained that, "the irresponsibly forceful nature of this stop and search, on a highway in full view of passing motorists, was anything but harmless. It presented the possibility of danger not only to this unarmed defendant, but also to innocent passersby.... The manner in which the stop and search were carried out is as much a part of that search as any other element. The overly intrusive nature of this law enforcement action requires us to suppress all the evidence so acquired." (*People v. Henry [1992] 591 NY.S.2d 1018.*)

Rights Depend on Who Conducts the Search

Constitutional rights provide protection only against actions by the *government* (federal or state) or its agents (the most obvious of which are police officers). There is no constitutional protection against unreasonable searches by *private* persons. This rule comes as a great surprise to many people without any legal training, and it is crucial to understand its effect.

Suppose a private citizen who is an anti-marijuana crusader suspects you of marijuana use. What if that person illegally breaks into your home, steals some of your marijuana, and gives it to the police? There are actual cases of this happening, and the answer is always the same. The marijuana turned over to the police will form the basis for a search warrant for your home. If a police officer's search under that warrant then turns up evidence of marijuana, you will be arrested despite the illegality of your neighbor's action. In addition, neither the exclusionary rule nor the fruit-of-the-poisonous-tree doctrine applies to searches or seizures by private people, and hence the marijuana removed by the thief will also be used against you in court. It does not matter that the person obtained the marijuana illegally by breaking into your home. (Of course, you can press criminal charges against your neighbor based on his illegal entry of your home, but that won't help you defend against the marijuana charge.)

Note, however, that the rule is different if the police arranged the break-in. In that case, a court would consider the private citizen an agent of the government; so the person's search of your home, and seizure of your marijuana, would be just as illegal as a police officer's. As a result, in such a situation the exclusionary rule would apply, and the marijuana found by the private person as well as the marijuana found during the execution of the search warrant would be excluded from evidence. Simply put, a private citizen who is working for the police *is* subject to the Fourth Amendment constraints and the exclusionary rule.

The Hotel-Maid Example

Bill was driving from Los Angeles to San Francisco but became tired as he approached Santa Barbara. Upon reaching Santa Barbara, Bill stopped and rented a motel room. Inside his room, Bill rolled a joint and smoked it while watching Dragnet. The next morning, Bill woke up and went out to get a bite to eat.

As Bill ate breakfast, he was unaware that a hotel maid was cleaning his room. The maid discovered Bill's personal stash of pot as well as the partially smoked joint. She rushed to the police with the marijuana, reporting that she found it while cleaning Bill's room. The police quickly obtained a search warrant and, upon searching Bill's room, discovered additional evidence that Bill was transporting marijuana. Bill was subsequently convicted of the crime of transporting marijuana.

In this example, the maid is not a government agent and hence is not limited by the Fourth Amendment. Therefore, even if she was in Bill's room without his permission, or digging through his belongings without his permission, her testimony on what she found in his room will be admissible in court. In this situation the exclusionary rule is inapplicable. Likewise, the search warrant is clearly valid, despite the fact it was based on the maid's theft of Bill's marijuana.

If Bill had been acting more cautiously and had understood the limits on the Fourth Amendment he would have removed all evidence of marijuana from his hotel room prior to leaving. Court cases indicate that the safest place for such items would have been in a closed opaque container locked in the trunk or glove box of his car.

Sending Marijuana Through Private Mail Carriers

Because the Fourth Amendment does not constrain searches by non-government agents, any packages sent through a private mail carrier, such as Federal Express or UPS, are subject to warrantless searches by the carrier's personnel, *for any or no reason at all*. In practice, private mail carriers have better things to do than dig through mail looking for drugs; therefore, such searches usually occur only when there is some indication that the package may contain drugs. In such cases, the carrier will usually notify the DEA or local law enforcement.

If a private carrier, like FedEx or UPS, notifies the DEA or a local police agency that they found a package believed to contain marijuana, the agency will send an agent to examine the package. There are many cases discussing the extent to which *the law-enforcement agent* can conduct a warrantless search of such a package. The rule that has evolved from these cases is that the law-enforcement agent must limit his warrantless search of the package to that already performed by the private carrier. The courts have reasoned that a person has no reasonable expectation of privacy in such a limited search, because the contents viewed by the private carrier are now public.

In the Supreme Court's words:

> Once frustration of the original expectation of privacy occurs,
> the Fourth Amendment does not prohibit governmental use of
> the now non-private information: this court has held repeatedly
> that the Fourth Amendment does not prohibit the obtaining of
> information revealed to a third party and conveyed by him to
> government authorities, even if the information is revealed on
> the assumption that it will be used only for a limited purpose
> and the confidence placed in a third party will not be betrayed.
> The Fourth Amendment is implicated only if the authorities
> use information with respect to which the expectation of
> privacy has not already been frustrated. *(US v. Jacobsen
> [1984] 466 US 109.)*

If the law-enforcement agent wants to go further than the search conducted by the private carrier, the agent must obtain a search warrant.

In a 1993 Georgia case, Ms. Hyatt was convicted of several marijuana offenses after Federal Express employees inspected two wooden crates and found that they contained marijuana. They called in DEA agents who made controlled deliveries of the crates, one of which was accepted by Ms. Hyatt.

In her appeal, Ms. Hyatt argued that the Federal Express employees violated the Fourth Amendment by searching the wooden crates without a warrant and without probable cause to believe that they contained contraband. However, applying the rule just discussed, the Georgia court of appeal rejected Ms. Hyatt's argument. The court explained:

> The Fourth Amendment did not apply due to the private
> character of the search of the crates. There was no evidence
> that the crates were opened through the intervention or direc-
> tion of law enforcement officers. Various law enforcement
> agencies became involved only after the corporate employees
> discovered the contraband and called an agent of the drug
> enforcement administration. The subsequent inspection of the
> contraband by law enforcement officers did not exceed the
> scope of the private search, and therefore did not amount to a
> violation of the Fourth Amendment. *(Hyatt v. State [GA.App.
> 1993] 436 S.E.2d 541.)*

State Constitutions vs. The Federal Constitution

Under our federalist system, there is a federal Constitution as well as fifty separate and distinct state Constitutions. State Constitutions may guarantee greater (but not less) individual liberties than those guaranteed by the federal Constitution. In fact, many state Supreme Courts have interpreted their state Constitutions to afford more expansive protection to the fundamental rights of their citizens particularly in the area of searches and seizures. A number of state Supreme Courts, for example, have held that a warrantless search of a citizen's garbage violates the *state* Constitution despite the fact that the United States Supreme Court has held that such searches do not violate the federal Constitution.

Double Jeopardy

Under the Double Jeopardy clause of the Fifth Amendment, the government is barred from bringing a second prosecution for the same offense following an earlier acquittal or conviction. As explained by the United States Supreme Court, "the basis of the Fifth Amendment protection against double jeopardy is that a person shall not be harassed by successive trials; that an accused shall not have to marshal the resources and energies necessary for his defense more than once for the same alleged criminal acts." *(Abate v. United States [1959] 359 US 187.)*

Under the Double Jeopardy clause, it is clear that the government is prevented from retrying a defendant after a jury has acquitted that defendant of the offense. In other words, if a defendant in a marijuana case wins at trial, by getting a jury to unanimously find him not guilty, the case is forever closed and the government is not permitted a second chance.

In many cases, however, the jury is unable to unanimously agree whether the defendant was guilty or not guilty. When one or more jurors cannot reach a decision as to guilt, the jury is said to be "hung." Because a "hung jury" is neither an acquittal nor a conviction, the Double Jeopardy clause does not bar a subsequent trial. Consequently, in any criminal case where the jury is unable to reach a unanimous decision, the government is free to prosecute the defendant again and again until a jury unanimously decides one way or the other.

A major exception to the double jeopardy rule is known as the doctrine of "separate sovereigns." Essentially, because of our federalist system, there are both federal laws and state laws. If a person commits a crime that violates only a state law, only the state can prosecute that person. If a person commits a crime that violates only a federal law, only the federal government can prosecute that person. It stands to follow that if a person commits a crime that violates *both* a state and federal law, *both* the state and federal government can prosecute that person in separate proceedings. Because each governmental power has an interest in enforcing its laws, the doctrine of separate sovereigns was created.

Under this doctrine, if you break a state law and a federal law in the *same* act, you can be prosecuted by either or *both* the state or federal government. *A win in either forum is no bar to a subsequent prosecution in the other*. The state and subsequent federal trials of the officers who beat Rodney King were a good example of this doctrine in action.

The Burden of Proof

Because of the severe consequences which can result from being convicted of a criminal offense, our legal system requires proof beyond a reasonable doubt in order to convict a person of a crime.

In theory, a judge or jury can convict a person of a marijuana crime only if it finds, beyond a reasonable doubt, that the person committed each and every element of the crime charged. (as discussed in Chapter One, all crimes are composed of "elements," and each element must be proven in order to find the defendant guilty of the crime.) In other words, if the judge or jury has any reasonable doubt concerning even one of the elements of the crime charged they cannot convict the defendant.

The definition of a "reasonable doubt" is explained in the instruction that the jury hears before it enters the jury room to decide upon its verdict. Unfortunately, for such an important principle, "reasonable doubt" is very poorly defined. In California, for example, the jury is instructed:

> A defendant in a criminal action is presumed to be innocent until the contrary is proved, and in case of a reasonable doubt whether his guilt is satisfactorily shown, he is entitled to a verdict of not guilty. This presumption places upon the people the burden of proving him guilty beyond a reasonable doubt.
>
> Reasonable doubt is defined as follows: it is not a mere possible doubt; because everything relating to human affairs, and depending on moral evidence, is open to some possible or imaginary doubt. It is that state of the case which, after the entire comparison and consideration of all the evidence, leaves the minds of the jurors in that condition that they cannot say they feel an abiding conviction, to a moral certainty, of the truth of the charge. *(CALJIC 2.90)*

The outcome in Dorothy Jackson's case is illustrative of the stringency of the "beyond a reasonable doubt" standard when properly applied. One day, Ms. Jackson was in her apartment when she heard a knock at her front door. Upon opening the door she was greeted by several police officers with a search warrant. Ms. Jackson, who happened to be carrying her purse at the time, stepped aside to allow the officers to enter. Then, without warning, she darted into her bathroom and locked the bathroom door.

One of the officers ran after her, pounded on the bathroom door and ordered her to open it. After a short hesitation, Ms. Jackson opened the door and was quickly handcuffed.

The officers searched her home pursuant to the search warrant but were unable to find any marijuana. However, as they searched the bathroom, one officer noticed that the bathtub appeared to have fresh footprints on its rim directly below an open window high on the wall. Suspecting that Ms. Jackson stood on the tub and tossed her marijuana out the window, the officer ran downstairs to see what he could find. Just as he suspected, among the debris below ms. Jackson's bathroom window he found a baggie containing marijuana. In addition, the baggie was dry whereas all the other debris in the area was wet from some earlier rains. All the evidence seemed to show that the marijuana had been tossed out of the bathroom window by Ms. Jackson.

When Ms. Jackson's case went to trial, her lawyer attempted to raise a reasonable doubt in the minds of the jury. He pointed out that as many as seven other apartments had windows located above the area where the marijuana-filled baggie was found. Additionally, he noted that it had not rained for two days, and hence, the baggie could have been deposited on the ground any time within the two days preceding ms. Jackson's arrest.

Although the jury rejected her lawyer's arguments and convicted ms. Jackson for possession of the marijuana, the conviction was reversed on appeal. The appellate court reversed her conviction after determining that, given the facts, it was impossible for a juror not to have a reasonable doubt that Ms. Jackson had possessed the marijuana. The officers never saw her with the baggie, and hence the jury could not possibly have found she actually possessed the baggie. Likewise, because the marijuana was not found inside her apartment, but rather outside, in a public place, the evidence was insufficient to prove that she exercised dominion and control over the marijuana. Therefore, the appellate court reversed Ms. Jackson's conviction, finding that a reasonable doubt did exist. *(People v. Jackson [1962] 178 N.E.2d 320.)*

The Jury's Power to Judge the Law

In a criminal case, the judge and jury have very separate and distinct roles. Once a trial in a marijuana case begins, it is the jury, not the judge, that holds the greatest power, and in whose hands a conviction will either stand or fall. Essentially, the judge's sole duties are to rule on the admissibility of evidence, and to instruct the jury on the laws relevant to the case. In contrast to the legal focus of the judge's role, the jury is charged with: (1) determining *the facts*, and then (2) applying those facts to the law as given to them by the judge. The above duties and responsibilities are spelled out to the jury at the beginning of every marijuana case. What the jury is not told (except in Indiana and Maryland), and in fact what is vehemently hidden from them, is the fact that they—the jury—have a long-standing and well established right to judge *the law* itself.

It is now fairly well-documented that in decades past government efforts at excessive social control via criminal laws were hampered by juries refusing to convict people charged under unjust criminal laws. For example, during the alcohol prohibition era in the 1920s and early 1930s, prosecutors had a very hard time gaining convictions for alcohol-related crimes because many jurors believed that alcohol prohibition was unjust and simply refused to convict those accused of alcohol trafficking. They judged the law itself, and found it unjust. In fact, the low rate of conviction was clearly a factor leading to the repeal of Prohibition. Similar circumstances helped end the fugitive slave law, when juries refused to convict people assisting runaway slaves.

The right of a jury to "nullify" a law is recognized in numerous court opinions. In fact, this power was itself purposefully created to give the *citizenry* the ability to combat tyranny by rejecting unconscionable laws similar to those currently outlawing marijuana. For example, the Fourth Circuit has written:

> If the jury feels the law is unjust, we recognize the undisputed power of the jury to acquit, even if its verdict is contrary to the law as given by a judge, and contrary to the evidence . . . . If the jury feels that the law under which the defendant is accused is unjust, or that exigent circumstances justified the actions of the accused, or for any reason which appeals to their logic or passion, the jury has the power to acquit, and the courts must abide by that decision. *(United States v. Moylan [4th Cir. 1969] 417 F.2d 1002.)*

Despite this concession, the Fourth Circuit has nevertheless concluded that the jury should *not* be told of its power to completely reject the law. To do so, said the court, "would be negating the rule of law in favor of the rule of lawlessness."

Therefore, if you are ever called as a juror in a marijuana case, you should know that you have a right to vote "not guilty" even if you believe the defendant committed the alleged marijuana crime. You can judge the law itself and refuse to lend your assistance to its implementation. As mentioned earlier, a single juror voting "not guilty" is all that is required for a hung jury. You cannot be punished for exercising this power and refusing to convict the defendant of a marijuana crime you believe is unjust. Remember, however, that although this right is well established, courts won't tell you about it. It is also considered misconduct for an attorney to bluntly inform the jurors of their power. Therefore, if you are the defendant in a marijuana case, all you can do is hope that someone on the jury knows of this power and has the courage to exercise his or her power.

A national organization known as the Fully Informed Jury Association is currently fighting for laws that would require judges to inform juries that they have the power to judge both the facts *and* the law. Tell your friends about their right to nullify laws as a jurors. If juries won't convict in marijuana cases, perhaps the anti-marijuana laws will go the way of Prohibition and the fugitive slave laws.

CHAPTER 3

GATHERING INFORMATION: BIG BROTHER IS WATCHING YOU

Thanks to technological progress, Big Brother can now be almost as omnipresent as God.
—A. Huxley, *Brave New World Revisited*

UNLIKE MOST OTHER CRIMES, marijuana crimes very seldom involve someone who could be considered a "victim." As a result, the police get very little information about marijuana offenses from alleged victims calling to report a crime. Rather, in most cases, the police must actively seek out information. There are numerous means by which law enforcement agencies gather information about marijuana growers, sellers, and users.

The Citizen Informer

Generally speaking, one of the best sources for information about marijuana crimes is the "citizen informer." This term refers to a supposedly disinterested person who is supposedly acting out of civic duty. In most crimes, the citizen informants are victims or witnesses who report the incident to the police. For example, a person who is robbed will call the police, report the robbery, describe the robber, and generally try to assist the police in catching the perpetrator. However, in marijuana crimes, citizen informers are often the concerned parents of a child who was sold or given marijuana or anti-marijuana crusaders who believe that marijuana use is evil or dangerous and that it is their civic duty to report any tips to the police. For example, the hotel maid in the last chapter was a citizen informer. There are many cases in which the citizen informer was a telephone repairman or a cable-television installer who notified the police after spotting evidence of a marijuana crime while inside a person's home. Similarly, a citizen informer could be your next door neighbor who smells marijuana emanating from your home.

Because citizen informers supposedly are not seeking personal gain from their tip, the Supreme Court has ruled that they are reliable unless there are circumstances indicating otherwise. This means that if a citizen informant calls the police and reports that she has seen evidence of a marijuana crime, the police may rely on that information without having to make any attempts to confirm it. How much reliability they can place on the tip depends on numerous factors most of which center around how the citizen says they obtained the information and the inherent reliability of information so obtained.

The Anonymous Citizen Informer

With the proliferation of programs like "Turn In Pushers" (T.I.P.) and Drug Abuse Resistance Education (D.A.R.E.), law enforcement agencies get a regular flow of anonymous telephone calls in which the unidentified caller tattles on a marijuana user, grower, or seller. Given the caller's refusal to identify himself or herself, such information is obviously suspect. It's quite possible, for instance, that the unidentified caller is making a false tip in order to get back at an enemy. Consequently, when police receive an anonymous report of a marijuana crime, they are required to perform some investigation before seeking a search warrant based on the tip.

In some cases, however, the courts have upheld search warrants based on anonymous tips when the police did very little to corroborate the caller's tip. For example in 1993 a federal court in Maine upheld the validity of a search warrant based on an anonymous tip that a man, referred to only as "John," was growing 40 *Cannabis* plants in his house. The tipster also stated that John's house "reeked" of marijuana, describing the house by noting that it had a new addition. Finally, the caller claimed that a search warrant had been previously executed at John's house and had resulted in the seizure of *Cannabis* plants, but that John had "beat the charge." Police officers verified that John had previously been the target of a search warrant that uncovered marijuana, and that his house had a new addition. They also discovered that power consumption records for John's home "revealed a pattern of usage consistent with indoor marijuana cultivation, with a dramatic drop in usage following the [earlier] search and substantial increases beginning in the fall of 1990." In upholding the validity of this search warrant the court explained that the police properly investigated and verified enough of the anonymous caller's statements and that the verification vouched for the reliability of the caller's allegations. *(U.S. v. Burke [1st Cir. 1993] 999 F.2d 59.)*

In contrast, in another 1993 case, this time in Kentucky, a detective with the Louisville Police Department of Narcotics received an anonymous telephone call from someone saying that he had been hired to do some work in a home and had observed a large stash of marijuana in the basement. The caller identified the home by its address. According to the affidavit for the ensuing search warrant, "when questioned about his knowledge of the smell and appearance of marijuana this person stated that in his younger days he had been a user of marijuana, but now that he was older with children he is very anti-drug." Before obtaining the search warrant, the detective staked out the home for about 2 hours but saw no signs of foot traffic in or out of the residence. Without any evidence corroborating the anonymous tip, a judge signed a search warrant for the home. Officers who subsequently executed the warrant seized over 300 pounds of marijuana from the basement.

The case against the man was dismissed because the search warrant affidavit failed to state probable cause that marijuana would be found in the man's home. The court explained that the officer's stakeout, other than confirming that the home appeared to have a basement, provided no evidence confirming the anonymous caller's accusations. The court explained that the caller was anonymous, and never gave the names of the people for whom he was supposedly working for. Also, the caller did not provide the dates upon which he saw the marijuana. For these reasons the court concluded that the search warrant was unconstitutional. As a result, the 300 pounds of marijuana were excluded from evidence, dissolving the government's case against the man for lack of evidence. (*U.S. v. Leake [CA 6 KY 1993] 998 F.2d* 1359.)

If an anonymous informer (or citizen informer) claims to have seen *Cannabis* plants on a suspect's property the police must present information showing that the tipster has the ability to identify *Cannabis* or marijuana. Since many anonymous tipsters aren't aware of this rule, they often fail to state the basis of their identification when they leave a message on a recorded tip line. In such cases, the police must themselves investigate the tip in an attempt to verify the tipster's identification of the supposed *Cannabis* plants. Failure to present such evidence in the application for the search warrant can make the search warrant invalid.

In one recent case in Idaho, for example, the police received an anonymous telephone call in which the caller reported seeing *Cannabis* plants growing in an outbuilding on the neighbor's property. The caller also said that the lights were always on in the outbuilding. The Idaho Supreme Court held that such information failed to establish probable cause supporting a search warrant for the building because the caller gave no information supporting his or her ability to identify *Cannabis* plants. The court noted that the search warrant might have been valid if the caller had given a description of the plant so that the magistrate could conclude that the plants were indeed *Cannabis*. Given the invalid warrant, all the evidence seized when it was executed was thrown out of court. (*State v. Josephson [Idaho 1993] 852 P.2d 1387.*)

The Confidential Informant

In 1692, the English parliament enacted the now infamous "Reward Statutes," promising cash rewards, known as "blood money certificates," to people providing the government with information leading to the conviction of criminals. The Reward Statutes were repealed in the mid-1750's after it was discovered that a group of career informants had framed absolutely innocent people (some of whom were executed!) in order to collect the cash rewards.

Despite such an opprobrious history, information supplied by paid confidential informants is regularly used by today's law enforcement agencies. There are often people who are working in concert to grow, harvest, transport, and sell marijuana. If a police officer can figure out a way to do it, he will try to use one such person to get incriminating information about one or all of the others. In other words, a confidential informant is someone, often part of formal or informal marijuana distributing chain, who trades information for personal gain. Confidential informants from the "criminal underworld" often have information that would be almost impossible for the police to obtain on their own.

Unlike the citizen informer, who acts out of a motive supposedly unrelated to personal gain, the confidential informant most often acts from a strong self-interest. These people are often paid money for their tips, or, just as commonly, are offered special deals on their own criminal cases in exchange for providing the police with incriminating information about someone else.

As we should have learned from the Reward Statutes of several centuries ago, the obvious problem with relying on the information supplied by confidential informants is that they may falsely accuse an innocent person in order to get whatever reward they are offered. The Supreme Court has therefore held that the police must try to verify the reliability and accuracy of information supplied by confidential informants. In other words, information supplied by a confidential informant is *not* presumed reliable. However, if an officer has used a particular informant in the past, and that informant has a record of providing accurate information, then the confidential informant will be presumed reliable just like a citizen informer.

Paid Confidential Informants and Conduct by the Government

Occasionlly, a specific operation or payment plan involving a confidential informer will strike a court as so outrageous as to violate due process. Reversals for outrageous governmental conduct in this context are very rare however. For example, courts have held that it was *not* outrageous conduct for the government to get an 18-year old drug rehabilitation patient to deal drugs, and it was also *not* outrageous for the government to purposefully introduce drugs into a prison in order to map the distribution network inside the prison.

What kind of government conduct with regard to paid informers is considered "outrageous?" Unfortunately, the term is not well-defined by the courts, which tend to describe the offending conduct vaguely as "fundamentally unfair," "shocking to the universal sense of justice," or "transgressing fundamental principles traditionally protected by our society."

The Ninth Circuit reversed the conviction of Bourne Thomas after finding that the DEA paid an informant in the case on a contingent basis and that the informant had played a central role in orchestrating the crime. Over the course of several months the informant had arranged to purchase drugs through the help of an initially reluctant Mr. Thomas. In fact, Mr. Thomas was not even going to make any money from the deal. The informant completely arranged the transaction and Mr. Thomas was arrested when it occurred. He was subsequently convicted and sentenced to 121 months in federal prison.

The Ninth Circuit found the government's conduct in employing the informant on a *contingent fee basis in a sting operation* to be so outrageous as to violate the Due Process Clause. For that reason, the court reversed Mr. Thomas's conviction. The Ninth Circuit pointed out that under the informant's agreement with the DEA, the amount of money he would be paid was dependent on several factors, including: (1) whether Mr. Thomas was convicted; (2) the amount of drugs involved, and; (3) the value of any assets that were seized. If no conviction resulted, the informant was to receive only *minimum wage* for his services. (In the course of the trial it was revealed that the informant had "earned" over $50,000 for his services.)

The Ninth Circuit was particularly upset that such a fee agreement was used in a sting operation of the kind employed against Mr. Thomas, explaining:

> The inherent danger of basing a paid informant's compensa-
> tion on the rate of conviction and the quantity of the drugs is
> exacerbated when the government engages in "sting opera-
> tions," which accord the government almost exclusive control
> over the information relating to the criminal activity. The
> danger is further exacerbated where the party with the financial
> incentive is the person orchestrating the crime. Unlike cases in
> which the paid informant merely provides information regard-
> ing ongoing criminal activities, in a "sting operation" of this
> kind the paid informant who structures the crime decides
> whether or not and at what time there will be witnesses present,
> which conversations will be recorded, whether to reveal any
> evidence of the defendant's reluctance to engage in the deal,
> and the like. Complete control over the "crime" makes "sting
> operations" an efficient law enforcement technique. However,
> this same feature creates enormous potential for abuse. When,
> as here, "sting operations" are combined with contingency fees
> designed to maximize the conviction rate and the amount of
> drugs, it is likely that this potential will become actual.

At a minimum, the Due Process Clause protects against the conviction of individuals on the basis of evidence that has such a high risk of being false. *(U.S. v. Thomas [9th Cir. 1994] 32 F.2d 418.)*

Controlled Buys

Rather than use an undercover police officer to purchase marijuana, law enforcement agencies often find it easier to use a paid informant to make a purchase. Such an informant is often a person who is already connected to the "marijuana underground," and who is quietly arrested one night. The prosecutor then "persuades" this person that he should help the officers in exchange for a dismissal of his charges or a lesser punishment than would ordinarily be expected. If the person agrees, the police have a multitude of options.

Often, informants are used to make "controlled buys" of marijuana. In the typical controlled buy, officers search the informant to ensure that he has no marijuana on him, and then give him some marked money. The informant is then instructed to go to his dealer and purchase as much marijuana as possible. Some officers usually park outside the suspect's home in an undercover car and observe the informant as he enters the seller's home. In high-risk buys (those involving a very large transaction or the possibility of violence), an undercover officer will often accompany the informant, posing as his friend. If the informant successfully completes a purchase, the police obtain a search warrant for the seller's home and raid it as soon as possible.

Undercover Cops and the Doctrine of "Misplaced Trust"

In addition to citizen informers and confidential informants, law-enforcement agencies collect information by conducting their own undercover operations. Undercover narcotics officers, commonly called "narcs," weasel their way into groups suspected of marijuana use, and attempt to gain information that will later be used in criminal prosecutions.

In order to facilitate the work of undercover police officers and confidential informants, the courts have developed what is known as the "doctrine of misplaced trust." Under this doctrine, there is no Fourth-Amendment protection when a person unwittingly invites an undercover officer or informant into his home under the mistaken belief that the person is really a fellow marijuana user, grower, or trafficker. As the Supreme Court puts it: "it is well settled that when an individual reveals private information to another, he assumes the risk that his confidant will reveal that information to the authorities, and if that occurs the Fourth Amendment does not prohibit the governmental use of that information." In other words, the courts universally conclude that individuals take the risk, in all their dealings, that their trust may be betrayed whenever they voluntarily speak with another person. Such rules not only debase individual liberties, but even more fundamentally undermine, in the words of Justice Harlan, a "sense of security in dealing with one another that is characteristic of individual relationships between citizens in a free society." *(US v. White [1970] 401 U.S. 745, dissenting opinion of J. Harlan.)*

In one case, Lewis invited a new friend into his home, not knowing that the person was an undercover federal narcotics agent. Lewis spoke freely with his new friend and even sold him marijuana on two occasions. When Lewis was arrested, he argued that the agent's actions were a violation of his right to privacy, and that he never knowingly consented to the agent's warrantless entry of his home.

The United States Supreme Court rejected Lewis' argument. The Court explained that whenever someone invites a guest into his home, he takes the risk that the guest will observe whatever is in plain view, and may divulge to the authorities what is seen. Likewise, the person has no assurances that the guest won't go out and repeat or report what was talked about inside. It makes no difference, says the Supreme Court, that the guest is really an undercover government agent.

As the Ninth Circuit stated, in a case where it upheld a federal agent's ploy of acting like a stranded motorist to gain invitation into a home:

> An officer may legitimately obtain an invitation into a home by misrepresenting his identity...if he is invited in he does not need a warrant, and, quite obviously, he does not need to announce his authority and purpose. Once inside the house, he cannot exceed the scope of his invitation by ransacking the house generally, but he may seize anything in plain view. *(U.S. v. Wright [8th Cir. 1981] 641 F.2d 602.)*

The cases indicate that police officers are happy to take advantage of any kindness commonly found among marijuana users. In fact, federal law enforcement agents are taught deceptive techniques for gaining entrance into homes by tricking the owner into consenting to the entry.

The *FBI Law Enforcement Bulletin* for January 1994 included an article on this very subject, bluntly titled "Obtaining Consent to Enter by Deception." In that article agents were taught numerous tricks including: "the Loyal Friend Deception" (where your friend, who is actually a police informant, gains entry by acting like he's your friend); "the Fellow Criminal Deception" (where a marijuana buyer, who is actually an undercover officer, knocks on your door and asks to come in so he can buy some marijuana); and "the Mundane or Ordinary Visitor Deception" (where a UPS delivery person, who is actually an undercover police officer, brings you a package and asks to come inside on the guise of receiving payment for a COD delivery).

After detailing these tricks, the article took special efforts to make clear that such techniques are especially helpful when there is not sufficient evidence against the person to establish probable cause for a warrant:

> Obtaining consent to enter through deception is an extremely
> useful law enforcement tool in certain circumstances, particu-
> larly when acquiring a search warrant is not possible because
> of insufficient facts for establishing probable cause.

What does this mean? It means that these deceptive techniques are employed in the very situations in which a court would ordinarily not permit a search! Needless to say, many innocent people must be subjected to such deceptions, never learning that their mundane visitor was actually an undercover government agent.

Another ploy is to pose as a stranded motorist who comes to your house asking if he can come in and use your phone. For example, in one 1993 case in Montana, the police received information from an informant that a man called "Cutter Bob" was growing *Cannabis* in his home. Several detectives drove out to "Bob's" home attempting to verify the information provided by the informant. They confirmed that the home matched the physical description given by the informant, but from outside they could detect no evidence of *Cannabis* cultivation. As explained by the court, the detectives used the following ruse to check their suspicions:

> At approximately 11:30 p.m., Detective Lenard [and two other
> officers] of the Gallatin County Drug Task Force drove back to
> the . . . area. Detective Lenard parked his car on Highway 191
> in a spot visible from the defendant's residence and left the
> emergency lights flashing. Wearing ski clothing and posing as
> a stranded motorist, Detective Lenard approached the resi-
> dence while the other two detectives waited out of sight in
> another vehicle.
>
> When defendant answered the door, Lenard told him that his
> car had broken down and asked the defendant if he could use
> his phone. The defendant led Lenard through an entryway and
> into a bedroom area in the main part of the residence . . . .
> Lenard testified that he . . . detected the odor of marijuana
> smoke in the air. *(State v. Holstine [Mont. 1993] 860 P.2d
> 110.)*

The court held that this ruse was perfectly legal under the doctrine of misplaced trust.

Direct Sales—Undercover Drug Agents—Entrapment

It is routine for narcotics officers to pose as a marijuana users seeking to purchase marijuana. Their hope is to make a hand-to-hand purchase from a marijuana seller. Often the seller is arrested immediately after such a transaction by a uniformed officer who appears out of nowhere. If the undercover officer has established himself in a particular area, the uniformed officer will also "arrest" the undercover officer so as not to blow his cover.

In some cases, however, an arrest is not made immediately after an undercover buy. Instead, an undercover officer might continue operating for many months compiling information about more and more people until the operation culminates with the coordinated arrests of all suspects on a single night. This technique is commonly used when a young-looking officer goes undercover in a school.

For obvious reasons it is very difficult to defend a marijuana case where the police have caught you in a direct sale to an undercover officer. Entrapment defenses are used very rarely, and are seldom successful. To argue entrapment, the defendant must admit he bought or sold marijuana, and for that reason alone, most defense attorneys use an entrapment defense only as a last resort. After admitting that the transaction occurred, the defense hinges on convincing a jury that the defendant was not "predisposed" to commit the crime. To win with an entrapment defense requires showing that the police practically forced the defendant to commit the crime.

There is no magic test to identify an undercover police officer. All states have laws that give police officers immunity from prosecution if they use drugs during an undercover operation. Therefore, the fact that someone smokes a joint with you does not prove he or she is not an undercover agent. For practical reasons, however, most undercover officers will not ingest true psychedelics such as LSD for fear that they might loose control of themselves and blow their cover. Also, any observations they might make while under the influence of a psychedelic are open to the possible attack that such observations were inaccurate or utter hallucinations.

Children as Informers

> *The children . . . were systematically turned against their parents and taught to spy on them and report their deviations. The family had become in effect an extension of the Thought Police. It was a device by means of which every one could be surrounded night and day by informers who knew him intimately.*
>
> —G. Orwell, *Nineteen Eighty-Four*

In Oceania of Orwell's *Nineteen Eighty-Four*, children educated by Big Brother were issued ear trumpets for listening through keyholes. In our country in 1994, the hysteria created by the government's "War on Drugs," has led to many elementary schools including antidrug "education programs" in their curriculum. The most popular program is "Drug Abuse Resistance Education," known more commonly by its acronym, DARE. Currently, the program is conducted in about a quarter of all elementary schools, reaching over five million students in school year 1991-1992.

The program instructors, who are almost all police officers (as of 1991 over 10,000 law enforcement officers had been trained to teach DARE), teach students that illegal drugs are very bad and that using them makes you a bad person. In addition to the general vilification of all illegal drugs, the officers ask students if they know anyone who uses drugs. Although the program states that no names are used in class discussions, DARE students have later confided in an officer that their parents or siblings smoke marijuana. For example, in one case in Colorado, a ten-year-old boy called the police to report that his parents smoked marijuana. He identified himself as "a DARE kid."

In another case, Mary, a fifth-grader in Maine, visited the police station following a DARE class and informed them that she knew two people who smoked marijuana: her parents. The police questioned Mary for nearly an hour, and then used her information to obtain a search warrant for her parents' home. The search uncovered some *Cannabis* plants growing in her parents' bedroom. As a result, Mary's parents were arrested and subsequently convicted of growing marijuana. Mary has required extensive psychological counseling for feelings of guilt and betrayal.

Mail Orders as Evidence

Many people wonder if it is risky to order equipment from companies advertising in magazines oriented toward marijuana users. Do law enforcement agencies monitor these companies? The details of just how much attention these companies draw from the DEA and other law enforcement agencies is shrouded in secrecy. What is known *for sure*, however, is that numerous people have been arrested and convicted based in part on their interaction with companies advertising in drug-oriented magazines.

It is known that in 1989 the DEA subpoenaed the records of companies that advertised hydroponic growing equipment or marijuana-seed catalogs in *High Times* magazine. Once the DEA obtained this information, they forwarded it to local law enforcement agencies across the country.

In one case, the DEA informed the Missouri State Highway Patrol that Mike had received two shipments of merchandise from Superior Growers Supply, Inc. The state police officer who was given the information drove by Mike's home and verified his address as the one receiving the two shipments. The officer also noticed that the windows of Mike's home were covered with blankets. The officer contacted the electric company and learned that Mike's home used almost four times more electricity than homes of similar size in his neighborhood.

With this information, the officer prepared an affidavit for a search warrant to search Mike's house for marijuana. The officer's affidavit stated:

> Superior Growers Supply, Inc., is a company who sells indoor hydrophonic [sic] growing equipment and grow lights. They advertise in *High Times* magazine, a magazine that specializes in marijuana-growing products and technology, and promotes growing of marijuana and concealment from law enforcement as well as the legalization of marijuana.

> As a law-enforcement officer trained in indoor marijuana-growing operations, I know that indoor-growing operations use large amounts of electricity to operate indoor grow lights and hydrophonic [sic] grow equipment. I also know that blankets are often used to conceal grow lights that are operated 24 hours a day and to obstruct the view of outsiders. The information obtained from the Drug Enforcement Administration identifying individuals who have placed orders with companies such as Superior Growers Supply, Inc. has resulted in indoor-growing operations being located in eight of eight cases that I am aware of.

Based on the above information, derived originally from the subpoenaed records of *High Times* advertisers, a judge issued a search warrant for Mike's home. The search uncovered an indoor-growing operation, and Mike was arrested and convicted.

There are very recent cases showing that the DEA still keeps an eye on people receiving shipments from such companies. In 1993, for example, the Third Circuit upheld the conviction of Tab Deaner for possession with intent to manufacture marijuana in violation of federal law. The following information was revealed in the court's opinion:

> Deaner became a suspect after the DEA learned that he had made mail order purchases of 244 pounds of supplies from Wormsway Organic Indoor/Outdoor Garden Supply ("Wormsway") between May 1987 and April 1991. Andrasi [the investigating DEA agent] related in the affidavit that he learned "[t]hrough additional intelligence information" that Wormsway was a supplier of cultivation equipment seized in various indoor marijuana cultivation operations, and that Wormsway was an advertiser in *High Times Magazine*, a publication devoted to promoting the growth and use of mari-

juana . . . . Andrasi cited a copy of an affidavit written by another DEA special agent as the source of his knowledge. That affidavit had been used to obtain a search warrant for Wormsway in October 1989. Andrasi also stated that undercover agents had discussed marijuana cultivation with Wormsway's owner and at least one of its employees "on numerous occasions," . . . and that the agents had purchased equipment from Wormsway after telling its owner that the purchase would be entirely used in marijuana cultivation.

The affidavit went on to say:

> [Andrasi] reviewed UPS shipping records . . . and they indicated that Deaner had received five packages from Wormsway at regular intervals [over an eight month period] . . . each weighing two pounds. Because he knew that marijuana growers must use a large amount of fertilizer over a long period of time, Andrasi said this regular flow of packages from Wormsway supported his belief that Deaner was cultivating marijuana. *(US v. Deaner [3rd Cir. 1993] 1 F.3d 192)*

In another case in 1993, an opinion from the Supreme Judicial Court of Maine revealed that Maine's Bureau of Intergovernmental Drug Enforcement "learned from the federal Drug Enforcement Administration (DEA) that a confidential source of information had supplied information of suspected shipments of hydroponic growing equipment used for indoor marijuana cultivation and marijuana seeds. Information from this source has led to dozens of arrests of indoor growers of marijuana." *(State v. Diamond [Me. 1993] 628 A.2d 1032.)*

Likewise in a recent case from the Fifth Circuit, the DEA focused on Brian McKeever after "McKeever received a shipment of merchandise from Dansco, an outfit engaged in the sale of equipment for use in Hydroponic gardening, and which advertised in *High Times*, a magazine that promotes the cultivation and use of marijuana." *(US v. McKeever [5th Cir. 1993] 5 F.3d 863.)*

Lastly, in a 1994 case, DEA agents and St. Louis, Missouri police began investigating Joseph Pinson after learning that he "received three United Parcel Service packages from companies that were known suppliers of indoor hydroponic growing equipment. These companies were also known to advertise is *High Times* magazine, a publication that promotes the cultivation and use of marijuana." Mr. Pinson was subsequently convicted of manufacturing marijuana and sentenced to the federal five year mandatory minimum. *(US v. Pinson [8th Cir. 1994] 24 F.3d 1056.)*

Garbage as Evidence

The various items you discard into your garbage actually provide a detailed record of your life. Your garbage contains evidence of your most private activities, including what you eat, what you purchase, where you shop, whether you have sex, and of course, whether you grow or even smoke marijuana.

In fact, one recent federal government publication gives the following advice to drug enforcement agents attempting to find hidden assets that might be forfeitable:

> In addition to the analysis of mail and telephone records . . . the legal pick-up and careful analysis of your target's trash, at either their residences or known businesses, should never be overlooked as a potentially important . . . source of intelligence. It must be stressed, however, that this must be accomplished in a totally legal manner to avoid tainting the evidence.

> If you are legally able to secure your target's trash, you may well obtain leads and information . . . . In addition, you may find notes written by your target regarding his involvement in some previously undisclosed business or investment. *(US DOJ, Asset Forfeiture, Public Record and Other Information on Hidden Assets, 2nd in a series, reprinted January 1992, pp. 3-4.)*

You might think that, given the clearly personal nature of garbage, the Supreme Court would have decided that a search warrant is required for government agents to search your garbage. However, the sad truth is that the Court has decided just the opposite. In a relatively recent case, the Court held that any garbage that a person places on the curb for pickup by his garbage collector can be seized and searched by the police without a warrant! In fact, the police do not even have to have a reasonable suspicion that you're involved in criminal activity before they seize your curb-side garbage. Rather, under the Supreme Court's opinion, a law-enforcement agent can snoop through your curb-side garbage for any reason whatsoever.

In the case that gave rise to this Supreme Court decision, a police officer received a tip from an informer that Billy Greenwood was trafficking in marijuana and other drugs. The officer investigating the tip drove by Billy's house and observed Billy's garbage on the curb in front of his house, ready for pickup. The officer suspected that Billy's garbage might contain evidence that would verify the informer's information. However, not wanting to tip off Billy by digging through the garbage himself, the officer contacted Billy's garbage collector, and requested that Billy's garbage be kept separate from the other garbage and turned over to the police. The garbage collector followed the officer's order, and upon receiving Billy's bags of garbage, the officer searched through them without first obtaining a search warrant.

By sorting through Billy's garbage, the officer found evidence that Billy was using drugs. This information was used to obtain a search warrant for Billy's home. When the police executed the search warrant, they discovered some hashish in Billy's home.

At the trial, Billy's attorney argued that the officer's initial warrantless search of his client's garbage was unlawful under the United States Constitution. The attorney argued that Billy had placed his garbage in a non-see-through bag, and that he therefore had a reasonable expectation that the contents would remain private. Therefore, his attorney argued, the Fourth Amendment protected Billy's garbage from a warrantless governmental search or seizure.

The Supreme Court disagreed. The Court explained that when Billy placed his garbage bags on the public curb for the garbage collector to take, he had no reasonable expectation that the contents would remain private. The Court reasoned that common experience indicates that plastic bags filled with garbage and left on the street for pickup are often torn open by dogs and their contents thereby disclosed to everyone. Likewise, such garbage is often snooped through by children and scavengers. In addition, the Court noted that Billy placed his garbage on the curb for the very purpose of turning it over to someone else. For these reasons, the Court concluded that a person has no reasonable expectation of privacy in the contents of garbage placed outside for the garbage collector. The Court concluded that the warrantless seizure and search of Billy's garbage was legal. *(California v. Greenwood [1988] 486 US 35.)*

Fortunately, some state Supreme Courts have decided that their state constitutions protect garbage placed on the curb for pickup even though the federal constitution may not. The Supreme Courts of New Jersey and of Washington have interpreted their own state constitutions as giving greater protection than does the federal constitution and an appellate court in Indiana made the same ruling under that state's constitution. In these and perhaps other states, police officers must obtain a search warrant before searching or seizing garbage.

Note, however, that because the protection in these states stems from the *state* constitution, a police officer's warrantless search of your garbage will be excluded only if you are prosecuted in *state* court. If the federal government chooses to prosecute, it is the *federal* constitution that will control the case rather than the state constitution. In that situation, even the state police officer's warrantless search of your garbage would be deemed legal, as in Billy's case above, and the evidence used against you in the *federal* prosecution.

A garbage search was instrumental in leading to the arrest and federal conviction of Tab Deaner (also discussed in the section on mail-orders), whom agents suspected was growing *Cannabis* indoors. During their investigation of Mr. Deaner on two separate occasions, a DEA special agent "examined the household refuse" of Mr. Deaner. The agent culled through Mr. Deaner's trash and located "marijuana stems and leaves mixed with soil on both occasions." This debris was reportedly "very fresh and green." The search of Mr. Deaner's garbage also uncovered several halves of one-gallon plastic jugs, which the DEA Special Agent claimed were often used by *Cannabis* producers for germination, and a Wormsway receipt for the purchase of fertilizer. *(US v. Deaner [3rd Cir. 1993] 1 F.3d 192.)*

A recent case in Idaho teaches that even if a garbage search is ruled constitutional, it might not provide sufficient evidence to establish probable cause that marijuana is *currently* within the suspect's home. The police in the case conducted a warrantless search of Terrance Josephson's garbage and found "two marijuana cigarette butts, an empty pack of *Zig-Zag* rolling papers, a bag apparently containing marijuana residue, and five plant stems ranging in length from one and one-half inches to two and one-half inches which field-tested positive for marijuana." Based on these discoveries, they obtained a search warrant for Mr. Josephson's home.

The Idaho Supreme Court, without determining whether the warrantless garbage search was constitutional under the Idaho constitution, ruled that even if the warrantless search was constitutional, it failed to provide probable cause that marijuana would be found in Mr. Josephson's home. The court reasoned that although the items found discarded in the garbage were "indicative of a conclusion that marijuana was at some point used at Josephson's residence and the refuse from such use discarded," the items, without more evidence of *current use* by Josephson, failed to support a conclusion that more marijuana remained in Josephson's home or that there was a grow operation maintained at his residence. Consequently, the court held that the search warrant was not based on probable cause and that all evidence seized as a consequence of the invalid warrant be excluded from court. *(State v. Josephson [Idaho 1993] 852 P.2d 1387.)*

Electric Bill as Evidence

In many cases, police officers investigating a suspected *Cannabis* grower obtain the suspect's electricity consumption records and examine them for any indication of a sharp rise which might suggest the use of high-intensity grow lights or other electrical equipment consistent with an indoor *Cannabis* growing operation. Courts have generally made clear that high electrical consumption is not by itself adequate to establish probable cause that the electricity user is growing *Cannabis*. However, as an Oregon court put it, "while high power usage is not alone sufficient to establish probable cause, it is an important factor to consider." *(State v. Russell [Or. App. 1993] 857 P.2d 220.)*

In a case decided by the Montana Supreme Court in 1993, the court upheld a man's possession conviction after police searched his home under a search warrant, and found marijuana as well as growing equipment. The search warrant was based in part on the man's "cyclic pattern of electric use...consistent with that commonly seen with indoor marijuana grow operations." The affidavit noted that the man's electrical consumption would jump from as low as 430 kilowatts to almost 1200 kilowatts, and was often much higher in the summer than in the winter time, contrary to the normal electric bill in Montana. *(State v. Mosley [Mont. 1993] 860 P.2d 69.)*

In one recent federal case from the Third Circuit, police were tipped off by the electric company that there had been "an abnormal consumption of electricity" at a farm in rural Pennsylvania. The electric company also informed the police that the doors and windows of the farm house were covered with dark plastic. Because the electric bill had not been paid on time, the company cut off service. A Pennsylvania Trooper accompanied the electric company employee to the farm after the resident paid the bill and requested the resumption of power. Testimony during the trial revealed that the trooper "intended to disguise himself as another utility company employee, if necessary." The electric company's information subsequently led to the seizure of over 900 *Cannabis* plants from the property and a 78 month sentence in federal prison for the grower. *(US v. Benish [3rd Cir. 1993] 5 F.3d 20.)*

Thermal Imaging Devices & Forward Looking Infrared Devices

The array of high-tech devices used by law enforcement agencies to fight the War on Drugs is frightening. Even local agencies now have equipment that allows them to see and hear through walls and locate items in almost complete darkness. One such device, known as a Thermal Imaging Device (TID) is essentially a temperature sensitive telescope. Viewed through a TID, relatively colder objects appear darker, and relatively warmer objects appear redder. Officers can use this device to spot a human being hiding in a field at night because his body temperature is warmer than the surroundings. It should be no surprise that such a device is quite capable of detecting a 1000 watt halide light hanging above someone's indoor garden.

A police officer's use of high-tech devices like TID's and similar functioning Forward Looking Infrared Scopes (FLIR's) raises numerous constitutional issues. Does an officer conduct a "search" by pointing such a device at a home? If so, does such a search require a search warrant? The use of these devices also raises questions regarding the accuracy and reliability of the evidence so obtained. The courts, which have examined these issues, have reached different conclusions.

In 1991, a federal district Court in Hawaii held that it did not constitute a "search" for officers to aim an FLIR at the defendant's home from a helicopter hovering 1200 to 1500 feet above the home. The court based its decision, in large part, on the manner in which an FLIR obtains information:

> [An FLIR is] a passive, non-intrusive instrument which detects differences in temperature on the surface of objects being

observed. It does not send any beams or rays into the area on which it is fixed or in any way penetrate structures within that area . . . [t]he instrument's sole function is to detect differences in surface temperatures of objects. Its being directed at objects in the early morning or evening, without direct sunlight present, shows man-made heat sources on those objects as shading from a white color for intense heat to shades of gray for cooler temperatures on the same objects.

The court pointed out that the homeowner used exhaust fans to vent heat from ten one-thousand watt lights. The court termed this "heat waste," and "abandoned heat," and compared such heat waste to curb-side garbage that the Supreme Court had decided can be searched without a warrant. In other words, the court reasoned that when the defendant fanned his heat waste outside into a public area, he relinquished any reasonable expectation of privacy with regard to it. It was, said the court, equivalent to placing garbage on the street for pickup.

Based on this reasoning, the court ruled that using an FLIR to detect the heat waste was not a "search" within the scope of the Fourth Amendment, concluding that an officer can use an FLIR any time and for any reason without first having to obtain a search warrant. (*U.S v. Penny-Feeney [D. HW 1991] 773 F.Supp 220, affirmed 984 F.2d 1053.*)

The Eighth Circuit, citing the above case, has likewise analogized the FLIR to a garbage search as well as to a dog sniff:

> . . . The use of the FLIR device is analogous to the detection of odors emanating from luggage or the search of garbage left outside for collection. Any subjective expectation of privacy [the defendant] may have had in the heat radiating from his house is not one that society is prepared to recognize as "reasonable." The detection of the heat waste was not an intrusion into the home; no intimate details of the home were observed, and there was no intrusion upon the privacy of the individuals within. None of the interests which form the basis for the need for protection of a residence, namely the intimacy, personal autonomy and privacy associated with a home, are threatened by thermal imagery. (*US v. Pinson [8th Cir. 1994] 24 F.3d 1056.*)

The Washington Supreme Court has ruled the opposite way, finding it a violation of the state's constitution to use a TID without a warrant. In the Washington case, the police received an anonymous written note claiming that Robert Young was operating "a big marijuana grow" in his home. The officers confirmed that Mr. Young lived at the address stated in the note and noticed that his basement windows were "consistently covered." They also obtained the power consumption records for his home for the previous six years and found that his electrical consumption had recently jumped to an abnormally high level. Based on this information, a group of officers and a DEA Special Agent drove by Young's home, parked on the street, and pointed their infrared thermal detection device at Young's home, detecting "abnormal heating patterns."

The officers then used the TID to check the heating patterns of other homes in the neighborhood. When these patterns were compared to the patterns detected from Mr. Young's home, the officers concluded that his pattern was unique and indicated (along with the other circumstantial evidence) that he was indeed growing *Cannabis* inside his home.

Based on an affidavit reciting the above facts, the officers obtained a search warrant, executed it, and seized a quantity of marijuana from Mr. Young's home. The case went all the way to the Washington Supreme Court, which ruled that "the infrared surveillance not only violated the defendant's private affairs, but also constituted a violation of the Washington State Constitution's protection against warrantless invasion of his home." While the court rested its opinion on the state constitution, it also ruled that the search also violated the Fourth Amendment. Consequently, the court excluded the illegally seized evidence and reversed Mr. Young's conviction.

In reaching its decision that the warrantless use of the TID was unlawful, the court made several important points that are worth quoting at length. First, with regard to whether the use of such a device is a "search," the court pointed out "as a general proposition, it is fair to say that when a law enforcement officer is able to detect something by utilization of one or more of his senses while lawfully present at the vantage point where those senses are used, that detection does not constitute a 'search.'" In the case of a police officer's use of a TID, however, the situation is much different.

> In this case, the police were positioned on the street, which is a lawful, non-intrusive vantage point. Therefore, the question is one of the intrusiveness of the means used and the nature of the property observed. The police used an infrared thermal detection device to detect heat distribution patterns undetectable by the naked eye or other senses. With this device the officer was able to, in effect, "see through the walls" of the home. The device goes well beyond an enhancement of natural senses. In addition, the nighttime infrared surveillance enabled the officers to conduct their surveillance without Mr. Young's knowledge. The infrared device thus represents a particularly intrusive means of observation that exceeds our established surveillance limits.

The nature of the property viewed was also a factor in finding that the surveillance unconstitutionally intruded on Mr. Young's private affairs. The infrared device was targeted at the outside of the home but allowed the officers to see more than what Mr. Young left exposed to public view. The device allowed the officers to draw specific inferences about the inside of the house:

> When directed at a home, the infrared device allows the officer to determine which particular rooms a homeowner is heating, and thus using, at night. This information may reflect a homeowner's financial inability to heat the entire home, the existence and location of energy consuming and heat producing appliances, and possibly even the number of people who may be staying at the residence on a given night. The device discloses information about activities occurring within the confines of the home, and which a person is entitled to keep from disclosing absent a warrant. Thus, this information falls within the "private affairs" language of [the Washington constitution].

The court was also outraged by the officers' conduct in pointing the TID at neighboring houses and recording the heating patterns of those homes:

> It is especially troubling that the police conducted thermal investigations not only on the defendant's home, but on the homes of his neighbors as well . . . There is no indication these neighbors were suspected of any criminal activity whatsoever. If we were to hold the use of the device does not constitute a search, no limitation would be placed on the government's ability to use the device on *any* private residence, on *any* particular night, even if no criminal activity is suspected. Such police activity is constitutionally offensive.

> Such unrestricted, sense-enhanced observations present a dangerous amount of police discretion. This kind of surveillance avoids the protection of a warrant issued upon probable cause by a neutral magistrate. Not only does this practice eviscerate the traditional requirement that police identify a particular suspect prior to initiating a search, but it also facilitates clandestine investigations by the police force, which are not subject to the traditional restraint of public accountability . . . . Such secret surveillance may not only chill free expression, but also may encourage arbitrary and inappropriate police conduct.

Finally, the court examined the validity of the argument that heat waste was analogous to garbage placed on the curb. The court rejected the validity of this analogy, explaining:

. . . It is difficult to say one voluntarily vents heat waste in the same way that one disposes of garbage. Heat, unlike garbage, automatically leaves a person's home without any deliberate participation by the homeowner. Even if some heat is vented to the outside, . . . the device detects all heat leaving the home, not just the heat directed out through the vent. Moreover, the [United States Supreme Court] also noted that one can avoid the risk by not placing private information in the garbage. On the other hand, the only way for a person to avoid the risk of exposure in this case would be to turn off all heat sources in the home, even in sub-zero temperatures. In addition, one could not stand near an open window or any part of the home constructed of material such as plywood because the device is capable of revealing the presence of human forms in these circumstances. *(State v. Young [WA 1994] 867 P.2d 593.)*

While courts remain divided on the constitutionality of warrantless FLIR and TID scans, the most recent cases seem to indicate a trend toward finding such police methods unlawful. For example, in addition to the Washington case just discussed, a federal district court in Texas, rejecting arguments making comparisons to garbage left on the curb as well as to dog sniffs, recently held that an FLIR scan is a search that is unlawful unless authorized by a search warrant. With regard to the dog sniff analogy, the court commented:

The comparison of dog sniffs and FLIRs fails on two levels. First the thermal imager cannot distinguish between "contraband heat," and "legal heat," so that the information garnered from such a technique is less limited, and thus results in more intrusion than a dog sniff. Second, a dog's sense of smell, while more acute than a human's, does not compare to a technology that can turn minute gradations in temperature into video tapes from 1500 feet away. *(U.S. v. Ishmael [E.D. Tex. 1994] 843 F.Supp. 205.)*

The DEA's NADDIS Database

The DEA maintains the Narcotic and Dangerous Drug Information System (NADDIS) which is a computerized compilation of the DEA's information on known and suspected drug traffickers. The government attempts to keep the details of the NADDIS system secret. Secondary literature depicts NADDIS as a disordered, unselective repository of unsubstantiated and often dated allegations. It's difficult to get much reliable information about the NADDIS database, but one recent case noted that in the auspicious year of 1984, the NADDIS database contained 1.5 million names obtained from debriefings of informants and suspects and from surveillance and intelligence reports.

At least one court (the Seventh Circuit) has ruled that an entry in the NADDIS system does not it itself provide probable cause to believe the person is a drug trafficker. *(US v. Ornelas-Ledesma [7th Cir. 1994] 16 F.3d 714; see also UPI Release, "VIP Names in Drug Agency's Computer Files," July 3, 1984; Vanessa Jo Grimm, "Behemoth DEA Database Tracks Drug Smugglers," Government Computer News, July 8, 1991, p. 85.)*

CHAPTER 4

ENCOUNTERS WITH POLICE

THE UNITED STATES SUPREME COURT, as well as all the state courts, have held that the reasonableness and hence the legality of an encounter between a police officer and a citizen must be judged by examining all the circumstances surrounding the encounter. Generally speaking, all encounters with police officers can be placed in one of three categories: (1)contact, (2) detention, or (3) arrest. Your legal rights during an encounter with a police officer will depend on how the encounter is categorized by a court.

Contact

The first level of many encounters with police is known as a "contact." A contact occurs when a police officer attempts to engage you in conversation. For example, if an officer asks you for directions, or asks you if you saw something or someone, he is merely "contacting" you. The essential characteristic of a contact is that you remain free to leave at all times. Because you are always free to leave, a contact is not considered a seizure. Since it is not a seizure, and obviously is not a search, the Fourth Amendment does not apply; therefore a police officer is free to contact a person for *any* reason. He does not need even a reasonable suspicion that the person is engaged in criminal activity.

During a contact with a police officer, you are free to behave as you would with any other citizen. You need not identify yourself. You may answer the officer's questions or ignore him and walk away. The United States Supreme Court has made this very clear, stating:

> Law-enforcement officers do not violate the Fourth Amendment by merely approaching an individual on the street or in some other public place, by asking him if he is willing to answer some questions, by putting questions to him if the person is willing to listen, or by offering as evidence in a criminal prosecution his voluntary answers to such questions. . . . The person approached, however, need not answer any question put to him; indeed, he may decline to listen to the

questions at all and may go on his way. . . . He may not be detained even momentarily without reasonable, objective grounds for doing so; and his refusal to listen or answer does not, without more, furnish those grounds. *(Florida v. Royer [1982] 460 U.S. 491.)*

Often, an officer will have a "hunch" that a person is "up to something," and hope that by talking to the person he might detect some concrete evidence of a crime, such as possession of marijuana. This commonly occurs in airports when drug-enforcement agents think a person may be transporting drugs, but have no real evidence. In such situations, the agents will often contact the person and inform him that they are conducting a narcotics investigation and would like to talk to him. In such a pressure-packed situation, many people (often those who actually *are* carrying drugs) foolishly agree to speak with the agents, perhaps believing that it would be more suspicious to decline to speak. These conversations often give the agent additional evidence that the person is in possession of drugs, leading to the person's arrest. In addition, if the person is prosecuted, any statements he made during the contact will be used against him.

Therefore, generally speaking, the cases teach that people who use marijuana should be on their guard whenever approached by a police officer interested in engaging in small talk. Numerous arrests make abundantly clear that, in the event of a contact, a person in possession of marijuana is usually well-advised to tell the officer that he or she is late for an appointment and then continue on his or her way. As will be explained in the next section, unless the officer has a specific reason to believe the person is involved in criminal activity, he must respect the person's wishes and allow him or her to leave.

Detention

The second level of citizen-police encounters is referred to as a "detention." A detention occurs whenever an officer's actions or words lead you to believe reasonably that you are *not* free to simply walk away. For example, any time an officer stops a vehicle, orders a person to stop, or orders a person to sit down, the officer's action constitutes a detention of the person.

Unlike a contact, a detention *is* a seizure, so the Fourth Amendment applies. As explained by the Supreme Court:

. . . A person has been "seized" within the meaning of the Fourth Amendment only if, in view of all of the circumstances surrounding the incident, a reasonable person would have believed that he was not free to leave. Examples of circumstances that might indicate a seizure, even where the person did not attempt to leave, would be the threatening presence of several officers, the display of a weapon by an officer, some physical touching of the person of the citizen, or the use of language or tone of voice indicating that compliance with the officer's request might be compelled . . . . In the absence of some such evidence, other inoffensive contact between a member of the public and the police cannot, as a matter of law, amount to a seizure of the person. *(U.S. v. Mendenhall [1980] 446 U.S. 544.)*

A recent issue of the *FBI Law Enforcement Bulletin* nicely summarized some of the factors that courts examine when determining whether a contact has escalated into a detention:

(1) Physical Contact
The slightest application of physical force for the purpose of stopping or holding a person is likely to constitute a seizure. While unintentional or accidental contact is generally not a seizure, officers should avoid physical contact until they have established reasonable suspicion to justify a detention.

(2) The Number of Officers
The threatening presence of several officers may transform an otherwise consensual encounter into a seizure. Thus, where officer safety is not jeopardized, an encounter is more likely to be deemed consensual if backup officers stay in the background where the citizen does not immediately recognize them as officers involved in the encounter.

(3) The Display of Weapons
The display of weapons is inherently coercive and is generally interpreted by citizens as compelling compliance. Thus, pointing guns or otherwise threatening a citizen with a weapon will in most cases transform a contact into a detention.

(4) Interference With the Citizen's Freedom of Movement
The manner in which officers position themselves or their vehicles and the extent to which they block a citizen's pathway or freedom of movement may communicate to that person that he is not free to leave. Officers wishing to keep an encounter consensual should position themselves to provide a clear path of exit for the citizen.

(5) Transporting From the Initial Site of the Encounter
Movement from the site of the initial confrontation to another location does not necessarily escalate a consensual encounter

into a seizure within the meaning of the Fourth Amendment. However, officers requesting a suspect to accompany them to another location should document that the citizen had a genuine choice and voluntarily agreed to the movement.

(6) Demeanor and Appearance of Officer

An officer's use of coercive or intimidating language or tone of voice may be interpreted by a reasonable person as compelling compliance. A uniformed officer repeatedly flashing a badge is intimidating conduct. Requests for a consent to search should be conveyed in a manner that makes it clear that the citizen has a choice and that compliance is not required or compelled. Advising suspects that they are suspected of transporting drugs is another factor courts assess in determining the coercive effect of police conduct. Since uncommunicated suspicions generally have no bearing on whether a particular encounter is consensual or a seizure, officers should consider delaying or avoiding the expression of such suspicions until a seizure is justified.

(7) Retention of Citizen's Personal Property

Although officers may request to examine a person's identification or tickets and ask questions about any discrepancies, such items should be promptly returned. The prolonged detention of personal items can transform a consensual contact into a detention.

There are strict rules governing the circumstances under which a police officer can legally detain a person. The courts have universally held that, with a few clear exceptions, an officer can detain a person only if he has a "reasonable suspicion" that the person is involved in criminal activity.

The legal definition of "reasonable suspicion" is ever-changing. The important thing to understand is that the reasonable suspicion standard is *lower* than what's termed "probable cause." In other words, it is quite possible that a police officer will have reasonable suspicion (sufficient to detain a person), but still not have probable cause to believe a person is engaging in criminal activity (needed to arrest the person). In fact, an officer's sole purpose in detaining a person is often to try to get enough additional evidence to establish the probable cause required to arrest the person.

Reasonable suspicion exists if an officer can point to some *specific facts* that, taken together, made it reasonable for him, with all his training and experience, to suspect that the person he detained was involved in some illegal activity. In other words, an officer's mere "hunch" is *not* sufficient to detain a person. Rather, the officer must be able to articulate the reasons underlying his suspicion, and the court must agree that his suspicion was reasonable.

The Supreme Court has explained that the purpose of a detention must be limited to conducting an investigation to find out if there is probable cause to arrest the person detained. Therefore, an officer is allowed to detain a person only for the length of time reasonably needed to confirm or dispel his suspicion. If a court finds that an officer detained a person for an unduly long period of time, the court will apply the exclusionary rule to any evidence that the officer found after he exceeded the reasonable time needed to conduct his investigation.

In almost all cases, it is a *series* of facts which, *when viewed in combination*, add up to a reasonable suspicion that a person is engaged in a marijuana crime. For example, in almost every state, smoking a hand-rolled cigarette is *not*, by itself, sufficient reason for an officer's detention of the smoker. However, when the officer states that he also smelled the odor of burning marijuana, or that the suspect seemed extremely nervous at the officer's approach, the totality of the factors may give rise to a reasonable suspicion of criminal activity (and maybe even probable cause sufficient to arrest), thereby allowing the officer to detain the person to investigate further. Similarly, most courts hold that the fact that a person runs when he sees the police is *not*, by itself, grounds to detain that person. However, when evasive conduct is coupled with other factors such as a "high-crime area" or an officer's observation of other suspicious actions, many courts will permit the officer to detain the person. Note, however, that if flight occurs *after* an officer has formed a reasonable suspicion to detain a person and has ordered the person to stop, the attempt to escape automatically transforms the reasonable suspicion into probable cause, and hence the officer can arrest the person.

Detaining Your Belongings

Not only can police detain *you* if they have a reasonable suspicion you are violating a marijuana law, they can also detain your belongings if they have a reasonable suspicion that they contain marijuana. Again, a common example occurs in airports when police stop and detain a person because they believe that his luggage may contain marijuana. In such a situation, the police can detain the luggage only for the reasonable time necessary to conduct their investigation. They cannot open the luggage without a search warrant or without the person's consent; therefore they must either quickly obtain a search warrant or release the luggage back to the person. Often in such a situation they will have a marijuana-detecting dog sniff the luggage, and return it to the owner if no drug is detected. If marijuana is detected by the dog, then the officer will arrest the person immediately and obtain a search warrant to open the luggage.

In one recent federal case in Colorado, the security police at Lowery Air Force Base received a telephone call in which the caller said he smelled marijuana while he was working in a particular building. An officer was dispatched to investigate. Inside the building, the officer smelled no marijuana and observed nothing out of the ordinary. The only people inside the building were two janitors.

Despite the lack of any reasonable suspicion that the men where involved in criminal activity, the officer told both men to "stand by" while he radioed for additional help. Three additional security police arrived with a narcotics dog. The additional officers smelled nothing, but ordered the dog to begin searching the area. The dog alerted to a coat lying inside an office. The officers asked the janitors if the coat belonged to one of them, and one janitor answered affirmatively. According to the janitor, the officer then ordered him to pull out whatever was inside the jacket, whereupon the janitor removed a small bag of marijuana from the coat.

The court excluded the marijuana after determining that the janitors had been unlawfully detained when the first officer told them to "stand by." The order to stand by was a detention because the men were not free to leave. The detention was unlawful because at the time the janitors were told to stand by there was absolutely no indication of wrongdoing. Moreover, when the first officer detained the men, he effectively also detained their property (the coat.) Since the janitor was not free to leave, he was obviously unable to remove his coat from the office. Since at the time the coat was effectively detained (which was prior to the dog sniff), there was no reason to suspect that it contained marijuana, the detention of the coat was also declared unlawful. The court held, therefore, that almost every action by the officer was unconstitutional. The proper remedy was to declare the unlawfully seized marijuana inadmissible evidence which meant that the case against the man had to be dismissed for lack of evidence.

In an aside, the court also noted that even had the detention of the coat been lawful, the order to remove the marijuana from inside the coat constituted an unlawful warrantless search. When a dog alerts to luggage or other property that might conceal marijuana, the constitutional procedure is for the officers to obtain a search warrant. (*U.S. v. Lumba [D.Colo. 1993] 825 F.Supp. 263.*)

Demanding to See Your Identification

If an officer legally detains you, most courts now permit the officer to demand to see proof of your identification. In such situations, it's usually best to politely provide the officer with your ID. Nothing is gained by attempting to conceal your identification once you have been legally detained. Similarly, it is not prudent to give a police officer a fake name once you have been lawfully detained or arrested. When a false name is given, the police almost always quickly discover that the person is lying and the person can then be charged with the additional crime of giving false information to a police officer. Furthermore, the person's evasiveness can later be used against him to show his consciousness of guilt. (See Chapter 1 on the "knowledge" element that must be proven to convict a person of possessing marijuana.) Remember, however, during a *contact* you do not have to identify yourself.

Frisks or Pat-Searches

If a police officer legally detains a person, the officer may have a right to "frisk" or "pat-search" the person. (The two terms are synonymous.) A frisk is intended only to protect the officer or the public, so an officer can conduct a frisk or pat-search *only* if he reasonably fears for his safety or the safety of others.

A frisk is therefore a *limited search* for the sole purpose of detecting a concealed weapon. When conducting a frisk, an officer can pat or feel only the *outside* of a person's clothing. The officer can reach inside a pocket only if he detects a hard object that he reasonably believes could be used as a weapon. The courts of every state have held that practically any hard object justifies the officer in reaching inside the person's pocket to find out if the object is really a weapon.

Courts will uphold a police officer's frisk whenever the officer can state specific facts that led him to reasonably believe the person was a threat and might possess a weapon. The Supreme Court has instructed that courts should find an officer's frisk illegal if the officer was really looking for drugs rather than weapons. Similarly, courts should find a frisk illegal if an officer went beyond the permissible scope of a frisk and removed *soft* objects or searched *inside* pockets without first detecting a hard object from the outside.

It is important to understand that if an officer, while conducting a frisk, feels a hard object that he believes to be a weapon, he can remove that object. If he happens to also feel something else in that pocket (such as a joint or baggie of marijuana), he can "accidentally" pull that item out as well. In fact, such "mistakes" are quite common, and the resulting incriminating evidence is often admissible.

For example, in one case, an officer in the Los Angeles Police Department stopped Larry Atmore because Larry allegedly met the description of a murder suspect. When the officer pat-searched Larry, he felt a round cylindrical object in Larry's jacket pocket. The officer had information that the murder suspect used a shotgun in the murder, and suspected that the cylindrical object was a shotgun shell.

For that reason, the officer reached inside Larry's jacket pocket and removed the object, which, in fact, turned out to be a lipstick case. However, as the officer removed the lipstick case, he also removed a joint that was in the same pocket. Although Larry was cleared as the murder suspect, he was subsequently convicted of possessing marijuana.

The court held that the officer's removal of the joint was legal because it occurred innocently and in conjunction with his removal of what he believed was a shotgun shell. The court stated, "There is no compelling evidence that [the officer] consciously seized the cigarette. A legitimate implication from the record is that his hand emerged with more than he intended to remove from the pocket.

We have all done the same thing when fumbling for keys or coins. There is nothing sinister about it. Once the cigarette was in plain sight, the officer did not have to ignore it."

The court found that the shotgun shell that the officer suspected to be in Larry's pocket would have legitimately been considered a weapon. The court reasoned that if the object had been a shotgun shell as the officer believed, Larry could have used it as a miniature bomb! In the court's words, "the officer could reasonably believe that any sharp object could be used as a detonator. He had not eliminated the possibility that [Larry] might be the person who was sought for murder and who, if caught, could face the death penalty. If he was the murder suspect, he might want to explode the shell even in a way that might entail considerable personal risk to himself, so long as he might escape in the ensuing confusion." Clearly, the lesson to be learned from Larry Atmore's misfortune is that it is not prudent to carry marijuana in the same pocket with a weapon or even a hard container.

Additionally, it sometimes happens that an officer who legally conducts a pat-search for weapons feels an object which, based on his experience and training, he believes to be marijuana or some other illegal drug. For example, in one case, Lee was legally stopped by an officer who suspected that he might be carrying a concealed weapon. As the officer pat-searched Lee, he felt a *soft* object that made a rustling and crumpling sound when pressed. Although the officer knew it was not a weapon, he suspected it was a baggie of marijuana. The officer reached into Lee's pocket and removed a baggie containing "green vegetable matter." The lab test later confirmed that the substance was marijuana, and Lee was charged with possession.

Lee argued that the officer's removal of the baggie was illegal because the officer knew it was not a weapon before he reached inside Lee's pocket. Therefore, Lee argued, the officer had exceeded the permissible scope of a legal pat-search for weapons and the illegally seized marijuana should therefore be excluded from evidence.

At the hearing on this issue, the officer testified that he was a 19-year veteran of the police force, and had received approximately 40 hours of education on identifying drugs, including marijuana. The officer stated that during his 19 years, he had arrested over 500 people possessing marijuana. The officer concluded that given all his training and experience, he was able to deduce, just by feeling the outside of Lee's pocket, that the object inside was a baggie of marijuana.

Based on such testimony, the prosecutor argued that the officer's pat-search, while initially conducted to detect weapons, unexpectedly turned up probable cause that Lee was in possession of marijuana. This probable cause permitted the officer to reach inside Lee's pocket and seize the marijuana even though he knew it was not a weapon. The court agreed with the prosecutor's argument. Therefore, the officer's search of Lee's pocket was deemed legal on the basis that the pat-search unexpectedly produced probable cause of marijuana possession.

The United States Supreme Court has been constantly expanding the permissible scope of an officer's search for weapons after detaining a suspect. At present, the Court permits police officers not only to pat-search the outside of a suspect's clothing, but also to search the immediate area surrounding the suspect. As will be explained in Chapter 6, an officer who legally stops a person's vehicle, and reasonably believes that an occupant is dangerous, can search the car's passenger compartment for weapons. Any marijuana they come across during the search can also be seized!

Legal Detentions Without Reasonable Suspicion

As explained above, the general rule is that an officer can only detain a person if the officer has a reasonable suspicion that the person is (or was) involved in criminal activity. There are, however, a few very important exceptions to this rule which it pays to know about. If any one of these exceptions applies, an officer can automatically (without reasonable suspicion) detain a person.

You may be automatically subjected to detention by a police officer if you fall into any of the following categories:

(1) you fit a "drug-courier profile,"
(2) you are stopped at a roadblock (discussed in Chapter 6),
(3) you are crossing a border, or are subject to a border inspection (discussed in Chapter 5), or
(4) you look young, and an officer reasonably believes you are a juvenile who is skipping school or violating a curfew.

The Drug-Courier Profile

In the early 1970's, the Drug Enforcement Administration developed what is referred to as the "drug-courier profile." This set of characteristics was derived from statistical information gained from numerous arrests of peoples attempting to transport illegal drugs. The courts have held that, for all practical purposes, resemblance to the DEA's drug courier profile is sufficient in and of itself to constitute reasonable suspicion of criminal activity, thereby providing grounds for an experienced officer to legally detain a person. (Of course, the courts have been very careful about the phrasing of this rule, noting that each case must be judged on its own merits.) In other words, if your appearance and behavior fit the drug-courier profile an officer has a free shot at legally detaining you.

When law enforcement agents spot a person meeting the profile characteristics, they will usually approach the person and try to engage him or her in conversation. As mentioned earlier, the courts have held that police can "contact" a person in public anytime and for any reason. During such an encounter, the agents are trained to ask a few questions without displaying force or otherwise implying that the person is not free to terminate the encounter and walk away.

A contact of this kind will escalate into a detention if the person fitting the profile does anything that the officer thinks is suspicious. In many cases, the officer contacting the person will ask if he can look in the person's luggage, hoping the person will foolishly consent to such a search.

Obviously, it is important for anyone desiring full protection against detentions by law-enforcement personnel to avoid resemblance to the profile. However the DEA has attempted to keep secret specifics of the profile. Fortunately, numerous cases have been litigated, and from the resulting court opinions one can deduce just what it is that the agents look for.

A careful analysis of the cases reveals that there are seven primary characteristics to the drug-carrier profile, and four secondary characteristics. The seven primary characteristics are:

(1) arrival from or departure to an identifiable source city for drugs
(2) carrying little or no luggage, or carrying several empty suitcases
(3) having an unusual itinerary, such as a quick return after a lengthy airplane trip
(4) use of an alias
(5) carrying unusually large amounts of currency (thousands of dollars)
(6) purchasing airline tickets with a large amount of small bills
(7) unusual nervousness beyond that ordinarily exhibited by passengers

The four secondary characteristics of the drug-carrier profile are:

(1) using public transportation, particularly taxicabs, in departing from the airport
(2) immediately making a telephone call after deplaning
(3) leaving a false call-back telephone number with the airline
(4) excessively frequent travel to drug source and distribution cities

The profile often varies. In fact, one court in New York remarked that "the profile has a chameleon-like quality; it seems to change itself to fit the facts of each case." This same court noted, "[o]ne agent candidly admitted that 'the profile in a particular case consists of anything that arouses his suspicions.'"

To make matters even more complicated, the profile changes depending on the airport or the area of the country. The specific profiles for the following airports and locations are derived from court opinions.

La Guardia Airport, New York City
(1) carrying little baggage
(2) nervousness
(3) checking to see if being followed
(4) attempting to leave the airport immediatcly
(5) unusual dress
(6) no tags on luggage
(7) attempts by individuals to conceal that they're traveling together

New Orleans
(1) ncrvousness
(2) little or no luggage
(3) large amounts of cash in small bills
(4) unusual itincrary
(5) arriving from drug-source city
(6) paying for ticket in small bills
(7) buying only a one-way ticket
(8) using an alias
(9) using a false telephone number on flight reservation
(10) placing a call immediately on arrival

Detroit Airport
(1) buying ticket with small bills
(2) travel to or from drug-source cities in short time period
(3) empty suitcases or luggage
(4) nervousness
(5) use of alias

Cleveland Airport
(1) purchase of round-trip ticket to and from drug-distribution city, with short stay between flights
(2) purchase of tickets with cash
(3) checking no luggage or empty bags
(4) use of alias
(5) suspicious or nervous behavior

While drug-courier profiles are used for justifying detentions at or near airports, in one recent case, a profile of this kind was used to justify the stopping of a vehicle and the subsequent arrest of its driver for transporting marijuana. In this case, DEA agents were driving an unmarked car on the coast of North Carolina in an area that they believed was used for drug trafficking. While on patrol, the agents observed two vehicles that appeared to be traveling together. They followed the vehicles for about twenty miles, during which time they observed that one of the vehicles was a pickup truck with a camper shell. In addition, the agents noticed that the truck appeared to be heavily weighed down. Lastly, the windows of the truck's camper shell were covered. Based on these observations, the agents suspected that the truck was transporting marijuana. They stopped the truck and, upon searching it, found a large quantity of marijuana.

The United States Supreme Court examined the legality of the agents' stopping the truck and concluded that it was constitutional. The court reasoned that the factors that aroused the agents' suspicion justified their belief that the vehicle was carrying marijuana. The Court emphasized that experienced DEA agents have learned that pickup trucks with camper shells are often used to transport large quantities of marijuana. Additionally, the truck appeared heavily laden, and its windows were covered with some material other than curtains. Accordingly, the vehicle matched the profile of one which is likely to be carrying marijuana, and hence, concluded the Court, the agents justifiably stopped it to investigate the nature of its cargo.

Juvenile Truants and Curfew Violators

In many states, if an officer reasonably believes that a truancy violation is occurring, he may legally detain the suspected youth and require him to identify himself. If the officer learns that the youth is indeed skipping school, he may return the youth to school or to his or her parents or guardian. The officer may *not* transport the juvenile to the police station or question him or her about unsolved crimes. Similarly, if a local government has established a curfew for juveniles, most states allow an officer who suspects a possible violation to detain the suspected violator and require proof of the person's age. The courts of most states have held that an adult's "youthful appearance" *is sufficient* for an officer to detain that person so long as the officer was reasonable in believing that the person was a juvenile violating a curfew or skipping school. However, once such a person shows proof that he or she is not subject to the curfew, the officer must immediately permit the person to continue on his way.

Arrest

The third and final level of citizen-police encounters is arrest. An arrest occurs when a police officer severely restrains a person's freedom, tells the person that he or she is under arrest, or takes the person into custody. Chapter 11 will discuss in detail what to do if you are arrested on a marijuana charge. For now, you need only know that in order to arrest a person an officer must have either an arrest warrant or *probable cause* to believe that the person has committed a crime. (If a person is inside *his* home, probable cause is not enough; the officer *must* have an *arrest* warrant. If the person is inside someone else's home, the officer *must* have a search warrant for the *host's* home.) Probable cause requires that the facts of the situation would lead a reasonable person to believe that the suspect was guilty of the crime for which he was arrested. Or, in the words of the United States Supreme Court, "probable cause exists where the facts and circumstances within [the police officers'] knowledge and of which they had reasonably trustworthy information [are] sufficient in themselves to warrant a man of reasonable caution in the belief that an offense has been or is being committed." As you can see, an officer's mere suspicion that you are breaking the law, even if reasonable, is insufficient to arrest you.

The courts like to say that "probable cause is a common sense, practical question" based on the "factual and practical considerations of everyday life on which reasonable and prudent men, not legal technicians, act." The test to determine whether probable cause exists is a gestalt one, based on the totality of the circumstances. "In dealing with probable cause ... we deal with probabilities ... Long before the law of probabilities was articulated as such, practical people formulated certain common sense conclusions about human behavior; jurors as factfinders are permitted to do the same and so are law enforcement officials." *(Illinois v. Gates [1983] 462 U.S. 213.)*

The gestalt nature of the probable cause test often places a great deal of weight on the police officer's claimed "experience and training." This is particularly true in marijuana cases, where an officer must sometimes act on his sense of smell or his quick view of some "green vegetable matter" (as they often state in their police reports). For example, if an officer sees some seeds which he thinks might be marijuana seeds, he will seldom have probable cause to arrest the person without some corroborating factors detected by his senses of sight or smell and all brought together by his training and experience that these factors combine to make it probable that the seeds are illegal marijuana seeds. (How he could possibly know they are viable is a question to be pursued on cross-examination, perhaps with the aid of a few sterilized *Cannabis* seeds from some bird food.)

Whether or not an officer has probable cause to arrest a person seen in possession of a hand-rolled cigarette also turns on what additional facts or circumstances indicate that it is a joint as opposed to a tobacco cigarette. In one California case decided in 1972, the court held that an officer's viewing of a person with a hand-rolled cigarette did not, by itself, constitute probable cause to arrest the person. The court, however, explained that there were no other factors that the cigarette contained marijuana as opposed to tobacco. The court said that its decision would have been different if

> . . . there was evidence of *other circumstances* such as at-
> tempted concealment of the item, the defendant's distinctive

manner of smoking it, the odor of burned marijuana, the defendant's evasiveness or abnormal physical condition, an admission by the defendant, or the arresting officer's expertise on the subject. *(Thomas v. Superior Court [1972] 22 Cal App.3d 972)*

CHAPTER 5

SEARCHES: WITH & WITHOUT WARRANTS

As WAS BRIEFLY EXPLAINED in Chapter 2, only *unreasonable* searches by police officers are illegal and result in the dismissal from court of evidence found during such a search. Therefore, officers who know the law will always try to make their searches appear reasonable. The best way for a police officer to guarantee that his search is reasonable is to obtain a search warrant prior to conducting the search. However, because obtaining a search warrant takes time as well as additional effort police officers seldom go to the trouble except in relatively important cases. Instead, they use one of several other ways to make warrantless searches appear reasonable to the judge who will eventually decide whether the search was legal.

As a general rule, searches conducted without a warrant are automatically *unreasonable* and hence violate the Fourth Amendment. This means that a court is predisposed to exclude from evidence anything that was found during a warrantless search. However, because judges generally dislike the exclusionary rule, they have fashioned a number of exceptions to the warrant requirement, anyone of which can make a warrantless search legal. If a warrantless search falls within one of these exceptions, then it will be deemed reasonable, and the exclusionary rule will not apply.

When dealing with warrantless searches, the crucial concept is whether the person searched had a "reasonable expectation of privacy" in the area searched. For example, homes and offices are considered very private and hence are highly protected against warrantless searches. In contrast, automobiles, trash cans, and public places, are considered less private and consequently receive less (and in some cases no) protection. Accordingly, a warrantless search of a home may be deemed illegal, whereas a similar warrantless search of a car is deemed legal.

When a Police Officer's Search or Seizure Is Legal Even Though He Doesn't Have a Warrant

As a general rule, a police officer can legally conduct a warrantless search or seizure under one or more of the following circumstances:

(1) The search was conducted after a peron was lawfully arrested. (See Chapter 9.)

(2) An automobile was searched, and the officer had probable cause to believe that the vehicle contained contraband. (See Chapter 6.)

(3) The person voluntarily consented to the search.

(4) The item seized was in plain view of the officer, and its illegal nature was immediately apparent.

(5) The search was conducted at a United States border.

(6) An immediate search was necessary to preserve evidence.

(7) The person or property searched belonged to a student at a public school, and the search was performed by a school official.

As noted above, the first two exceptions are discussed in later chapters. This chapter will examine the remaining five exceptions.

Consenting to a Search

The law concerning consent is widely misunderstood among the general public, and this misunderstanding can have dire consequences. As a general rule if a person consents to a warrantless search, *the search automatically becomes reasonable and therefore legal.* Consequently, whatever an officer finds during such a search can be used to convict the person. Simply put, if a person consents to a search, he has waived the primary protection offered by the Fourth Amendment!

Don't expect a police officer to tell you about your right not to consent. Although your consent must be voluntary in order to be valid, the courts have made clear that police officers do *not* have to tell people that they can refuse to consent. In other words, a police officer does not need to read you your rights before asking you to consent to a search. Also, despite the widespread myth to the contrary, an officer does *not* need to get your consent in writing. Oral consent is completely valid. Do not, therefore, act under the misconception that because you never "sign" anything, your consent is not valid.

Police officers are often pretty tricky about trying to get someone's consent to a search. They know that most people feel intimidated by police officers and are predisposed to comply with any request by a police officer. For example, the average motorist stopped by a police officer who asks them, "Would you mind opening the trunk, please?" will probably consent to the officer's search without realizing that they have every right to deny the officer's request.

It is absolutely astounding how many people get arrested only because they consent to a search and the officer finds some marijuana. Evidently these people do not understand that they have a constitutional right to refuse to consent. In most cases, without even knowing it, people relinquish a substantial portion of their Fourth-Amendment rights by consenting to an officer's request to search. You should never hesitate to assert your constitutional rights, particularly when they are all that stand between freedom and arrest on a marijuana charge.

The sad fact is that most people believe that they are under some kind of obligation to acquiesce when an officer contacts them and asks permission to search them or their belongings. The truth is the exact opposite — you have a right to associate with, and speak to, whomever you please. In this respect, there is nothing special about a police officer. Assuming you would not let a complete stranger look through your purse or search your pockets, why would you allow a police officer to do so — especially if you knew you were in possession of marijuana? Just say "no!"

For example, if Officer Martin Marietta approaches a person and asks, "Do you mind if I look in your backpack?" he is asking the person to consent to a search. His question is no different from asking, "Would you please give up your Fourth-Amendment right and allow me to look in your backpack?" If, *for any reason* you don't want the officer digging through your belongings, you should refuse to consent by saying something like, "Yes, I do mind. I have private, personal items in my backpack and do not want you looking through them." If you're really squeamish about standing up to a police officer, keep the wallet cards in Appendix B with you and simply hand the appropriate card to an officer who asks you to waive a constitutional right. Simply present the card to the officer and say something like, "I've been told to use this if a police officer ever asks me to consent to a search."

The point, to repeat, is that whenever a police officer asks your permission to search, you are under no obligation to consent. The only reason he's asking is that he doesn't yet have enough evidence to search forcibly. By consenting you are giving up one of the most important constitutional rights you have.

Though you are almost always best served by refusing to consent to any search, you should know that if you do chose to consent, your consent need not be absolute. It is perfectly appropriate to tell a police officer that he can search one particular area, but not another. The way you phrase your consent sets the boundaries on the officer's search. Provided that the officer does not turn up probable cause while searching the area that you have consented to have searched, he must go no further than you explicitly state. If the officer starts to search beyond the bounds of your consent you must politely, but forcefully, tell him to stop—that you did not consent to a general search—and that you will now be continuing on your way unless he is lawfully detaining you.

Generally speaking, a person gains nothing by consenting to a police officer's request to conduct a warrantless search. The many court cases on the subject reveal the great danger that often accompanies the waiver of the constitutional right to remain free from such searches. Just remember, *any officer who asks your permission to search is looking for evidence that he doesn't have—yet*. The whole point of the search is to look for, and hopefully find, incriminating evidence! Little is to be gained and much can be lost by waiving a constitutional right.

If an officer hassles you when you refuse to consent to a search, just tell him that you have personal items and you object to his violating your constitutional right to privacy. (Or give him the card in Appendix B.) If the officer still proceeds to search you and find marijuana, your attorney can argue that the marijuana was discovered through an illegal search and hence should be thrown out of court.

How Mr. Puff Asserted His Constitutional Rights

The following story illustrates the proper use of the constitutional right to withhold consent to a warrantless search. Officer Eli Lilly stopped Mr. Puff's vehicle because his registration was expired and asked Mr. Puff, "Would you please empty the contents of your pockets?"

Mr. Puff said, "Are you asking me to empty my pockets, or are you ordering me to empty my pockets?" When Lilly said he was simply *asking*, Mr. Puff said, "No thanks, and I really must be going."

Mr. Puff's question to Officer Lilly was entirely appropriate. In fact, Mr. Puff's response was an effective method of turning the tables on the officer. If Lilly had told Mr. Puff that he was ordering him to empty his pockets, Mr. Puff could have properly responded, "Get a search warrant. I do not consent to your search and would like to continue on my way." If the officer had proceeded to search Mr. Puff's pockets without a warrant, Mr. Puff's lawyer could argue that the search was illegal. If Mr. Puff had consented, his lawyer would have no argument.

The Plain-View Rule

As was briefly explained earlier, a "search" occurs whenever a government agent accesses an area in which a person has a reasonable expectation of privacy. A clear example of a "search" occurs when an officer opens someone's purse and looks inside for marijuana. In such a case, the owner of the purse clearly has a reasonable expectation of privacy regarding its contents, and hence the officer's opening of the purse is considered a "search." The next question would be whether the officer had a warrant to search the purse or whether his search fell within one of the exceptions to the warrant requirement. On the other hand, if an officer's conduct is *not* considered a "search," the Fourth Amendment does not apply.

For example, suppose the purse in the above example was made of a clear, see-through plastic that exposed the contents of the purse to public view. In such a case, if an officer looked through the outside of the purse and (similar to looking through a car window) saw some marijuana in the purse, the marijuana would be in plain view, and the officer would immediately have probable cause to arrest the person and search the purse. A court would hold that the officer's observation of the marijuana was *not* a search, since it invaded no reasonable expectation of privacy.

However, as discussed in greater detail in Chapter 7, if marijuana is seen *inside* a *home* in plain view by an officer who is *outside* the home, the plain-view sighting gives the officer only probable cause to believe that marijuana can be found in the home. The officer still needs either a warrant, exigent circumstances, or consent to enter the home. In contrast, if an officer sees marijuana in plain view *inside* an *automobile*, and the officer is *outside* the automobile, the automobile exception (see Chapter 6) allows the officer to enter the car without a warrant and immediately seize the contraband. The reason for the different rules? A person inside a home has a greater reasonable expectation to privacy than a person inside a car.

The primary limit on the plain-view rule is that the officer's view must have been legally obtained. In other words, in order for the plain-view rule to come into play, the officer must have had a legal right to be in the place from which he saw the contraband. For example, if an officer is in your home with your consent and he happens to see some marijuana on your kitchen table, a court would consider the officer legally entitled to his view of the marijuana and uphold the officer's warrantless seizure of the marijuana. In contrast, if the officer was *illegally* inside your home when he saw the marijuana, a court would find that although the marijuana was in plain view, the officer was not legally entitled to that view. In that case, his warrantless seizure of the marijuana would be considered illegal, and the exclusionary rule would apply.

The plain-view rule is really a matter of common sense. It's simply the Law's way of saying that it won't protect your privacy if *you* don't protect your privacy. The bottom line: always keep your private items private—*out of view*. There will be more examples showing the operations of the plain-view rule in the chapters to follow.

How Wayne Learned about the Plain-View Rule

Officer Philip Morris stopped Wayne's car because Wayne's brake lights were not working. The officer approached Wayne's car and asked Wayne to step out. Officer Morris then asked Wayne for his driver's license and vehicle registration. When Wayne opened his wallet to remove his driver's license, Officer Morris saw a joint in Wayne's wallet. Officer Morris immediately searched Wayne, as well as the inside of his car. Inside Wayne's glove box, the officer found more than 100 marijuana joints. Wayne was arrested and convicted.

In the above scenario, Officer Morris observed the first joint in plain view when Wayne opened his wallet. The fact that Wayne possessed even a single joint gave the officer probable cause to search the rest of Wayne's person as well as the passenger compartment of his car.

The moral of the story is obvious. First, people who smoke pot are less likely to be stopped if they keep their cars in working order. Second, those who have a special relationship with plants that the government has declared illegal would be prudent to keep preparations of those plants away from their driver's license, registration, and any other objects or areas into which they might have to reach if stopped by a police officer. You'd be surprised how many people keep marijuana on top of their sun visor right next to their car registration, never stopping to think about the problem that could ensue if they are stopped by the police.

Plain-View Paraphernalia

Not only can a police officer seize marijuana that he sees in plain view, but he can also seize any items that he has probable cause to believe are used for criminal activity. Examples of specific items that many states allow an officer to seize on sight include identifiable items of marijuana paraphernalia, such as pipes and roach clips.

Most states allow an officer to seize a pipe only if something about it indicates it is used to smoke marijuana. (For example, it's small, has a screen, has a vent, or contains marijuana residue.) Likewise, most state courts have ruled that a roach clip, by itself, is usually not seizable unless it holds the remnants of a joint or is accompanied by other signs of marijuana use.

Distinct Drug-Carrying Devices

Keeping marijuana and smoking aids out of plain view is common sense. Courts, however, have extended the plain view rule to encompass what they call "distinct drug-carrying devices." If you observed someone walking down the street carrying an electric-typewriter case, it would be reasonable to assume that the case contains a typewriter. In a similar vein, courts have held that certain containers are "distinct *drug*-carrying devices." If an officer observes such a container, the courts of most states allow the officer to immediately seize and search the container without a warrant.

In most states, the following containers have been held to be distinct drug-carrying devices that can be searched and seized without a warrant: small glassine envelopes, clear baggies filled with leafy substances, paper bindles, small party balloons filled with a powdery substance, and large blocks wrapped with dark garbage bags and taped with duct tape. Clearly, when at all possible, a person should not have in his or her possession such items, nor should marijuana ever be stored or transported in such containers. To do so simply screams out to the police, "I'm in possession of illegal drugs, feel free to search and arrest me!"

In one case, a Florida police officer detained Torin Thompson. The officer asked Torin for identification. Torin stated that his identification was inside a shaving case. The officer pat-searched the outside of the case, and after detecting no weapon allowed Torin to reach inside to retrieve his identification. When Torin pulled his billfold from the case, a small brown manila envelope fell out onto the hood of his car, and Torin quickly but quietly attempted to brush it to the ground. The officer saw the envelope, picked it up, opened it, and found marijuana inside it. The Florida court held that the officer's warrantless opening of the manila envelope was *illegal*, because, although some brown manila envelopes may contain marijuana, "It cannot be said that most brown manila envelopes contain marijuana. There could have been any number of items in the envelope other than marijuana that Torin would wish to keep private." The court also stated that Torin's conduct in attempting to hide the envelope by brushing it to the ground "was no different than if he had simply told the officer that he did not want him to look into it without a search warrant." Torin was saved because he wisely put his marijuana in an opaque envelope rather than in a clear baggie. Most courts would probably agree with the Florida court that brown manila envelopes are not distinct marijuana-carrying devices.

The Arizona Supreme Court has, in effect, held that brick-shaped, dark plastic garbage bags are distinctive marijuana-carrying devices. In this case, Dennis Million and two of his friends were observed late one evening "carrying dark-colored garbage bags and packing them in various compartments within a [motor home]." After loading the motor home, the men began driving toward the California border. As they approached the border between Arizona and California, DEA agents stopped the vehicle, conducted a warrantless search, and recovered a total of 1,238 pounds of marijuana.

Dennis argued that the agents' warrantless search of the plastic garbage bags was illegal because those bags were not distinct marijuana-carrying devices. However, the prosecutor defeated this argument by careful questioning that

convinced the court that, to an experienced DEA agent, the plastic bags were
recognizable as distinct drug-carrying devices:

> (Q) What type of garbage bag—you have used the word
> garbage bag—what type of garbage bags were they carry-
> ing that you observed at first?
>
> (A) They were the dark large type that you would put in an
> outside garbage can. Dark green or black. They appeared
> very dark.

> (Q) Did they appear to be empty or full?
>
> (A) No, sir, they appeared to contain various objects in them
> that were—that they would bend when they would carry
> them. The garbage bags would bend and loose objects
> inside them could be observed.

> (Q) How would you describe these objects you saw in the bags?
>
> (A) Well, they were individual objects, not large. I would
> describe them, as from prior experiences, as brick-shaped
> objects.

> (Q) Have you seen these types of garbage bags on prior
> occasions?
>
> (A) Yes, sir.

> (Q) How many prior occasions?
>
> (A) A 100 or 150 times.

> (Q) Have those been in connection with investigations of
> marijuana?
>
> (A) Yes, sir.

> (Q) Is there anything unusual, anything common about the
> garbage bags, put it that way?
>
> (A) In this area, it is most common to find garbage bags of this
> type to contain marijuana contraband. They are available
> everywhere.

> (Q) Is there some reason why garbage bags are used instead of
> cardboard boxes?
>
> (A) One thing, they contain the smell better. Second, they are
> waterproof. They are able to pack them on different con-
> figurations very readily by pushing and shoving them into

different locations in the compartment. They put talcum on them to deaden the odor.

The rule about distinct drug-carrying devices is a good example of one which, if known, can be used in the public's favor. For example, there are two favorable aspects to the courts' defining what containers can be searched on sight. First, the public is put on notice never to hold or transport "private items" in such containers. Second, in deciding some of these cases, the courts have clearly stated that certain items are *not* distinct drug-carrying devices. For example, most courts have held that opaque film canisters (the little ones with black bodies and black or light-gray caps) are *not* considered distinct drug-carrying devices, so they cannot be searched without a warrant. Other such "safe" containers include opaque pill bottles, eyeglass cases, purses, and any other containers commonly used to carry legitimate items.

Abandoning Marijuana

In many marijuana cases, police officers have claimed that as they approached a suspect they saw him drop a baggie containing "green leafy vegetable matter believed to be marijuana." The officers then report that he or she picked up the baggie and found that it did in fact contain marijuana. It is interesting to note that, following the Supreme Court's 1961 ruling that the exclusionary rule applies in state courts (initially it was only applied in *federal* courts), there was a significant increase in the number of cases in which police officers claimed that a person dropped drugs as the officers approached. For example, one study of New York City police officers showed a near 80 percent increase in the number of cases in which people allegedly abandoned drugs. Either people suddenly began abandoning marijuana in droves, or police officers were fabricating the alleged abandonments in order to escape the exclusionary rule following what was really an illegal search.

The general rule on these cases (known as "dropsy" cases) is that an officer can retrieve the marijuana based on either the plain-view rule or on the theory that the drugs were abandoned. The officer can then arrest the person for possession because he has probable cause to believe that the person did possess marijuana. For example, Paul was a musician in a band playing at a local bar. It was late in the evening and he stepped outside for some fresh air and smoked a joint between sets. As he stood there enjoying his respite, he noticed a car slowly driving toward him. Not particularly worried, he took another drag on his joint and suddenly noticed that the car was in fact a police patrol car. In shock, and without thinking, Paul threw his joint to the ground and stood there looking at the patrol car.

Officer Monsanto, inside the patrol car, observed Paul throw down a lit cigarette (littering) and, suspecting he might turn up some other evidence of crime, got out of his car to speak with Paul. As Officer Monsanto bent to retrieve the cigarette, he discovered it was actually a marijuana joint. Because the officer had observed Paul toss the joint on the ground, the officer had probable cause to arrest Paul and search him for additional marijuana. Inside the pocket of Paul's jacket, the officer found a small vial of hash oil. Paul was convicted for possession of marijuana and concentrated *Cannabis*.

If Paul had known the law, he would have known that he should never throw marijuana down on the ground when he is the only person in the area, and a police officer is nearby. Paul's best move would have been to quickly place the joint into an empty pocket and casually walk back into the bar. In that case, Officer Monsanto would have simply seen a man smoking a cigarette outside a bar. Such observations would not have given the officer probable cause to search Paul, nor even a reasonable suspicion to stop and detain him.

In another case, police in Arizona received information that a man had sold marijuana to two out-of-town women and was driving them to the airport. The police observed the man helping the women carry two suitcases. When the suitcases were passed through the x-ray machine, the officers observed what appeared to be bricks of marijuana on the x-ray picture. The officers asked the man for consent to search the suitcases. The man replied that the suitcases were not his, but rather belonged to the women. The women likewise denied ownership of the suitcases, claiming they were taking them for a friend. The police seized the suitcases, opened them, and discovered a large amount of marijuana inside. The man was convicted of possessing marijuana for sale. The court held that the man had voluntarily abandoned the suitcases when he denied ownership. Accordingly, he had no right to complain that the warrantless seizure and search of the suitcases violated *his* reasonable expectation of privacy.

In a rather strange case, a man in Maryland was hospitalized because an overdose of hashish oil had leaked from balloons he had swallowed. While in a semiconscious state, the man had a bowel movement into a hospital bed pan. The police, without a warrant, looked through the man's excrement and removed several balloons containing hashish oil. The man was subsequently convicted of possession after the court found that he maintained no reasonable expectation of privacy in his excrement that had been deposited in a bed pan rather than in the privacy of his own bathroom at home. In effect, the court held that the man had abandoned his own excrement and hence a warrantless search and seizure was fully permissible under the Fourth Amendment!

In another case, a woman in Louisiana who had several marijuana joints in her purse became nervous and began to run as a police officer approached her. At one point, out of either anger or nervousness, the woman threw her purse at the officer. The court held that the officer's subsequent warrantless search of the purse, which led to his discovering marijuana cigarettes, was entirely legal because the woman had abandoned the purse, and its contents, by throwing it at the officer.

The Marijuana Aroma

The distinctive aroma of marijuana, burning or not, is recognizable by much of the population. Additionally, most police officers are trained to recognize the odor. Therefore, as a general rule, an officer who detects the odor of marijuana has probable cause to search the person or place from which he believes the odor is emanating.

In one recent Florida case, an off-duty police officer who was working security at Funtastic Skating Center "smelled a very strong odor of smoked *Cannabis*" emanating from a young man who entered the rink. The officer identified himself as a police officer and took the minor into a nearby office where he proceeded to search the boy's pockets. He found a partially smoked joint and arrested the minor.

The boy argued that the mere smell of marijuana did not give the officer probable cause to believe that the boy was then, and there, in possession of marijuana. The Florida court of appeal disagreed. The court explained that the officer was trained to recognize the aroma of marijuana and that the aroma could not be confused with any other legal substance. The court commented:

> The sense of smell is perhaps not as keen in humankind as in other animals, but some odors such as burned *Cannabis* are very strong and very distinctive. A person who is trained to recognize the odor of marijuana and is familiar with it and can recognize it has probable cause, based on the smell alone, to search a person or a vehicle for contraband. *(State v. T.T. [Fla.App. 5 Dist. 1992] 594 So.2d 839.)*

Most courts agree with the Florida court that a trained police officer's detection of the marijuana aroma is sufficient to establish probable cause necessary to immediately search a person. It's often possible, however, for defense counsel to later attack the officer's claimed olfactory abilities. In particular, some cases have been won by cross-examining the officer about what training he has received (usually none) with regard to the period of time that it takes for the aroma to dissipate. Defense counsel should try and show that the marijuana aroma can linger for a considerable period, and hence, its mere detection does not make it *probable* that the person is *currently* in possession of marijuana as required for probable cause. Likewise, the officer can be cross-examined about what training he has received (again, usually none) to distinguish, based on odor alone, a person who has been in a room with others who smoked marijuana, versus the person himself smoking or possessing marijuana.

Note, that with respect to *containers* that smell of marijuana, the courts have looked at the nature of the container from which the aroma was emanating. Generally speaking, if the container was one that judges would consider private, such as a briefcase, the courts have required that the officer obtain a search warrant before searching, despite the detection of the marijuana aroma. On the other hand, if the container is less private in the eyes of a judge (such as a brown paper bag), the courts are more likely to allow a warrantless search.

As is explained in Chapter 6, most courts permit an officer to conduct a warrantless search of a car if the odor of marijuana is detected. However (as explained in Chapter 7), without exigent circumstances or consent to enter, an officer cannot conduct a warrantless search of a home simply because he can smell marijuana coming from inside.

The Marijuana Aroma and Dog Sniffs

The Supreme Court, as well as most state courts, has held that using a dog to sniff *containers* or *persons* suspected of possessing or transporting marijuana is not a "search" and, therefore, does not require a search warrant or probable cause. The Supreme Court has explained its reasons for permitting warrantless dog sniffs of containers such as luggage:

> We have affirmed that a person possesses a privacy interest in the contents of personal luggage that is protected by the Fourth Amendment. A "canine sniff'" by a well-trained narcotics-detection dog, however, does not require opening the luggage. It does not expose non-contraband items that otherwise would remain hidden from public view, as does, for example, an officer's rummaging through the contents of luggage. Thus, the manner in which information is obtained through this investigative technique is much less intrusive than a typical search. Moreover, the sniff discloses only the presence or absence of narcotics, a contraband item. Thus, despite the fact that the sniff tells the authorities something about the contents of the luggage, the information obtained is limited. This limited disclosure also ensures that the owner of the property is not subjected to the embarrassment and inconvenience entailed in less discriminate and more intrusive investigative methods . . . We are aware of no other investigative procedure that is so limited both in the manner in which the information is obtained and in the content of the information revealed by the procedure. Therefore, we conclude that the particular course of investigation that the agents intended to pursue here—expo-sure of respondent's luggage, which was located in a public place, to a trained canine—did not constitute a "search" within the meaning of the Fourth Amendment. *(US v. Place [1982] 462 US 696.)*

This means that an officer with a marijuana-sniffing dog is entirely free to approach you with his dog and let it have a sniff. A citizen is, of course, under no obligation to allow this to happen. An approach by an officer with a dog is merely a contact, and as discussed earlier a person is absolutely free to walk away and avoid the officer and dog completely. As explained earlier, the officer can detain a person only if he has a reasonable suspicion, based on objective facts, that the person is involved in criminal activity.

Most courts hold that if a marijuana-sniffing dog alerts to a package or person, that alone establishes *probable cause* that the package or person is concealing marijuana. However, if challenged in court, the prosecution must prove that the dog was properly trained and has proven reliable in the past. In most cases, the issue of a dog's reliability is easily resolved by the prosecutor introducing proof that the dog is certified as a drug detection dog. A defense attorney can attack this by introducing, or eliciting, evidence that the dog has not been recertified on a yearly basis; has performed very few drug sniff searches; has a poor record of accurately detecting the presence of marijuana; or that the dog's handler has a poor record of distinguishing when the dog is alerting to marijuana versus when the dog is barking for some other reason, such as unconscious cueing by the handler. *(US v. Diaz [6th Cir. 1994] 25 F.3d 392)*

As a final note, at least one state court (New York) has held that under the *state constitution*, the use of man's best friend to sniff for drugs *is* a "search" and hence may be conducted only pursuant to a warrant or under an exception to the warrant requirement.

Canvassing Dog Sniffs

In several recent cases, courts have upheld the use of a drug-sniffing dog in a *general* canvassing operation (as opposed to having a dog sniff a *particular* person or package). In one case in the town of Truth or Consequences, New Mexico, for example, a Border Patrol agent regularly began walking a trained marijuana-sniffing dog through the parking lot of the town's Super 8 Motel. The Border Patrol suspected that this motel was a general staging area for drug smugglers. One morning while walking the dog through the parking lot, the dog alerted to the trunk of a Chevy Impala parked in front of one of the motel rooms.

The agents watched the car until Keith Ludwig approached it. The agents contacted Mr. Ludwig, identified themselves as Border Patrol agents, and requested his consent to search the car's trunk. When Mr. Ludwig refused to consent, one of the agents took Mr. Ludwig's keys and opened the trunk. Inside were several large bags of marijuana.

The Tenth Circuit upheld the canvassing dog sniff on the theory that the motel parking lot was not a private area, and hence anyone, including law enforcement agents, had a right to walk through it. Given the agents' legal right to be in the parking lot, the Tenth Circuit reasoned that under the Supreme Court's ruling that dog sniff's are not "searches," the agent was entirely within the law to allow a drug-sniffing dog to do its thing.

Finally, the Tenth Circuit held that given the dog's alert to Mr. Ludwig's trunk, the agent had probable cause to search Mr. Ludwig's trunk. Consequently, the agent did not need Mr. Ludwig's consent, and under the automobile exception to the warrant requirement, he did not need a warrant. The Tenth Circuit explained: ". . . a dog alert usually is at least as reliable as many other sources of probable cause and is certainly reliable enough to create a 'fair probability' that there is contraband. We therefore have held in several cases that a dog alert, without more, gave probable cause for searches and seizures." The court noted that a dog alert might not provide probable cause if the particular dog had a poor accuracy record. The court noted, however, that the dog in question had never falsely alerted. *(US v. Ludwig [10th Cir. 1993] 10 F.3d 1523.)*

Border Searches

Because the federal government has the authority to exclude aliens from the country, courts have granted law-enforcement agents broad powers to conduct searches at or near borders. In 1992, in fact, the U.S. Customs Service seized over 462 thousand pounds of marijuana, about twenty thousand pounds more than the DEA seized that same year.

The United States Supreme Court has held that an officer does *not* need a warrant, probable cause, or even reasonable suspicion to search you, your car, or your belongings, at a border. Therefore, any time you cross a U.S. border, you in effect consent to a search. Most people are aware of this rule and plan accordingly.

Two aspects of border searches are not as well-known. First, the rule has been extended to allow the opening and search of mail coming into or out of the United States. The inspectors do not need a warrant, probable cause, or even a reasonable suspicion that the mail contains marijuana before opening it. Note that this rule applies only to *international* mail. As discussed shortly, mail traveling within the United States is given much greater protection.

Second, the definition of "border" has been expanded to include airports that receive nonstop flights from foreign countries. Therefore, if a person flies into or out of any U.S. airport directly from a foreign country, that person is subject to a warrantless search even though he or she may be a thousand miles from the closest geographical border.

Border Strip Searches And Body Cavity Searches

With respect to the scope of a border search, the Supreme Court has made clear that "routine" border searches may be conducted without probable cause or justification of any kind. However, if the search or detention of a traveler is beyond the scope of a routine customs search or inspection, it must be justified by at least a *reasonable suspicion* that the person is involved in criminal conduct.

So far, no case has explicitly defined a "routine" border search. The cases make clear, however, that the degree of intrusiveness is critical factor in distinguishing routine from non-routine border searches. For example, a strip search at a border cannot be conducted without at least a reasonable suspicion that the person is concealing contraband beneath his or her clothing. Similarly, in order to conduct a body cavity search or subject someone to an involuntary X-ray search at a border, there must be a "clear indication that the suspect is carrying contraband in a body cavity." *(US v. Ramos-Saenz [9th Cir. 1994] 36 F.3d 59.)*

Exigent Circumstances

An officer may conduct a warrantless search or seizure if "exigent circumstances" exist. Exigent circumstances were described by one court as "an emergency situation requiring swift action to prevent imminent danger to life or serious damage to property, or to forestall the imminent escape of a suspect or destruction of evidence." As the quote indicates, this exception to the warrant requirement is very broad. Courts created the rule out of concern that some emergency situations require immediate action by the police, and that such actions would be hindered if an officer had to delay acting to obtain a search warrant.

The exigent-circumstances exception to the warrant requirement is often applied in marijuana cases to uphold an officer's warrantless search. As mentioned earlier, when police officers make a warrantless search that turns up evidence of a marijuana crime, many judges are reluctant to find the search illegal and suppress the evidence. As a result, judges often invoke the "exigent circumstances" exception to the warrant requirement whenever there are the slightest grounds for doing so, theorizing that if the officer had to delay his search to obtain a search warrant, the suspect would have either destroyed, moved, or sold the marijuana.

For example, in one case an officer thought that a particular home was being burglarized. He checked the home's windows and front door, but saw no evidence of forced entry. He then decided to knock on the front door just to check that everything was all right. Doug, the resident of the home, came to the door and opened it a few inches. Out flowed the overwhelming aroma of burning marijuana. When Doug saw that it was a police officer on his doorstep, he quickly tried to close his door. The officer used his foot to block the door and gain entry to Doug's home. Once inside, the officer arrested Doug and his friend for possession of marijuana.

A California court noted that in most cases an officer must have a warrant to enter a person's home. However, the court held that the officer's warrantless entry of Doug's home was legal under the "exigent circumstances" exception to the warrant requirement. The court explained that the odor of burning marijuana is unmistakable to a trained officer, and hence, established probable cause that Doug was in possession of marijuana. Ordinarily, an officer needs a search warrant to enter a home even if he has probable cause that marijuana is located inside. Here, however, the court explained that Doug saw the officer when he opened the door, and was aware he was in trouble. The officer's immediate warrantless entry of the home was necessary, said the court, to prevent Doug from destroying the marijuana.

One well-established exigent circumstance justifying a warrantless entry by a government agent is when a building is on fire. Obviously, such an exception makes sense, unless we want buildings to burn to the ground while firefighters track down a judge to issue a warrant permitting them to enter a burning home and fight the fire. The problem is, however, that some courts, adrift in the hysteria of the War on Drugs, have stretched the exigent circumstances exception to dangerous limits, finding almost any "emergency" justifies the warrantless entry of a home.

For example, in one 1993 case from MacDonald County, Missouri, deputy sheriffs arrived at Larry Taylor's home to arrest him on a misdemeanor arrest warrant. Deputy Sheriff Perkins parked his patrol car about ten feet from a metal shed near Larry's home. As Perkins exited his automobile, he thought he smelled something burning. The aroma was emanating from Larry's shed. He also heard "a motor or something running." Perkins went to the shed door; it was locked. Although he did not have a search warrant authorizing the search of the shed, Deputy Perkins found a closed window and opened it. A blanket hung on the inside of the window. Perkins pushed the blanket aside and poked his head inside to look around. He testified: "It was kind of hazy in there, and I seen this motor, looked like a heater, or something, blowing down there. And I also seen what appeared to be marijuana on some screens. Looked like screens off of the window...."

About a *half hour* later, and still without a search warrant, Perkins removed the door to the shed and went inside. Inside, he found marijuana suspended on screens above a heater. Deputy Perkins seized the marijuana and Larry Taylor was later convicted of possession.

Larry argued that Deputy Perkins performed an unlawful warrantless search when he opened the window, pulled the shade up and looked inside the shed. Claiming that a danger of fire existed, the prosecutor used the exigent circumstances exception to the warrant requirement to defeat Taylor's argument. The prosecutor put Deputy Perkins on the stand and asked him, "Why did you look into the shed?" Perkins replied, "Because I was afraid something was on fire in there."

The court held that Perkins had lawfully entered the building because he thought he smelled something burning and needed to take swift action in order to prevent possible disaster. Consequently, the court held that exigent circumstances excused the need to obtain a search warrant, and hence no constitutional right was violated by Deputy Perkins' warrantless entry of the shed. *(State v. Taylor [Mo. App. S.D. 1993] 857 S.W.2d 482.)*

Swallowing Incriminating Evidence

It's relatively common for individuals in possession of illegal drugs to become terrified at the approach of a police officer and attempt to dispose of evidence by swallowing the drug. Often the police officer will immediately attempt to force the person to spit out the contraband. As a general rule, police officers may reach into a person's mouth to recover evidence if there is probable cause to believe a crime is being committed. No warrant is required for such a search, because, under the exigent circumstances rule, immediate police action is necessary to prevent the destruction of evidence. As stated by the California Supreme Court, "the mouth is not a 'sacred orifice' and there is no constitutional right to destroy or dispose of evidence."

The Fourth Amendment does place some restrictions on how police can attempt to seize swallowed contraband. Police officers attempting to remove contraband from a person's mouth must act reasonably and may use only as much force as is necessary to remove the object. In other words, the police may not use brutal or excessive force, or engage in a removal technique that "shocks the conscience." Most courts have held that police officers cannot "choke" a person to prevent the person from swallowing marijuana. For example, in one case an officer who had been surveilling an apartment unit suspected of being a "drug house" observed Michael Jones leave the unit carrying a tiny toy balloon suspected to contain heroin. When the officer approached, Michael panicked and attempted to swallow the balloon. The officer grabbed Michael's lower jaw and, for ten or fifteen seconds, applied pressure to Michael's jaw and throat in an attempt to prevent him from swallowing the balloon. In the struggle, Michael was shoved to the ground, the balloon was expelled, and was later found to contain heroin.

The court held that, "a suspect may not be choked or abused in order to force evidence from his person or to prevent its disposal by swallowing.... choking a man to extract evidence from his mouth violates due process." The court rejected the prosecution's argument that a "reasonable amount of choking" is permissible. The court stated:

> California law . . . has not recognized distinctions in a degree of choking, but rather has drawn the line of illegality at choking . . . . When illegality is shown the law does not recognize degrees of illegality and inquire whether the conduct was grossly or only mildly illegal. No object that is forced from an accused by means of choking should ever be received in evidence.

After stating the above rule, the court held that the officer's forceful action on Michael's throat and lower jaw was indeed "choking," and hence was illegal. As a result, the balloon and its contents were excluded from evidence. *(People v. Jones [1989] 209.Cal.App.3d 725.)*

In another case, police officers tackled an amputee in a wheel chair, after observing him place a "two-inch wad" of masking tape into his mouth. After knocking the man out of his wheel chair, several officers grabbed the man's chin and placed pressure on his neck to prevent him from swallowing the wad. When the man refused to spit out the wad, another officer pushed his Bic pen into the man's mouth and successfully pried the object out. The court held that this action was *legal* because there was no evidence that the officers attempted to choke the man.

Searches at School If You Are a Student

If you are a student at a public school, it is important to understand that the Supreme Court has reduced the level of protection you have against searches conducted at school by a school official. The case in which the Court created this exception involved a female student, referred to by the Court as "T.L.O." who was reportedly smoking cigarettes in the school bathroom in violation of school rules. She was called into the principal's office and questioned by the assistant principal. Although T.L.O. denied smoking, the assistant principal did not believe her.

The assistant principal reasoned that if T.L.O. did smoke, then she probably carried the pack of cigarettes in her purse. Without any more evidence, and without a search warrant, the assistant principal snatched T.L.O.'s purse, opened it, and found a pack of cigarettes. Along with the cigarettes, he also saw a package of rolling papers, which he associated with marijuana use. After finding the rolling papers, he emptied T.L.O.'s purse and carefully searched for more evidence of marijuana use. In among T.L.O.'s personal belongings, he discovered additional evidence of her use, and possible sale, of marijuana.

Clearly, had this been a search of an adult's purse by a government agent, the Court would have held that it was illegal because it was not based on a warrant. However, because the search was of a child, and on school property by a school official, the Court created a special exception to the warrant requirement. This exception permits a public school official to search students and their belongings, if the official has a *reasonable belief* that the student possesses contraband. Under this rule, school searches by teachers and principals will almost always be upheld as legal. Remember, however, what little protection this rule gives to public school students is *not* available to students at private schools. Private school officials are not constrained by the Fourth Amendment. Therefore, officials at private schools may legally search a student for *any* reason. Reasonable suspicion is not required. (*New Jersey v. T.L.O. [1985] 469 US 325.*)

Marijuana and Your Telephone

The Supreme Court has held that people are reasonable in expecting the contents of their telephone conversations to be private. For this reason, the Court has held that a police officer must obtain a search warrant in order to tap a person's phone. Unfortunately, there is one main exception to this rule which is often used in marijuana investigations. Specifically, no search warrant is needed if *one* party to the telephone conversation agrees. This often occurs in marijuana cases when the police apprehend a small-time marijuana user and promise to give him a break if he helps them catch his supplier. The police will often instruct the user to call his supplier and set up a buy. As part of the deal, the police will obtain the user's "consent" to tape the telephone conversation. The contents of the conversation will be used against the supplier.

Likewise, telephone companies routinely monitor conversations to perform maintenance, to monitor employee performance, and to prevent fraud. If such monitoring results in the interception of a conversation concerning a marijuana crime, the company can disclose the intercepted comments to the police, despite the fact that the information was obtained without a search warrant. Remember, the Fourth Amendment does not protect you against searches by private people or private companies.

An additional exception to the search warrant requirement concerns telephone communications involving pagers and cordless phones. These broadcasts are easily intercepted with a radio. In fact, many radio buffs make it a hobby to eavesdrop on cordless phone calls. Most courts hold that, because such conversations can be intercepted by almost anyone, and often are, a person has no reasonable expectation of privacy in such communications. Therefore, the police are free to listen in on them without having to get a warrant.

It's interesting to note that nearly half of the 95 million households in the United States use cordless telephones, with the figure growing by leaps and bounds each year. As one court recently noted:

> If, as some experts predict, we are moving inexorably toward a completely cordless telephone system, the decision as to whether cordless telephone conversations are protected by the Fourth Amendment may ultimately determine whether *any* telephone conversations are protected by the Fourth Amendment.

As just mentioned, the general rule is that conversations carried by land-based telephone lines are protected by the Fourth Amendment, while pure radio communications are not. Although most people who use a cordless telephone probably feel more like they're using a telephone rather than a radio, courts have routinely ruled that because cordless transmissions can be fairly easily intercepted by widely available radios, it is not reasonable for a person to expect them to be private. Consequently, the police may intercept them without a warrant. "Broadcasting communications into the air by radio waves," asserted one court "is more analogous to carrying on an oral communication in a loud voice or with a megaphone than it is to the privacy afforded by a wire."

Fortunately, at least one federal court (the Fifth Circuit) has noted that today's cordless phones are providing more and more privacy protection through such features as automatic frequency selection and cycling, and even scrambling. The court intimated that it might soon be reasonable for a person using such a high-tech cordless phone to expect his conversation to be just as private as one carried by wires. In that case, the person might be able to challenge warrantless interception of such a communication as an unreasonable search that invaded his or her reasonable expectation of privacy. For now, however, most courts which have examined the issue of intercepted cordless telephone conversations have refused to find that the caller had a reasonable expectation of privacy. The lesson is obvious: sensitive topics should never be discussed on a cordless phone.

Pen Registers and Trap & Trace Devices

The Supreme Court has held that police officers may install "pen-registers" and "trap-and-trace" devices without obtaining a search warrant. A pen-register is a device that records all the telephone numbers that are dialed from a particular residence. A trap and trace device is similar, but it records all the telephone numbers of incoming calls. With both devices, the numbers are recorded at the instant they are dialed or received, and hence, the information is extremely up-to-date. The Court has held that installation of such a device is not a search; so the Fourth Amendment is inapplicable, meaning that police can install such devices for any reason and need not obtain a warrant.

In the case that created this rule, the police suspected that Mr. Smith was involved in a robbery. The officers, without first obtaining a search warrant, attached a pen-register to Mr. Smith's telephone line at the central telephone office. The device recorded every number dialed out of Mr. Smith's home, and in so doing, provided some incriminating evidence against Mr. Smith.

At a pretrial hearing, Mr. Smith asked the court to exclude all evidence derived from the pen-register, arguing that it was a warrantless search and hence unreasonable under the Fourth Amendment. The case went all the way to the Supreme Court, which held that installation of the pen-register was not a search. The Court reasoned that because the pen-register was installed at the phone company, Smith could not claim that *his* property was invaded or that the police intruded into a "constitutionally protected area." The Court rejected Smith's argument that the pen-register infringed on his legitimate right of privacy, explaining that the register only recorded the *numbers* dialed and not the *contents* of his conversation. The Court reasoned that telephone users realize that such information is a used by the phone company to calculate the subscriber's monthly bill, and hence, subscribers have no reasonable expectation of privacy in the information. For these reasons, no warrant is required before law enforcement officers install a pen-register. *(Smith v. Maryland [1979] 442 US 735.)*

The reasoning in the *Smith* case is unsound. A person's awareness of the phone company's access to such information does not necessarily entail consent to have that information made available to the general public or the police. As Justice Marshall commented, "Privacy is not a discrete commodity, possessed absolutely or not at all. Those who disclose certain facts to a bank or phone company for a limited business purpose need not assume that this information will be released to other persons for other purposes."

There is a federal law placing some restrictions on when officers can attach such a device to a person's phone line. Under this statute officers seeking to install a pen register or trap and trace device must at least submit a form to a judge and, under oath, declare that the information likely to be obtained is relevant to an ongoing criminal investigation.

Clone Pagers

Another device used by law enforcement agents to track communications is known as a clone pager. This device is a telephone pager with the same telephone number as the suspect's. An officer with a clone pager simply wears it around and, when it beeps, records the telephone numbers of the people who page the suspect. In other words, every time the suspect gets paged, so does the officer. In many cases, the person calling the pager uses a public phone. Once officers record enough incoming calls originating from a particular pay-phone, they often put the pay-phone under surveillance, based on the calling patterns documented by using the clone pager. By using this technique they can often identify the person that has been paging their suspect, even if the person has been using a pay phone and using only a code for identification.

Marijuana and the U.S. Mail

In 1992, a total of almost 2000 people were arrested after the U.S. Postal Inspection Service found that their mail contained a controlled substance. The law concerning marijuana and the mail is similar to that regarding the government's eavesdropping on telephone conversations. Like the *contents* of a telephone conversation, the *contents* of a letter or package are considered private by most reasonable people. The Supreme Court has held that United States *first-class* mail, whether a letter or package, is protected by the Fourth Amendment. Therefore, the government cannot open first-class mail on the mere hunch that it contains marijuana. Rather, the government must obtain a federal search warrant based on probable cause that marijuana will be found inside the letter or package. (A federal search warrant is required because state courts do not have jurisdiction over U.S. mail.)

Once a warrant has been obtained, officers can obtain the contents of your mail, either from the mail stream or straight out of your mailbox. A government agent's failure to obtain a search warrant before opening first-class mail will result in the exclusion from court of any marijuana found during such an illegal mail search. Remember, however, only first-class mail is protected. Mail not sent first class does not receive the same stringent protection. Moreover, mail sent through a *private* mail carrier, such as Federal Express or United Parcel Service, receives *no* protection under the Fourth Amendment if opened by employees of the private carrier. To repeat, the Fourth Amendment protects you against unreasonable searches *only* by the government or its agents — there is no protection against searches by private individuals.

The courts have held that the border exception to the warrant requirement allows government agents to open international mail if they suspect, *for any reason*, that it contains marijuana or other drugs. No warrant is required for such a search. One recent case decided in 1995 held that mail coming into the U.S. from a recognized "drug source country" (in this case Turkey) *and* addressed to a post office box, was automatically suspect and could be opened without a warrant.

Besides getting a hold of your mail and reading it, law enforcement agents sometimes contact mail delivery people to try and learn more about a particular suspect. In one federal law enforcement manual, for example, agents are instructed:

> Private mail-receiver agents, may be willing to talk with law enforcement personnel, so they should not be overlooked. Nor should Postal Service mail carriers be overlooked as information sources. Carriers tend to have regular routes, and thus may have useful information. Discretion in contacting mail carriers is advisable, especially in small towns and rural areas, as the carrier may be friendly with the target. *(US Dept. Of Justice. Asset Forfeiture, Informants and Undercover Investigations, 13th in a series, reprinted January 1992.)*

Mail Covers

In contrast to the protection given the contents of first-class mail, the Supreme Court has held that you have no reasonable expectations of privacy regarding the information featured on the *outside* of your envelopes. For this reason, the courts have held that the police may conduct "mail covers" without the need for a warrant. During a mail cover, the authorities record all the information on the outside of your envelopes, including the names of the addressee and sender, return address, postmark, and anything else you, or your correspondent, write on the envelope.

To conduct a mail cover, the police do not need a search warrant, probable cause, or even a reasonable suspicion that you're involved in criminal activity. Rather, law enforcement officers simply fill out a simple form and submit it to the office of the regional postal inspector which coordinates mail covers with the local delivery station. The information is recorded by postal employees at the local post office before delivery. Officers can obtain a mail cover on all classes of U.S. mail. The information obtained can be used against you if the police find that you sent or received mail from another person who is a known marijuana grower or user.

The "Drug Package Profile"

The U.S. Post office has developed what is known as the "drug package profile." If a package matches the profile and an alert postal worker sees it, it is pulled from the mails and usually presented to a drug-sniffing dog. If the dog alerts to the package, or if other factors rouse the inspector's suspicion, the inspector prepares an affidavit and obtains a search warrant. Under the authority of such a search warrant, the package is opened and searched.

According to one recent case, postal inspectors specifically target Express Mail because history has shown Express Mail has been used in the majority of cases involving mailed contraband. As with the "drug courier profile" discussed earlier, the characteristics making up the drug package profile are not absolute. The following factors, however, seem to be primary:

(1) The package is sent from or to a known "source state" for drugs.
(2) The package is sent from one individual to another individual.
(3) The mailing labels are hand written.
(4) The return address is fictitious or inaccurate.
(5) There are unusual odors coming from the package.
(6) The package is heavily taped to seal all openings.

Private mail carriers, such as Federal Express, employ a similar drug package profile. However, because they are private companies they do not need to obtain a search warrant before opening packages. In fact, all packages sent via Federal Express can be opened for any reason pursuant to a fine-print agreement that all senders sign when shipping a letter or parcel *via* Federal Express.

The "No Knowledge" Defense for Marijuana Received In The Mail

As discussed in Chapter One, one of the elements required for conviction of marijuana possession entails that the government prove that the defendant knew the substance he possessed was marijuana. In cases involving a defendant arrested after receiving marijuana in the mail, this element is sometimes difficult for the government to prove.

When the authorities intercept a package or letter found to contain marijuana, they often deliver it to the addressee and then, moments after the person has retrieved the package, they knock on the door and announce that they have an arrest warrant. Occasionally, the police act prematurely, arresting the person before he or she has opened the package and taken some action that circumstantially shows he or she knows it contains marijuana. In many cases, however, when the police burst in, some circumstantial evidence will show that the person knew the package contained marijuana. In some cases, knowledge was established by showing that the person placed the package in the refrigerator or gave evasive answers when the police asked for the package. In other cases, knowledge has been established by showing that the person possessed paraphernalia for smoking marijuana.

CHAPTER 6

MARIJUANA & YOUR CAR

When Can a Police Officer Stop Your Car?

THE BEDROCK RULE is that an officer can pull over a vehicle only if he has at least a *reasonable suspicion* that the driver or occupant committed a crime or traffic violation. A very large proportion of marijuana arrests occur in conjunction with the suspect being stopped for a traffic violation. There are numerous court cases in which people were convicted of marijuana crimes following an officer's stop of their vehicle due to: double parking, expired registration tags, dirty windshield that obstructed the driver's view, faulty muffler, polluting car, no registration tag, headlights out, broken tail light, failure to dim high beams, no brake lights, bald tires, no license plate, illegible license plate, no license plate light, speeding, driving over a double line, unsafe lane change, and weaving. If your car has any such defects, or if you violate any traffic laws, you are inviting a police officer to pull you over at any time.

Roadblocks

As just mentioned, the general rule is that an officer must have reasonable suspicion in order to legally stop a person driving a vehicle. One major exception, however, pertains to roadblocks. Currently, the most common use of roadblocks is to detect and deter people driving under the influence of alcohol or drugs. When the police properly conduct such a roadblock, they may stop vehicles without any reason to believe that the driver is under the influence. Usually they employ some system such as stopping every third car. If a vehicle is stopped at a roadblock, the stop must be very short. The officers must quickly allow the driver to pass through unless they observe facts that create a reasonable suspicion that the driver is intoxicated or otherwise violating the law. This is usually accomplished by asking the driver a question or two and judging his response. If the driver slurs his speech, or exhibits any other signs of alcohol or drug use, the officer will be provided with a reasonable suspicion sufficient to extend the driver's detention and order him or her to get out and perform some field sobriety tests. If the driver fails the field sobriety tests, the officer will then have probable cause to arrest the driver for driving under the influence.

In short, a police roadblock only allows the officers to *stop* your vehicle. They cannot *search* you or your car without probable cause to believe that you are violating the law. For example, sometimes roadblock detentions are extended because an officer smells marijuana when he talks to the driver. Likewise, even at a roadblock, you retain every right to refuse to consent to an officer's request to search.

Ordering You Out of Your Car

If a police officer legally stops a vehicle, he has the right to order the driver out of the car. This is a routine procedure which most courts have allowed for "officer safety reasons." Upon ordering a person out, the officer may conduct a pat-search of the person's outer clothing *only* if he sees a bulge or has some other reasonable basis for believing that the individual may be armed or dangerous.

When Can a Police Officer Search Your Car Without a Warrant?

There are several conditions that can grant an officer the right to search your car without a warrant. Specifically, an officer can conduct a warrantless search of your car if:

(1) the officer reasonably believes you may have a weapon in the vehicle; *or*
(2) the officer has probable cause to believe there is marijuana or other contraband inside the car; *or*
(3) the officer arrests you; *or*
(4) your car has already been impounded.

Vehicle Search for Officer Safety

As noted above, if a police officer legally stops a vehicle and reasonably believes an occupant may be armed with a weapon or dangerous, the officer can order the occupant out of the car and search the passenger area of the vehicle for weapons.

In one famous case, police officers on patrol late at night observed a car speeding and weaving. As they watched, the driver of the car lost control and swerved into a ditch. When the officers got to the car, the driver, Mr. Long, was already out of the car. He exhibited all the classic symptoms of intoxication. When the officers asked to see his vehicle registration, Mr. Long walked back to his car to retrieve it. At that moment, the officers saw a large hunting knife on the floor board of Mr. Long's car and immediately ordered him to freeze. They pat-searched Mr. Long, but found no weapons. The officers then directed their flashlights inside the car to look for any other weapons in plain view. Although they saw no weapons, they did see a large open pouch in the front seat. The pouch appeared to contain a large amount of marijuana. Based on their observations, the officers arrested Mr. Long for possession of marijuana, and after searching the car found 75 pounds.

The Court concluded that the officers acted constitutionally when they looked into Mr. Long's car with their flashlights. The Court explained that even when a suspect has been removed from his vehicle for questioning, the police may still conduct a "protective search" of the vehicle's interior. The Court reasoned that a suspect might break away and enter his vehicle, thereby obtaining a hidden weapon. In addition, the Court explained, if a suspect is not arrested following a detention, he will be allowed to return to his car and could retrieve a weapon at that time. Therefore, for "officer safety reasons," whenever a police officer reasonably believes a suspect may be dangerous, the officer can search the *passenger compartment* of the suspect's vehicle. Moreover, when such a search for weapons is conducted, the officers may seize any illegal drugs found during the search. *(Michigan v. Long [1983] 463 US 1032.)*

Vehicle Searches Based on Probable Cause

Although a police officer can stop your vehicle with only a *reasonable suspicion* of criminal activity, he cannot typically search your vehicle unless he has *probable cause* to believe you are or were engaged in criminal activity. In other words, if a police officer stops you for speeding, he ordinarily cannot search your car. However, if an officer stops your car, and somehow probable cause develops to believe that there is marijuana in the vehicle, the Supreme Court has held that the officer can immediately conduct a *warrantless* search of you and your vehicle's passenger compartment. The twin justifications for warrantless searches of automobiles are their mobility and the lesser expectation of privacy which an individual has in a vehicle as compared to a home. *(US v. Ross [1982] 456 U.S. 798.)*

Air Fresheners

Juan Garza was stopped for speeding as he drove from Texas to Chicago. While the officer and Mr. Garza chatted, the officer asked Juan whether he was carrying marijuana in the car. Juan denied transporting any marijuana and told the officer he was welcome to search his car. As mentioned earlier, a police officer will almost always accept such a gracious offer, and this officer proved not to be unique.

The officer searched Juan's car, beginning with the front seat. There was a jacket lying on the seat and when the officer lifted it he found a can of air freshener underneath it. The officer asked to look in the trunk and again Juan consented. The officer later testified that in the trunk he found "a box of Downy dryer sheets laying on top of a spare tire and a hang-up air freshener." At that point, the officer began to get very suspicious and intensified his search of the trunk. He noticed that the back of the rear seat looked like it had just recently been spray painted and seemed to be covered with an adhesive material. He pushed on the back seat and discovered it was harder than would be expected. When the officer entered the back seat area of the car and pulled the back seat forward, he discovered a secret compartment and was overcome with the aroma of marijuana. Inside the secret compartment were numerous packages containing marijuana.

In court, Juan's attorney argued that when the officer pulled apart Juan's back seat, his search exceeded the scope of Juan's consent. He argued that no one stopped for speeding reasonably expects a police officer to tear his car apart even if he consents to a search. The court disagreed, explaining that while, in general, a person who consents to a search of his car does not necessarily consent to the officer damaging his car, the rule changes if the person is present during the search and does not object to the officer's actions. In such circumstances, said the court, the damage can be considered to be within the scope of the person's consent.

The court, however, did not rest its decision on the scope of Mr. Garza's consent. Rather, the court found that the officer had uncovered probable cause *before* he removed the back seat. Therefore, armed with probable cause of wrongdoing, the officer did not need Juan's consent and did not need a warrant. As the court explained:

> Defendant was en route from Texas to Chicago–a frequent pathway for drug trafficking–without luggage. Items for disguising odors were in the trunk and the passenger area. When the officer looked in the trunk, the adhesive material and spray paint in the rear of the trunk were apparent. When he pressed in the area behind the back seat arm rest, it was "very hard." These items, combined with the officer's knowledge and experience, established the probable cause necessary for the officer to proceed to look for the compartment behind the back seat. *(State v. Garza [Mo.App.S.D. 1993] 853 S.W.2d 462.)*

Aroma, Hand-Rolled Cigarettes, Seeds & Roach Clips

In one case in Arizona, the officers stopped Mr. Lynch's vehicle for reckless driving. When the officer reached into the car to take Mr. Lynch's driver's license, he detected the aroma of fresh marijuana. Without obtaining a warrant, the officer searched Lynch's vehicle, discovering marijuana, hashish, and some pipes. The

Arizona court upheld the warrantless search, holding that the aroma of marijuana provided probable cause that Lynch was in the process of transporting marijuana in his vehicle. *(State v. Lynch [1978, Az.App.] 587 P.2d 770.)*

After Nebraska police officers stopped Mr. Daly's truck for speeding, one officer detected a "faint odor of marijuana" that seemed stronger near the back of the truck. The officer advised Mr. Daly of the odor and "requested" that Mr. Daly open the rear door of the truck. When Mr. Daly complied, the officer smelled a strong aroma of marijuana, and proceeded to search the truck without a warrant. Inside the truck, the officer found more than 500 pounds of marijuana. A Nebraska court upheld the officer's warrantless search, finding that the officer had made approximately 50 similar arrests in the past after detecting the aroma of marijuana. Therefore, given the officer's experience, his detection of the marijuana aroma gave him probable cause to believe that Daly's vehicle contained marijuana. *(State v. Daly [1979] 274 NW2d 557.)*

Occasionally the courts have held that an officer's detection of a marijuana aroma is *not* sufficient to establish probable cause for a warrantless search of the vehicle. However, in those cases it was either because the officer simply lacked experience or training to positively identify the aroma as marijuana, or because the source of the aroma could not be pinpointed or its "freshness" determined.

For example, after Michigan state police officers had legally stopped Mr. Hilber's car, one officer detected the aroma of burnt marijuana emanating from the vehicle. For that reason, the officer performed a warrantless search of the vehicle, recovering marijuana and other drugs. A Michigan court held that the officer's warrantless search was illegal, saying that the aroma alone did not establish probable cause. The court based its holding on the fact that this particular officer had no training in determining how long the aroma of marijuana can linger. Therefore, the officer could not reasonably infer that the driver had just been smoking marijuana or that the car currently contained marijuana. Consequently, he did not have probable cause to search the car for marijuana. *(People v. Hilber [1978] 269 NW2d 159.)*

In a similar case in Montana, a court refused to find probable cause for a warrantless vehicle search after an officer detected the combined aroma of incense and marijuana following a vehicle stop. The court referred to the officer's own testimony that the aroma of marijuana can linger in a vehicle for more than a day. Therefore, because the officer did not actually see the vehicle's occupants smoking, and did not observe any other evidence of marijuana, the aroma alone was insufficient to establish probable cause that the vehicle *currently* contained marijuana or that the driver was currently under the influence of marijuana. *(State v. Shoendaller [1978] 578 P.2d 730.)*

The Supreme Court of New Hampshire has held that an officer's observation of a hand-rolled cigarette by itself was *insufficient* evidence of marijuana use to entitle the officer to reach into a vehicle and retrieve the hand-rolled cigarette without a warrant. In this case, New Hampshire state troopers stopped a vehicle driven by Forrest Ball. As one trooper approached the vehicle, he observed in the ashtray "several partially smoked manufactured cigarettes, as well as a partially smoked hand-rolled cigarette." Unable to identify the contents of the hand-rolled cigarette by sight, the officer reached in, removed it from the ashtray, and smelled it. He concluded that the cigarette contained marijuana, and arrested Mr. Ball. A search of Mr. Ball led to the discovery of additional contraband.

The New Hampshire Supreme Court held that the officer's warrantless seizure of the hand-rolled cigarette was *illegal*, even under the plain-view rule, because the incriminating nature of the cigarette was not immediately apparent. The court stated:

> Not all hand-rolled cigarettes contain contraband. Consequently, we cannot say that observation of a hand-rolled cigarette, by itself, would lead a reasonable and prudent person to believe that the cigarette contained an illegal substance. To transfer a mere suspicion about the contents of the hand-rolled cigarette into a reasonable belief based on probable cause, the officer must articulate additional corroborating facts. For instance, it might be shown that the arresting officer had the ability to distinguish hand-rolled marijuana and tobacco cigarettes by sight, or that he perceived the odor of marijuana, or that the defendant made a furtive gesture in an attempt to conceal the cigarette, or that the defendant's conduct was otherwise incriminating. *(State v. Ball [N.H. 1983] 471 A.2d 347.)*

Most courts agree that the mere observation of a hand-rolled cigarette is not sufficient to provide probable cause that it contains marijuana. However, once an officer spots a hand-rolled cigarette, very little further evidence *will* establish probable cause. For example, courts have routinely found that hand-rolled cigarettes establish probable cause where other elements (such as furtive acts by the suspect, the presence of drug paraphernalia, or the odor of marijuana) are present to justify the officer's suspicions. After stopping a vehicle driven by Julian Franklin, a New York state police officer observed a roach clip on Julian's key ring, that had a "charred residue" on the end but did not hold the remnants of a joint. Based on his observation of the roach clip, the officer conducted a warrantless search of Julian's car and discovered several plastic baggies of marijuana. A New York court held that the officer's observation of the roach clip did not give rise to probable cause to search Julian's car. Why? Because the officer "had no indication that the roach clip had recently been used for smoking marijuana by reason of its being hot or by the presence of smoke in the vehicle." Therefore, the court dismissed the case against Julian, ruling the officer's illegal search required the exclusion of all evidence.

In many states, any amount of marijuana seen in a car establishes probable cause to search the car's interior. In one case, officers stopped a car and spotted a single seed and a few stems on the back seat. The court held that was sufficient to permit the officers to search the car's passenger compartment.

Trunks vs. Passenger Compartments

In another case, Officers Moffett and Najera were on routine patrol when they observed a vehicle speeding and occasionally swerving out of its lane. The officers stopped the vehicle for speeding, suspecting that the driver might be tired or under the influence. Officer Najera approached the vehicle and spoke with the driver, Steven Wimberly. Officer Moffett approached the passenger side, where Richard Harrison was seated. As he approached, Moffett shined his flashlight into the vehicle and saw, among other things, a smoking pipe and twelve dark seeds on the floor near Richard's feet.

The general characteristics of the seeds, coupled with their proximity to the pipe, led Moffett to conclude they were *Cannabis* seeds. Moffett ordered Richard to hand him the pipe, and Richard complied. The officer sniffed the pipe, detecting the odor of burnt marijuana. He also observed a burnt residue, including some seeds and stems, inside the pipe.

At this point, the officers ordered Richard and Steven out of the car and searched the passenger compartment. Inside, they detected the aroma of burnt marijuana. Additionally Officer Moffett found a plastic bag containing a small amount of marijuana inside the pocket of a jacket found in the car. The officers then used Steven's keys to open the vehicle's trunk. Inside the trunk they found a suitcase which they proceeded to open, revealing several pounds of marijuana and hashish.

The California Supreme Court held that Officer Moffett's search of the vehicle's *passenger compartment* was legal. The Court explained that Moffett had probable cause based on his observation of the pipe and the seeds. The Court pointed out that Moffett's observation of the seeds alone was sufficient to establish probable cause to search the vehicle's passenger compartment and any container within the compartment such as the jacket. Therefore, all the evidence found in the car's *passenger compartment* was admissible against Steven and Richard.

The Court went on, however, to hold that the officer's search of the vehicle's *trunk* was *illegal*. The Court explained that the officer's discovery of the pipe, seeds, and small bag of marijuana was indicative of the casual use of marijuana. Nothing indicated that the two men were transporting marijuana in the trunk. In other words, although there was probable cause to search the *passenger compartment*, the officer's further intrusion into the vehicle's *trunk* was unlawful because there was no probable cause that marijuana would be found therein. As a result, the Court held that the large amount of marijuana and hashish found in the trunk was inadmissible in court.

This decision makes an important distinction. Unlike a vehicle's passenger compartment, which is surrounded by see-through windows, a vehicle's trunk normally cannot be seen into from outside. Accordingly, the courts have found that it is reasonable for a person to expect more privacy for items placed inside a vehicle's trunk than for items placed in a vehicle's passenger compartment.

Therefore, the rule has developed that probable cause sufficient for searching a vehicle's passenger compartment may not be sufficient to justify the search of the vehicle's trunk. Rather, in order for an officer without a warrant to search the trunk of a vehicle for marijuana, he must have probable cause to believe that marijuana is concealed *in the trunk*.

In one case, probable cause to search a vehicle trunk was held to exist when the drivers attempted to outrun the police. When the car was finally stopped, a kilo of marijuana was seen in plain view on the back seat, and three joints were seen on the floorboard. The court held that the plain-view observations, coupled with the desperate attempts to avoid apprehension, gave the officers probable cause to believe the occupants were transporting a large amount of contraband in their vehicle. Therefore, the trunk search was legal.

In another case, officers stopped a vehicle and discovered a baggie of marijuana in the passenger compartment. In addition, the officers smelled a very strong aroma of fresh, unburned marijuana that could not be attributed to the baggie. The court held that this gave the officers probable cause to believe that additional marijuana was in the trunk.

One court nicely summarized the rule for probable cause to search a vehicle's passenger compartment versus probable cause to search a vehicle's trunk compartment:

> The lawful observation of marijuana debris on a seat or the floor of the interior of the car, or in the clothing of the occupants, or the smell of burned marijuana emanating from the interior of the car would give probable cause to believe that marijuana might be found in the areas adjacent and immediately accessible to the occupants, such as ashtrays, a passenger console, a glove compartment and underneath and between the seats . . . . Similarly, if a substantial quantity of marijuana is found inside the automobile or on the person of an occupant, it reasonably may be inferred that additional contraband may be concealed in areas of the car not immediately accessible and adjacent to the occupants, such as the trunk or under the hood. A substantial quantity of marijuana in the interior of the car would give rise to a logical inference that the car was being used to transport marijuana. *(People v. Gregg [1974] 43 Cal.App.3d 137.)*

Opening Your Trunk

As the above cases indicate, it is often possible for officers to have probable cause to search a vehicle's passenger compartment without probable cause to search the vehicle's trunk. Often, in such cases, the officers will put pressure on the driver to consent to a search of the vehicle's trunk. Obviously, a driver in such a situation who has a large amount of marijuana in his trunk would be foolish to waive his Fourth Amendment rights and consent to the search of his trunk. Unfortunately, the practical reality in such circumstances is that the officers will likely open the trunk anyway, hoping that a judge will later find that they did have probable cause to believe it contained marijuana.

On the other hand, if officers find marijuana in the passenger compartment *and the driver knows there is no more in the trunk* consenting to the search of the trunk might be the most financially sensible action. As mentioned above, it is quite likely the officers will search the trunk even without the driver's consent, in the hopes that a court will find they had probable cause to do so. In such a situation, if the driver does not consent, the officers will likely cause some severe and costly damage to his car by breaking open the trunk.

As one court explained:

> If the officers have the right to engage in a warrantless search of the entire car they may do so by any means reasonably available; thus, if the trunk key cannot be located they may break open the trunk. Carried to its logical end, if the officers have the right to search the entire car and it is necessary to accomplish their purpose, they may rip apart any part of the car in which they should suspect that additional contraband may be found. *(People v. Gregg [1974] 43 Cal.App.3d 137.)*

Vehicle Searches-Incident to Arrest

The United States Supreme Court has held that whenever a police officer legally arrests a person in an automobile, the officer can search the person as well as the entire passenger compartment of the vehicle. Moreover, the officer's search can include the opening of closed containers found inside the passenger compartment.

In the case in which the Supreme Court created this rule, Officer Nicot, a New York State police officer, was driving an unmarked police car when he was passed by a speeding car. Officer Nicot gave chase and pulled the vehicle over. Inside were four occupants, including Roger Belton, who was riding in the back seat.

When Officer Nicot approached the car to write a speeding ticket, he smelled the aroma of burnt marijuana. In addition, as he spoke with the driver, he noticed an envelope on the floorboard of the car marked, "Supergold." In the officer's experience, such factors added up to probable cause that marijuana was inside the envelope and that the occupants had been smoking marijuana as they drove.

Therefore, under the New York rule which presumes all persons in a car to be in possession of any marijuana found in the passenger compartment, Officer Nicot ordered all four occupants out of the car and arrested them for possession of marijuana. Then, incident to the arrest of the men, the officer picked up the envelope and found that it did, indeed, contain marijuana. The officer searched the entire passenger compartment of the vehicle. On the back seat, where Roger Belton had been sitting, Officer Nicot found a black leather jacket. He unzipped the jacket's pockets and inside found additional illegal drugs. Roger was subsequently convicted of possessing narcotics.

Roger argued his case all the way to the Supreme Court. His position was that the officer had no right to search the closed pocket of his jacket without a search warrant. Roger argued that because Officer Nicot failed to get a search warrant, the search was illegal; hence all evidence of drugs found in the jacket should be excluded from court.

The Supreme Court rejected Roger's argument. The Court held that any time a police officer legally arrests the driver of a car, the officer automatically has the right to immediately search the passenger compartment of the car. Moreover, the officer may open and look inside any containers that he finds inside the passenger compartment. The Court broadly defined "containers" as:

> Any object capable of holding another object. It thus includes closed or open glove compartments, consoles, or other receptacles located anywhere within the passenger compartment, as well as luggage, boxes, bags, clothing, and the like. *(New York v. Belton [1981] 453 US 454.)*

The Court did place one very important limit on the vehicle search, stating that the arrest of a vehicle's occupant does *not*, by itself, permit the police to search the vehicle's *trunk*. Therefore, while an officer's arrest of a driver allows him to search the vehicle's passenger compartment, he cannot search the vehicle's *trunk* unless he has probable cause to believe that marijuana is inside the *trunk*.

Throwing Marijuana from a Moving Vehicle

As discussed earlier, a person retains no reasonable expectation of privacy for abandoned property. For this reason, a person cannot complain of an officer's warrantless search or seizure of the property once it has been abandoned.

In one case, narcotics officers received a tip that a man would be transferring some marijuana from his home into his truck. The officers staked out the man's home and, just on schedule, observed the man exit the home with a package and place it in the truck. The man then got in the truck and drove away. One of the officers tried to stop the truck by driving alongside it and flashing the driver his police badge. Rather than pull over, however, the driver accelerated, and the agents gave chase. During the chase, the man tossed a package out the window. The officers recovered the package, searched it without a warrant, and discovered it contained marijuana.

The court held that because the man abandoned the package, the officer's retrieval and discovery of the marijuana inside the package was neither a "search" or a "seizure." Consequently, the warrantless search of the package was entirely legal under the Fourth Amendment.

In another case, police officers performing a routine traffic stop of a speeding vehicle observed the passenger toss a bag out the window. The police recovered the abandoned bag and found marijuana inside. The court upheld the passenger's conviction for possessing marijuana.

Automobile Inventory Searches

Often, when a person is arrested following a vehicle stop, the arresting officer will have the person's car towed away and impounded. This is often done if the driver is alone when arrested and his vehicle is stopped on a public street.

When a car is impounded by the police, most states permit the police to "inventory" the contents of the vehicle to avoid a lawsuit in which the owner might claim that property inside the car was not returned to him. This is known as a "vehicle inventory search." The scope of an inventory search is very broad. In fact, in most states, the police can open a vehicle's *trunk* as well as closed containers found anywhere in the car. In other words, a vehicle inventory search is even broader than the search permitted incident to the arrest of a vehicle's driver.

In one case that went all the way to the Supreme Court, a Florida Highway Patrol trooper stopped Martin Wells' vehicle for speeding. After smelling alcohol on Martin's breath, the trooper arrested him for driving under the influence of alcohol and impounded his vehicle. At the police impound facility, an inventory search turned up "two marijuana cigarette butts in an ashtray and a locked suitcase in the trunk." The police forced open the suitcase and discovered a garbage bag containing marijuana.

The Supreme Court upheld the warrantless search of the ashtray, trunk, and suitcase, noting that the search was reasonable in order "to protect an owner's property while it is in the custody of the police, to insure against claims of lost, stolen, or vandalized property, and to guard the police from danger." *(Florida v. Wells [1990] 495 US 1.)*

In another case, a man named Bill had grown a very robust *Cannabis* plant inside the closet of his city apartment. However, because of the plant's rapidly increasing size and aroma, Bill decided he and the plant would be better off if he moved it to the backyard of his secluded summer cabin in the country. One night, Bill carefully covered the plant with a bed sheet and quietly carried it outside to his van. Bill then began the long drive to his cabin.

Along the way, Bill stopped at his favorite restaurant and had dinner. As he left the restaurant he was mortified to see that his van was gone. After running around the parking lot in a panic, he came to the awful realization that he had mistakenly parked in a "No Parking" zone and the police had towed his van. When Bill arrived at the police impound lot, he was arrested on numerous marijuana charges, including cultivation, transporting, and possession of marijuana.

Bill should not have parked in a "No Parking" zone. Since the police impounded his van, they were legally authorized to conduct an inventory search which revealed the *Cannabis* plant.

Since an inventory search is permitted only if your car is impounded, it stands to reason that you can avoid such a search if you can prevent the officer from impounding your car. There are several strategies you can use. First, if you have a passenger in the car when you are arrested, and that person is legally able to drive, you can try turning your keys over to the passenger and giving him or her permission to drive your car home for you.

Second, some people have been able to appeal to the officer's goodwill by being very polite during the arrest and then asking the officer if he would be so kind as to move the vehicle off the road and into a private parking lot. (Obviously, you do not want to use this tactic if you think the officer will smell or see marijuana when he enters the car.) Some officers understand that impounding a vehicle costs the owner a lot of money, and if you can engender their sympathy, they may move your vehicle to give you a break.

Lastly, you may be able to avoid impoundment if you, yourself, pull your vehicle into a private parking lot. If you suddenly realize that an officer is pulling you over, and you suspect you are going to be arrested, you should immediately look for an upcoming parking lot to pull into. The goal is to get your car off the public roadway, thereby making it much less likely that the officer will have it impounded. Of course, you must be very careful when using this tactic. If you drive too far after the officer turns on his overhead lights or siren, you could face an additional charge of fleeing a police officer.

Containers in Cars

Using a marijuana case as the platform for narrowing all people's rights, in 1991 the United States Supreme Court announced a new rule that severely reduced the right to privacy in regard to closed containers taken into an automobile. In this case, Officer Coleman of the Santa Ana, California, Police Department received word from a DEA agent that the agency had intercepted a Federal Express package containing marijuana addressed to a person in Santa Ana. Officer Coleman was told to take the package to the local Federal Express office and secretly wait for the addressee to come and claim the package. Officer Coleman did so, and observed a person retrieve the package. He followed the person to his home and staked out the house with several other officers.

After a few hours, the officers observed another individual (later identified as Steven) arrive at the home. Steven left about ten minutes after arriving, and carried a brown paper bag that was the same size as the marijuana package sent through the mail. Steven placed the bag in the trunk of his car and drove away. The officers followed him, stopped him, opened the trunk, opened the bag, and found marijuana inside. Steven was then arrested.

At his trial in California, Steven's attorney successfully argued that the officers' search of the bag was illegal because the officers failed to get a search warrant for the trunk or the bag. The prosecutor, however, appealed the case to the Supreme Court, which held that the officers' search was legal.

The peculiar nature of this decision becomes clear when it is contrasted with the explanations in Chapter Five of the conditions under which search warrants are usually required. To review, if an officer sees a person walking down the street with a closed container such as a briefcase, and has probable cause to believe the briefcase contains marijuana, he cannot open the briefcase without first obtaining a search warrant (unless, of course, the person consents to the warrantless search, or another exception to the warrant requirement applies). The officer must obtain a search warrant even if he has probable cause to believe that the briefcase contains marijuana.

However, under the rule created by the Supreme Court, if that person gets into a car, carrying that same briefcase, an officer is able to search the container *without* first getting a search warrant! Once a container is placed in an automobile, it loses a great deal of its protection against warrantless searches.

Your Car and the Plain-View Rule

If a police officer has stopped your vehicle for a valid reason, he can seize any objects which he sees in plain view so long as their illegal nature is immediately apparent. A common example of the plain-view rule in action arises when a person is stopped for a simple traffic violation. When the officer comes up to write the traffic ticket, he sees some marijuana on the dashboard or in the ashtray. In such cases, it is not an illegal search or seizure for the officer to reach into the car and seize the marijuana without first obtaining a warrant. Other arrests have occurred because a person consented to an officer entering their car to obtain their driver's license or vehicle registration and, in so doing, the officer spots a see-through baggie of marijuana in the glove-box. Ordinarily, such marijuana would not have been in "plain-view" since it was inside the glove box. However, since the officer had a right to be in the car and look where people ordinarily keep their vehicle registration (inside the glove-box), his spotting and seizing of the marijuana was legal under the plain view rule.

Furtive Movements

A recurring issue in many auto searches are what have come to be know as "furtive movements." A furtive movement gives the appearance that the person is attempting to retrieve or conceal contraband. An example of a furtive movement would be when an officer lawfully stops a vehicle and sees an occupant bend down or reach behind the seat.

Occasionally, when an officer performs a search of a vehicle that he later believes may have been illegal, he will try to beef up his report by indicating that "the suspect made a furtive movement as if he was retrieving a weapon," or "as I pulled over the suspect's vehicle, I observed him bend down as if to retrieve a weapon from under his seat."

As previously explained, a police officer ordinarily can't search a vehicle or its occupants following a routine traffic violation. However, if the officer sees the driver or occupant make a furtive movement, the officer has a legitimate concern for his safety and is therefore permitted to search the area into which he saw the person reach. Moreover, if some other factor, in combination with the person's furtive movement, gives the officer probable cause to believe the person is transporting marijuana, the officer has a right to arrest the person and search the entire passenger compartment of the car, including closed containers.

Consenting to a Search of Your Car and Withdrawing Consent

If a police officer is unable to establish probable cause to search a car, he can still search if the car's driver gives consent. The officer will usually say something like, "Would you please open your trunk?" or, "Do you mind if I look in your trunk?" Remember, as explained earlier, the officer is hoping the person will foolishly waive his or her constitutional right to be free from unreasonable searches. In this situation, a person desiring to assert his constitutional right to be free from unreasonable searches and seizures is wise to politely withhold consent and to inform the officer he would like to continue on his way. If for some reason the person does consent to a search, he may still withdraw his consent during the search, so long as he does so *before* the officer finds something illegal.

As an example, Officer Rockwell legally stopped Ernie's car because of its cracked windshield. Rockwell had a hunch that Ernie was a marijuana smoker, but had no probable cause to search his car. Rockwell asked Ernie, "Would you mind if I looked in your trunk?" Ernie, not wanting to offend the officer, handed Rockwell the key to his trunk and stepped out of his way. Officer Rockwell opened the trunk and began searching.

Suddenly Ernie remembered that he had a small bag of marijuana inside the first-aid kit in his trunk. Ernie quickly but calmly told Officer Rockwell, "O.K., stop your search. That's good enough. I've gotta get going now."

Ernie was foolish to consent to the trunk search. However, withdrawal of his consent was valid, since Officer Rockwell had not yet found anything illegal or anything that would establish probable cause. If Officer Rockwell had continued searching after Ernie withdrew his consent, any marijuana found should have been excluded from court.

Whose Pot Is It?

If marijuana is found *hidden* in your car (rather than on one of the passengers), a presumption arises that the marijuana was possessed by you because you control the vehicle. In most states, a passenger in a vehicle is not presumed to be in control of the vehicle, and hence is rarely convicted of possession when marijuana is discovered hidden in a car. To convict a passenger in such cases, the prosecution must produce evidence that links the passenger with the marijuana.

In one case, Texas police officers stopped a car and discovered more than 400 pounds of marijuana in the vehicle's trunk. The driver, as well as a passenger named Lawrence McCullough, were arrested and subsequently convicted of possessing marijuana. They each received a five-year sentence in state prison. Lawrence appealed his conviction, arguing that he was simply a passenger in the car and that the evidence was insufficient to prove that he knew that marijuana was inside the vehicle's trunk. The prosecutor argued that the arresting officer smelled marijuana inside the car and that so must have Lawrence. The officer also observed the vehicle's spare tire in the back seat, which, the prosecutor argued, should have given Lawrence reason to believe that something was inside the trunk. Lastly, the prosecutor argued that during the stop Lawrence "was nervous, with a rapid heartbeat, breathing heavily, and appeared to be excited and trembling."

The court found that these factors were *insufficient* to convict a passenger of possessing marijuana found inside a vehicle's trunk. The court agreed with Lawrence's arguments that the fact that trained police officers could smell marijuana is no evidence that a layperson, like Lawrence, could do so; that the tire in the back seat also failed to prove that Lawrence knew *marijuana* was in the trunk; and that nervousness is an appropriate response to a confrontation with police officers and, again, did not necessarily indicate Lawrence knew that there was marijuana in the trunk.

However, a trend may be starting in the other directions. A New York law has been passed holding that any drugs found in the passenger compartment of a car (except those found on an occupant) are presumed to be possessed by each and every person in the car at the time the drug was found. Under the New York law, every occupant must prove his or her innocence if marijuana is found in the passenger compartment. This extremely harsh law permits prosecutors to obtain several convictions in cases where previously they would likely have gotten only one.

Driving Under the Influence of Marijuana

In every state, it is a crime to "drive" or "operate" a motor vehicle while under the influence of marijuana. There are basically two elements to the crime: (1) driving or operating a motor vehicle, and (2) being under the influence of marijuana at the time of such driving.

The various states differ regarding the precise action outlawed. At last count, seven states make it illegal to "drive" a motor vehicle while under the influence. In these states, the courts originally interpreted the word "drive" as requiring actual *movement* of the vehicle. Those states which outlaw "operating" a vehicle when under the influence interpret their law more broadly than for "driving." In most such states, "operating" is often defined as simply having access to the physical controls of the vehicle. However, the recent trend is to broaden the crime of "driving" under the influence; hence some courts have interpreted "drive" to be the same as "operate." Therefore the difference between the two types of laws is really insignificant, because nearly all those states which outlaw "driving" under the influence are now broadly interpreting that word to include simply "operating" a motor vehicle. A very good and surprisingly common example of the long-arm of this law is illustrated by the following case.

Gene, a constant marijuana smoker, was on a solo road trip on a relatively unused state route. As midnight approached, he decided to pull off the road, onto the shoulder, and sleep a few hours. He turned off his headlights as well as his engine. However, because it was rather chilly outside, he left his keys in the ignition and turned them to the position that would allow him to run his heater and listen to the radio.

As Gene was drifting off to sleep, he was awakened by bright headlights directly behind him. When he peeked out his back window, he was greeted by the local sheriff, who was stopping just to see if Gene needed some assistance. When Gene rolled down his window to speak with the sheriff, the sheriff smelled marijuana and, after giving Gene some field sobriety tests, arrested Gene for operating a motor vehicle while under the influence of marijuana.

Gene's attorney argued that Gene's action did not constitute "operating" a vehicle. Needless to say, the court disagreed. The court held that Gene was indeed operating the vehicle by placing his keys in its ignition and turning on the electrical components. Therefore, Gene's conviction for driving under the influence of marijuana was upheld.

The states are split on the issue of whether a crime is committed if the driving or operating of a vehicle occurred only on *private* property. In some states, the law explicitly states that the conduct is only outlawed "on a *public* highway." However, the clear trend is toward outlawing *any* driving under the influence, whether on public or on private property. California has just such a law, representative of the recent trend, which states: "It is unlawful for any person who is under the influence of an alcoholic beverage or any drug, or when under the combined influence of an alcoholic beverage and any drug, to drive a vehicle."

Under such a law, it is clear that a person can be arrested and convicted of driving under the influence when backing out of his driveway, driving a tractor on farm lands, or driving in a private parking lot.

If a police officer has reason to believe you are driving under the influence of *any* drug (including legal drugs), he can stop your vehicle and require you to complete some sobriety tests. These tests involve physical tests, such as walking heel-to-toe, touching your nose, and balancing on one foot, as well as mental tests, such as counting backward.

In addition to giving you these tests, an officer who suspects you of driving under the influence of marijuana will likely shine his flashlight in your eyes, measure the responsiveness of your pupils, and take your pulse. After the officer administers any or all of these tests, he can arrest you if your poor performance gives him probable cause to believe that you were driving or operating a vehicle under the influence of marijuana.

Often, the real proof that a person was "under the influence" of marijuana comes by way of a blood or urine test. In most states, any person who applies for and receives a driver's license implicitly consents to submit to a breath, blood, or urine test if an officer reasonably suspects him or her of driving under the influence of alcohol or a drug. However, because most breath-testing machines cannot detect marijuana, most state laws require a person suspected of driving under the influence of marijuana to take a blood or urine test. In California, the penalty for refusing to take such a test is an automatic, minimum one-year suspension of driving privileges.

If you take a blood or urine test and marijuana is detected, the prosecution will introduce the results of that test into evidence, and have an expert testify that the level of marijuana in your blood or urine was sufficient to impair your driving ability to an appreciable degree. Your attorney may be able to counter this argument by presenting other expert testimony or by cross-examining the prosecution's expert.

In addition, if you are ever charged with driving under the influence of marijuana, you should advise your attorney of a little-known study conducted by the California Highway Patrol. In this study, the CHP tested the correlation between marijuana smoking and a person's ability to competently operate their vehicle. To the CHP's surprise and despair, they discovered that *some* people actually drive *better* after smoking marijuana. The study is reported in un article titled "Marijuana and Alcohol: A Driver Performance Study — A Final Report." It was published in 1986 by the California Department of Justice.

CHAPTER 7

MARIJUANA &
YOUR HOME

A Home Is Entitled to Maximum Protection

SINCE THE FOUNDING of our country, the Supreme Court has held that a person is reasonably entitled to the highest degree of privacy when inside his or her home. An excerpt from a recent opinion by the Court makes it very clear that the Court is prepared to severely scrutinize all searches and seizures that occur inside a person's home:

> The Fourth Amendment protects the individual's privacy in a variety of settings. In none is the zone of privacy more clearly defined than when bounded by the unambiguous physical dimensions of an individual's home — a zone that finds its roots in clear and specific constitutional terms: "The right of the people to be secure in their . . . houses . . . shall not be violated." That language unequivocally establishes the proposition that "[a]t the very core of the Fourth Amendment stands the right of a man to retreat into his own home and there be free from unreasonable government intrusion." In terms that apply equally to seizures of property and to seizures of persons, the Fourth Amendment has drawn a firm line at the entrance of the house.

Because the home is considered a person's most private retreat, the United States Supreme Court made clear long ago that even if an officer has probable cause to believe that marijuana is inside, he may not enter the home without first obtaining a search warrant. As the Court explained, "the search of a private dwelling without a warrant is, in itself, unreasonable and abhorrent to our laws . . . Belief, however well founded, that an article sought is concealed in a dwelling house, furnishes no justification for a search of that place without a warrant. Any such searches are held unlawful notwithstanding facts unquestionably showing probable cause." *(Agnello v. United States [1925] 269 U.S. 20.)*

Given the very strong right to privacy that is compromised when police search a home, the Court has made clear that the only exceptions to the search warrant requirement are: (1) when exigent circumstances exist, or (2) when the occupant consents.

A Home's Outdoor Private Areas Also Receive Maximum Protection

In addition to cloaking the interior of your home with a great deal of protection against the prying eyes and grabbing hands of the government, the courts have developed the legal concept of a home's "curtilage." The term 'curtilage' refers to those areas immediately surrounding the home that most people consider to be just as private as the interior of their home. This concept was created to afford those areas the same level of protection as the inside of a home. Because most curtilage issues discussed in this book involve *Cannabis* gardens, the details of what is and isn't considered part of a home's curtilage are discussed in the next chapter. For now, you need only understand that all the rules in this chapter that apply to the *home* itself also apply to the home's *curtilage* .

The Front Door is Usually *Not* Part Of Curtilage

At least one court has made clear that unless rather extraordinary precautions are taken to keep strangers at a distance, the front door of a home is *not* within the home's curtilage. This case holds that without a locked gate keeping people from approaching your front door, and signs stating that they are trespassing by encroaching on your doorstep, a police officer does not need a warrant to approach your front door and knock on it. The rationale for this rule is that although a front door is an integral part of a home, it is widely accepted for strangers to approach it. Distinguishing a home's *front* door from it's *back* door (which is generally considered to be within the home's curtilage and hence entitled to increased protection), an Oregon court explained:

> Going to the front door and knocking [is] not a trespass. Drivers who run out of gas, Girl Scouts selling cookies, and political candidates all go to front doors of residences on a more or less regular basis. Doing so is so common in this society that, unless there are posted warnings, a fence, a moat filled with crocodiles, or other evidence of a desire to exclude casual visitors, the person living in the house has implicitly consented to the intrusion . . . Going to the back of a house is a different matter. Such an action is both less common and less acceptable in our society. There is no implied consent for a stranger to do so. (*State v. Mcintyre [Or. App. 1993] 860 P.2d 299.*)

The Oregon court was not being overly facetious when it mentioned placing a crocodile-filled moat around your home. Access to the front door of the home at issue in this case was protected by a tall wooden fence *and* a metal gate crossing the driveway. The court claimed, however, that these constructions are not sufficient to signal that the resident expected privacy because neither the fence nor the gate were locked and because there were no signs telling strangers to keep out.

Human Sniff At Garage Door

In one case in 1993, the Texas Court of Appeals in Houston upheld a *police officer's* marijuana-detecting sniff outside Roberto Delosreyes, Jr's, home. In court, the officer testified that when he arrived at Roberto's house, he walked up to the garage area "to see if I could detect any smell of any drugs." He sniffed by the edge of the garage door and supposedly detected the aroma of "unburned, fresh marijuana." This sniff, coupled with evidence from a "reliable informant" that Roberto had received a large delivery of marijuana, gave police officers probable cause to arrest Roberto.

Following his arrest, Roberto consented to the search of his garage and the officers found 71 packages of marijuana, totaling over 900 pounds. He was sentenced to 75 years in prison and fined $100,000.

In his appeal, Roberto argued that the officer's sniff at the garage door was an unlawful warrantless search because the sniff violated Roberto's reasonable expectation of privacy for the contents of his closed garage.

The court of appeal rejected his argument. The court explained that when the officer approached the garage he walked only on the driveway, and nothing blocked his passage. For example, there was no fence or any other obstruction around the residence or across the end of the driveway. There also were no signs prohibiting people from walking on the driveway. The driveway led to the front door of the house and the garage. In short, there were no fences, gates, signs or other notices to the public that the driveway leading to the garage was not open to the public. For these reasons, the garage door did not qualify as part of the home's curtilage. Therefore, the court explained, the officer had a right to walk up near the garage just like any other person. Moreover, there was no reason for the officer to hold his nose. He was free to smell the area, just like any other passerby. *(Delosreyes v. State (Tex.App. Houston [1st Dist. 1993] 853 S.W.2d 684.)*

Search Warrants

As discussed earlier, a search conducted under the authorization of a search warrant is presumed to be reasonable and hence legal. The method of obtaining a search warrant is relatively straightforward. A police officer simply writes out an affidavit explaining to a judge why he has probable cause to believe that a search of a particular place will produce marijuana. If the judge is persuaded by the officer's affidavit, he will sign the warrant and the officer will be authorized to conduct the search.

The purpose of requiring a search warrant is to take some power away from the police and vest it in a *neutral* judge. In one case, Judge Green in California received information that his tenant was cultivating *Cannabis* on his property. The judge investigated and confirmed that 15 *Cannabis* plants were growing on his rental property. He took Polaroid pictures of the plants and immediately notified the police. The police officer who received the information prepared an affidavit for a search warrant and brought it back to Judge Green, who quickly signed the search warrant authorizing the officer to search the Judge's rental premises and to seize the *Cannabis* plants. A higher court held that the search warrant issued by Judge Green was invalid because the judge, as the owner of the targeted property, was anything but a "neutral and detached magistrate" as required by the Fourth Amendment. (*Grimes v. Superior Court [1981] 120 Cal.App.3d 582.*)

Not only must the judge be neutral, but *he or she*, as opposed to the police officer, must be the one who concludes that probable cause exists for the search. For that reason, a police officer's affidavit must not simply state conclusions. Rather, the officer must present facts that allow the *judge* to conclude that marijuana will be found in the place to be searched. Search warrants are often attacked by defense counsel for having invalid affidavits which state only the officer's conclusions rather than facts.

There is a great deal of law governing search warrants. However, only a few key points are relevant to the person who hears a knock at his or her door accompanied by the bone-chilling words, "Police officers, we have a search warrant."

If you or your home are the target of police officers with a search warrant, the following scenario will likely be played out. First, the officers will knock on your door and announce their identity as police officers; they will also announce their purpose, such as "narcotics" or simply "search warrant." Immediately upon entry they will run from room to room and, at least initially, bring all the occupants together in one room. One officer will usually show the search warrant to the homeowner and then begin a thorough search of the premises.

There is not much you can do if police arrive at your home with a search warrant. The best thing to do in such a situation is to take several deep breaths and try to remain calm. Do not admit *anything*. Ask to see the search warrant and check it to see if your correct address is listed. Occasionally, sloppy police work will result in an error on the face of the warrant. If you discover such an error, immediately bring it to the attention of the officer in charge and demand that he or she immediately stop searching and leave your premises. You should also check to confirm that it has been signed by a judge. Again, if no signature appears, bring this fact to the attention of one of the officers and demand that they stop searching and leave your home.

Again, aside from checking the validity of the warrant and demanding an attorney, the best advice in such a situation is to remain silent. Do not admit anything and do not answer questions.

If It's Nighttime You're Probably Safe

Under the laws of most states, search warrants may be executed only during daylight hours. In these states, an officer may execute a search warrant at night only if the warrant contains a specific clause that authorizes a nighttime search. Such clauses are rare. The general rule is that a judge can authorize a nighttime execution of a search warrant only if he is presented with facts that indicate a nighttime execution is required to prevent the removal or destruction of evidence.

A recent Arkansas case illustrates this rule in operation. Arkansas law enforcement agents received evidence that Elmer Ramey was selling marijuana out of his home. The officers conducted "surveillance activities" around Ramey's home for approximately two months during which time they observed a pattern of activity they believed indicative of drug dealing. One day, after observing a suspected deal, the officers stopped the buyer and seized a baggie of marijuana which the man said he purchased from Ramey's nephew.

With this information, the officers obtained a search warrant for Ramey's home and, with warrant in hand, rushed over to Ramey's home. They arrived at about 10:30 p.m. and searched his home. The search uncovered a relatively small amount of marijuana, over $3,000 cash, a scale, and some rolling papers.

Ramey was convicted on numerous charges, including: delivery of a controlled substance; possession of a controlled substance with intent to deliver; possession of drug paraphernalia; operating a drug premises; and conspiracy to deliver marijuana. He was sentenced to 39 years in state prison, with 15 years suspended.

His conviction, however, was reversed in 1993 because of the officers' unauthorized nighttime execution of the search warrant. Under Arkansas law, search warrants can only be executed between 6 a.m. and 8 p.m., unless the warrant affidavit sets out facts showing reasonable cause to believe that unusual circumstances exist to justify a nighttime search. The Arkansas Court of Appeals noted, "the nighttime intrusion into a private home is a violation of an important interest." After examining the search warrant affidavit, the court determined that the affidavit failed to state any facts showing that a nighttime search was justified. Consequently, the court concluded that the evidence seized as a result of the intrusion should have been suppressed, and hence, Ramey's conviction had to be reversed. *(Ramey v. State [Ark.App. 1993] 857 S.W.2d 828.)*

Some courts, faced with an unauthorized nighttime search, use an "exigent circumstances" rationale to justify the search. For example, in one case in Vermont, police arrested a man who was cultivating *Cannabis* on public property. There was sufficient evidence to establish probable cause that more evidence would be found in the man's home, and a judge issued a search warrant. The warrant was signed by the judge at 10:00 p.m. and authorized the search "at any time." The officers arrived at the man's empty home at 1:00 a.m., entered the home pursuant to the search warrant, and found additional incriminating evidence.

The man argued that it was illegal for the officers to execute the search warrant after nightfall. He cited Vermont law, which explicitly states, "the warrant shall be served between the hours of 6:00 a.m. and 10:00 p.m. unless the warrant directs that it may be served at any time." He noted that the Vermont courts had interpreted this law as justifying a nighttime search only when evidence exists that unless the warrant is executed at night, there will be a danger that the evidence sought will be destroyed or hidden. He argued that there was no danger of destruction of evidence because he was in jail at the time the search warrant was executed, and so could not possibly have destroyed evidence located at his home.

The Vermont Supreme Court rejected the man's argument. The court explained that although the man was in jail when the search warrant was obtained and executed, he was married. Therefore, an exigent circumstance existed permitting the nighttime execution of the warrant at his home:

> The very real possibility existed that appellant's fate had become known or would become known before the night was over, and that this would prompt removal of the incriminating evidence by others. The judicial officer [who authorized the nighttime search] knew from the affidavits that [the appellant] had a wife. He could have reasonably concluded that the spouse might upon learning of her husband's apprehension seek to destroy any incriminating evidence and that an immediate search was warranted. *(State v. Weiss [VT 1990] 587 A.2d 73.)*

Consequently, the Vermont Supreme Court upheld the warrant's nighttime execution as well as the man's conviction for cultivating *Cannabis*.

The Knock-Notice Rule

Even with a warrant, a police officer may not enter a person's home without first knocking and announcing his presence. This is known as the "knock-notice rule." Under this rule an officer executing a search warrant for a residence must knock on the door of the residence to be searched, and give notice that he is a police officer. The officer must also give the occupants a reasonable amount of time to open the door. If no person answers, or the officer hears rustling inside that might indicate that the people are getting weapons or disposing of contraband, he may immediately enter the home by force.

In many states, when a warrant is issued to search a residence believed to contain marijuana or other drugs, courts will routinely authorize the officers to execute the warrant without first knocking and giving notice of their search because to do so might give the occupants time to flush marijuana down the toilet or arming themselves. These courts, however, usually require that the search warrant affidavit include some factual basis for believing that notice to the occupants would result in them destroying the marijuana, arming themselves, or escaping.

Warrants and the Plain-View Rule

The plain-view rule is not as simple as its name suggests. Remember, what is or is not in plain view depends upon the position of the viewer (i.e., the police officer). Ordinarily, a baggie of marijuana inside a desk drawer is not in plain view. However, if a police officer has a right to open the drawer (e.g., he has a search warrant or your consent) its contents are suddenly in plain view. This aspect of the plain view rule often comes into play when officers search a home under the aegis of a search warrant. If police officers are legally searching a home pursuant to a warrant, they may seize any illegal items which they find while searching, so long as the criminal nature of the items is immediately apparent. If, for example, a search warrant authorizes a search for marijuana and during that search the officers find some cocaine, they may seize the cocaine because it is clearly illegal. Likewise, if a search warrant authorizes a search for a gun, and the officers find marijuana while searching, they may legally seize the marijuana.

People on the Scene

What about visitors who happen to be present when the police unexpectedly arrive with a search warrant? Can the police search them? In most situations the answer is "no." In most states the officers are restricted to searching only those persons or places specifically listed in the warrant. In most cases, a search warrant authorizes the search of only named individuals who reside at the residence to be searched. In such cases, the police can not search other people who happen to be present when the police execute the search warrant. The police can, however, detain and *frisk* all persons present, but only for the purpose of detecting weapons, not for the purpose of finding contraband.

Occasionally, the police will have information leading them to believe that a particular home is used exclusively for growing or "manufacturing" marijuana. In such cases, some courts will permit the search warrant to contain a rather general authorization permitting the police to search "any or all persons on the premises." Of course, the police can also search any person who consents to a search.

Police can also search a visitor who is not named in the search warrant if, during the search, an officer uncovers evidence establishing probable cause to believe that the visitor is concealing contraband or involved in unlawful activity. In this case, the officer can arrest that person and search him or her incident to arrest.

For example, in one case, Mary Lou was visiting her friends Bob and Larry at their penthouse apartment. As they spoke, they were suddenly interrupted by a loud pounding at the door. Thinking it must be another friend, Bob yelled out, "Come in, it's open." At that moment the door flew open, and five police officers ran into the apartment. The officers ordered them to get on the ground with their hands out to their sides.

The three followed the officers' orders and hit the ground. The officers quickly ran through the apartment to check for other occupants. One officer advised Larry and Bob that he had a search warrant for their apartment authorizing a search for marijuana and evidence of its sale. Because Bob and Larry were listed in the search warrant, the officers searched their pockets, finding a half-smoked joint and $350 in Bob's possession. The officer confiscated the joint and the money. The officers found nothing on Larry. Last, the officers pat-searched Mary Lou but felt no hard objects.

Inside Bob's bedroom, the officers found 13 vacuum-packed ounces of marijuana. Inside Larry's room, the officers found a professional-quality scale, $950 in cash, and a well-used vacuum-packaging machine. The officers confronted Bob and Larry with their discoveries, but the two men remained silent.

As the search warrant authorized, the officers checked the apartment for a telephone answering machine and found one in the kitchen. They played back the last message and heard a female voice leave the message, "Hey, you guys, it's Friday 3:00 p.m. If it's O.K., I'll drop by around 5:00 p.m. with the money. I really need the stuff for the weekend. See you later." The officers checked their watches. It was 5:20 p.m. on Friday. Putting these facts together, the officers confronted Mary Lou, and asked her if she left a message. Mary Lou refused to answer. One of the officers then grabbed Mary Lou's jacket and searched inside its pockets. Inside the left pocket he found a vacuum-packed ounce of marijuana very similar to the 13 recovered in Bob's room. The officers then arrested Mary Lou, Bob, and Larry.

Mary Lou's attorney argued that the officer's search of Mary Lou's jacket was illegal, because she was not named in the search warrant, and did not even live at the apartment. The court rejected the argument. The court reasoned that the tape-recorded message in a female voice, the time correspondence between the message and Mary Lou's presence at the apartment, and the $350 found on Bob, all combined to give the officers probable cause to believe that Mary Lou had just purchased marijuana from the two men and was currently in possession of the marijuana. Therefore the court held that the officers' search of Mary Lou was legal, despite the fact that she was a visitor to the apartment and was not listed in the search warrant.

If It's Your Home, It's Presumed to Be Your Marijuana

In situations where officers execute a search warrant and find several visitors at the home, as well as some marijuana, the question often arises as to whether the visitors can be convicted of possessing the marijuana merely because they were at the premises. If the police find a resident and a nonresident in a room in which concealed marijuana is also found, the resident will be presumed to be the one in possession of the marijuana. The visitor can still be convicted of possessing the marijuana, but the prosecution must present evidence linking the visitor to the marijuana as well as establishing the other necessary elements of the crime of possession.

As a general rule, any concealed marijuana found on premises which you control is presumed to be in your possession. (You may be able to disprove or rebut that presumption if you can show facts which indicate that either you were not aware of the marijuana's presence or had no control over it.) This rule makes sense because, as the owner or renter of a room, you have the most control over the items concealed in the room.

In one case, the police entered a home pursuant to a search warrant and found a visitor and the homeowner in the bedroom. Underneath a chair on which the visitor was sitting, the officers found marijuana. The court held that in such circumstances there was *insufficient* evidence to convict the visitor of possession. The court stated:

> Where a person is present in premises where marijuana is found, but does not have exclusive access, use or possession of the premises, it may not be inferred that he had knowledge of the presence of marijuana and had control of it unless there are additional independent factors showing his knowledge and control.

Most courts agree with the above quote, and require more than a visitor's mere presence to convict him or her of possessing marijuana found concealed on someone else's premises. A case from Texas gives a good example of the sort of additional evidence needed to convict a visitor in such a situation. In this case, police officers entered a home with a search warrant and found four people seated at a table playing cards. Approximately four feet from the table, the officers found a shoe box containing two bags of marijuana. In addition to the marijuana inside the box, the officers also found a letter addressed to one of the visiting card players. Although the player was a visitor to the residence, and although the marijuana was concealed from view, the court upheld the visitor's possession conviction on the reasoning that the letter linked him to the concealed marijuana.

One final note regarding visitors: if the police search a person's home and find marijuana concealed on the person of a visitor, the above rules work to protect the home owner. In other words, the home owner is *not* presumed to be the possessor of marijuana which is found concealed on the person of a visitor.

The Plain-View Rule and Your Home

Because of the plain-view rule it is unwise to leave marijuana out in the open, even inside one's own home. If an officer is legally inside a person's home, any marijuana seen therein may be lawfully seized without a warrant. In fact, many arrests for marijuana result from police officers' inadvertently discovering evidence of marijuana use when they legally go to a home for some other reason.

One common situation that often results in an arrest on a marijuana charge occurs when police go to a home to break-up a party or respond to a noise complaint. When the occupants allow the police inside, an officer spots a baggie of marijuana in plain view. As this example indicates, the plain-view rule only comes into play if an officer is *legally inside* your home when he spots the marijuana.

If an officer is *outside* a person's home, and from a lawful viewpoint observes through a person's window that there is *Cannabis* inside the home or its curtilage, the plain-view rule establishes only probable cause that *Cannabis* can be found inside the home. Yet, as explained earlier, probable cause is *insufficient* for an officer to conduct a warrantless entry of a home if he has neither exigent circumstances nor consent. In other words, an officer's observation of marijuana in plain view does not entitle the officer to *enter* the home without a warrant. (In contrast, if an officer sees marijuana inside a car, the officer *is* legally entitled to conduct a warrantless search of the automobile. The automobile is considered less private than a person's home, and hence, as discussed in Chapter 6, probable cause *is* sufficient for an officer to search a vehicle without a warrant.)

If a police officer is outside your home and sees *Cannabis* through a window of your home, he will usually use his observation to obtain a search warrant for your home. It is not uncommon, however, for an officer who makes such an observation to attempt to obtain consent to enter your home so that, once inside, he can seize the plant under the plain-view rule and arrest you. As stressed earlier, a police officer does not need a warrant to enter your home if you consent to his entry.

Police Use Of Binoculars

In some cases, police are unable to positively identify *Cannabis* plants without resorting to the use of binoculars. The courts have analyzed the legality of this practice by examining whether or not the plants could have been identified with unaided vision. In cases were the binoculars allowed an officer to identify plants which he could not have identified with the naked eye, the courts have generally held that use of the binoculars constituted a "search" within the meaning of the Fourth Amendment. In cases, where the plants could be identified without using binoculars, courts have found that no search occurred by reason of an officer's use of binoculars.

In one Oregon case, the state police received information that Chris Blacker was growing *Cannabis* in his home. In order to corroborate the informant's information, the police observed Mr. Blacker's home from a vantage point along a rural highway adjacent to Mr. Blacker's house. A state trooper parked along the highway an estimated 50 yards from Blacker's home. From that location, and with the aid of a spotting scope which magnified 16 to 36 times, the trooper examined the premises. Using the scope to look into a second story window of the home, the trooper saw what he recognized as a *Cannabis* plant. Based on these facts, he obtained a search warrant, searched Mr. Blacker's home and seized some plants.

Mr. Blacker's case was dismissed after the court ruled that the officer's use of the spotting scope violated Mr. Blacker's reasonable expectation of privacy, and hence constituted a search without a warrant. The court explained that the officer used the scope to intrude upon Mr. Blacker's home — a place which, as already discussed, receives the highest level of protection under the Constitution. Quoting from another case, the court pointed out:

> The vice of telescopic viewing into the interior of a home is that it risks observation not only of what the householder should realize might be seen by unenhanced viewing, but also of intimate details of a person's private life which he legitimately expects will not be observed either by naked eye or enhanced vision.

The court was quick to point out that without the aid of scope, the officer would have been unable to see the *Cannabis* plant. The outcome would have been different if the plant was viewable with the naked eye. *(State v. Blacker [Or.App. 1981] 630 P.2d 413.)*

In those cases where the courts find a search occurred by reason of an officer's warrantless use of binoculars, they must then determine whether or not the search was unreasonable and hence a violation of the Fourth Amendment. A New Jersey court analyzed the question as follows:

> Is a "search" with the use of binoculars an invasion of one's privacy that society is prepared to accept without the necessity of obtaining a search warrant? We believe it is.

> In an age where the possession and use of binoculars by the average citizen, as well as the police, is so common it is unreasonable for property owners to expect that objects within their curtilage not shielded by a fence or other barrier will not

be observed by persons passing their home on the road or
sidewalk . . .

The use of devices to enhance vision and other senses has been
sanctioned in the past. For instance, eyeglasses enhance
vision, yet no one can reasonably argue that observations made
by a police officer wearing glasses constitutes an unreasonable
search. Moreover, courts throughout the nation, including this
state, accept without question the admissibility of electronically intercepted statements made by a defendant which he
intended to remain private even when made in the privacy of
one's home. The philosophy underlying the admissibility of
such evidence is that those involved in illegal activities should
anticipate the use by police of scientific devices commonly
used by and available to the general public, and we should
neither shield defendants from the risk that their illegal activities may be observed with the use of commonly used scientific
devices, nor should we be too ready to erect constitutional
barriers to relevant and probative evidence which is also
accurate and reliable . . . .

Patently, binoculars are commonly used scientific devices and
provide information which is accurate and reliable. *(State v.
Citta [N.J. 1990] 625 A.2d 1162.)*

Another court upholding a police officer's warrantless use of binoculars to
look through a person's window and observe what appeared to be a *Cannabis*
plant, explained "the use of binoculars is not an unexpected occurrence in today's
society. They are used, not only by law enforcement officers, but by citizens for
hunting spotting game, bird watching and other ordinary, lawful purposes."

These cases are alarming for the Orwellian world that they could manifest.
Any time a police officer uses a high-tech device, even binoculars, to obtain
incriminating evidence without first obtaining a warrant, the action should be
attacked as an unreasonable warrantless search, analogizing use of the device to
use of an eavesdropping device.

Consenting to a Search of Your Home

How is it that, if most searches occur without warrants—and homes cannot be
searched without warrants even if probable cause already exists—police find so
much marijuana in people's homes? Well, the sad fact is that people, usually
without thinking, invite the police into their homes. Simply stated, and as
explained earlier, consenting to a police officer's request to enter or search
automatically makes the entry or search legal. The courts reason that if you allow

a police officer to come into your home and conduct a warrantless search, then you cannot later argue that the warrantless search was an unreasonable invasion of your privacy. Moreover, *unintentional* consent is considered valid. For example, in one case, a police officer knocked on the door of a suspected marijuana user. From inside came the response, "Yeah, come in." The officer walked in and immediately saw a *Cannabis* plant on the kitchen floor. The court held that the homeowner's consent was valid, even though he was unaware that it was a police officer who sought entry. The court noted that the officer did not make any fraudulent statements nor was the occupant under any duress when he consented to the entry. Therefore, the occupant's consent was voluntarily given, even though he did not know that it was a police officer who sought entry.

Occasionally a police officer, suspecting a person of marijuana use, will go to the person's home in hopes of pressuring the person into consenting to the officer's entry into and search of the home. If the officer does this by making some false or misleading claim under the authority of his badge, courts hold that the occupant's consent was invalid; hence the officer's entry and search are deemed illegal. For example, the courts have routinely held that it is illegal for police officers to gain entry to a home by telling the occupant that they have a search warrant or arrest warrant when they actually do not. The trick used by the police officer in the following Illinois case was also found to invalidate the homeowner's consent.

Richard Daugherty reported to the police that some money was missing from his home. A police officer was dispatched to the Daugherty household and made a report of the apparent theft. A few days later, the parents of the Daugherty's baby-sitter called Mr. Daugherty to report that their daughter had taken the money one night while baby-sitting. The police were notified of this information and questioned the baby-sitter regarding the theft. During the questioning, the baby-sitter volunteered that she had seen evidence of marijuana use while baby-sitting at the Daugherty home.

Officer Barts of the local police department was given this information, and set out to try to arrest Richard Daugherty for possession of marijuana. However, Officer Barts did not get a search warrant. Rather, several days after taking the information from the baby sitter, Officer Barts arrived unannounced at the Daugherty household, and asked for permission to come in, "to conduct further inspection regarding the theft." Daugherty's wife, Karen, consented to the officer's entry for such purpose. Once Barts was inside the home, he began asking Karen questions about the theft that were designed to get her to show him around the home so he could look for marijuana.

The officer asked her to show him the place from which the money had been taken. Next, he asked her to show him where else in the home the Daugherty's kept money. Just as the officer hoped, when Karen took him into the kitchen, Barts saw some marijuana in plain view on the kitchen countertop. He seized the marijuana, arrested Karen and Robert Daugherty, and called for backup. Under the pressure of the situation, the Daughertys confessed that more marijuana could be found in several places in the home. Robert Daugherty also turned over a scale and several pipes used to smoke marijuana.

Fortunately, the Daugherty's lawyer heard what happened and how Officer Barts tricked Karen into consenting to the officer's entry. The lawyer argued that the officer's warrantless entry was illegal, because Karen's consent was procured through a trick by Officer Barts under the authority of his badge.

The Illinois Court of Appeal found that Barts went to the Daugherty's residence to gain entry and search for evidence of marijuana use, and that the theft investigation was a subterfuge to trick Karen into consenting to his entry of the home. Therefore, the court agreed with the Daugherty's attorney and ordered the reversal of Richard Daugherty's conviction. (The charges against Karen had already been dropped.) The court explained that when a person gives consent to a police officer's warrantless entry of their home, the consent must be *voluntarily* given. The court reasoned:

> Where, as here, the law-enforcement officer without a warrant uses his official position of authority and falsely claims that he has legitimate police business to conduct in order to gain consent to enter the premises when, in fact, his real reason is to search inside for evidence of a crime, we find that this deception under the circumstances is so unfair as to be coercive and renders the consent invalid. This police conduct offends the Fourth Amendment and is fundamentally unfair when compared with the need for effective police investigation. *(People v. Daugherty [Ill. App.2d 1987] 514 NE.2d 228.)*

The importance, and potential value, of refusing consent to a warrantless search of your home is demonstrated by the experience of Alberto Wallace and Jonathan Jolly. Officers from the Winston-Salem Police Department received information from an informant that indoor *Cannabis* cultivation was occurring in a certain house. The officers were not able to confirm the information, so they decided to go to the house and ask a few questions of the occupants. When the officers knocked on the door, a man who identified himself as Jonathan Jolly answered. The officers identified themselves as police officers and explained that they received some information that someone was growing *Cannabis* in the home. Mr. Jolly kept his cool, and exited the residence, closing the door behind him. The officers spoke with Mr. Jolly and then asked him to consent to a search of his residence. Before Mr. Jolly could answer, his roommate, Alberto Wallace, came outside and wisely shut the door behind himself. The officers again asked for consent to search the home and both men refused to consent. After a some more discussion the officers once again asked for consent to search and once again were denied.

Despite both men's refusal to consent to a search, the officers decided to search anyway, telling the men that they had a right to make a "protective sweep" without a warrant. After a final protest by Mr. Jolly and Mr. Wallace, the officers proceeded to enter the home and search it. After searching for about five minutes, the officers located some *Cannabis* plants. The officers then secured the home and requested other officers to apply for a search warrant based on the information discovered during the warrantless "protective sweep" search. Some time later, more officers arrived with a search warrant, removed the plants, and arrested Mr. Jolly and Mr. Wallace.

Before their trial, Mr. Jolly and Mr. Wallace argued that the officers' warrantless entry was unlawful since the men never consented to the search and no exigent circumstances existed. The court agreed, finding that when the men refused to consent, they denied the officers the only legal means by which the officers could gain entry to the home. No exigent circumstances existed, and there was no legal justification for making a warrantless "protective sweep" of the residence. Therefore, because the officers' search violated the constitution, the court suppressed the evidence against the men, and the case was dismissed — all because Mr. Jolly and Mr. Wallace knew their rights and had the courage to exercise them. *(State v. Wallace [N.C.App. 1993] 433 S.E.2d 238.)*

Officers Who Threaten to Obtain a Warrant

It is possible that some day a police officer will come to your home without a search warrant and accuse you of some sort of marijuana crime. The officer will tell you that he wants to search your home for marijuana, and that you should have nothing to worry about if you are innocent. He will also tell you that if you do not consent to a search, he will get a search warrant. He will tell you to "make it easy on yourself" and just consent.

Although such coercive circumstances might later cause a court to rule that your consent was involuntary and hence invalid, *don't depend on the court!* You should never consent under such conditions. This tactic is almost always used when an officer knows that he does not have enough evidence to get a search warrant. (Obviously, if the officer really did have sufficient evidence against you, he would have obtained a search warrant already.) Therefore, you can and should refuse to consent to the officer's entry and search in the absence of a search warrant. Once the officer leaves consider eliminating all evidence of marijuana for at least the next two weeks. However, be careful when performing such a cleanup. In one case, an officer parked outside a person's apartment after being refused consent to enter witnessed the person running out of his apartment toward the dumpster with a large amount of marijuana in his hands!

Who Can Consent to a Search of Your Home?

The issue arises as to whether someone else can consent to the search of your home. For example, can your landlord or roommate consent to the search of your apartment? To a large extent, the answer depends on the relationship between the person consenting and the home to be searched.

Landlords and Hotel Employees

So long as you are legally entitled to the premises, your landlord has no authority to consent to the search of your apartment. In other words, if you have paid your rent or are not in the process of being evicted, your landlord has no authority to consent to an officer's request to search your apartment. Any consent your landlord might give will be considered ineffective by a court, so anything an officer finds during such a search should not be used to convict you. The rule with respect to landlords also applies to hotel owners and hotel employees. In other words, a hotel clerk, janitor, or maid has no authority to consent to an officer's request to search your hotel room.

Roommates and Spouses

For roommates the answer is slightly more complicated. If your roommate is home alone when the police arrive, he can consent to a search of any area that he shares with you. Courts have held that you maintain no reasonable expectation of privacy in such common areas because your roommate has an equal right to invite his friends or guests into them. However, your roommate cannot consent to a search of any areas that you alone inhabit. For instance, if you have a separate private bedroom, then your roommate may *not* consent to a search of that room.

Suppose both you and your roommate are home when the police arrive. Can your roommate consent to a search of the common areas over your objection? Under a Supreme Court decision, the answer seems to be that your objection is irrelevant. The police may search the common areas based on the consent of your roommate alone. Accordingly, you should be aware that when you decide to have a roommate, you are potentially giving up a portion of your Fourth Amendment privacy rights, at least in the common living areas. The same rule applies to your spouse and anyone else you allow to live with you.

In contrast, most courts hold that your roommate or spouse may not consent over your objection if he or she is away from the apartment. In one case, for example, the police lawfully arrested Charles for possession of marijuana after stopping him for a traffic violation. Charles denied possessing any other marijuana and gave the police his key to the apartment, telling them that they could search it to confirm that he possessed no other marijuana.

When the officers arrived at the apartment, Charles' roommate, Roger, was home and refused to allow the police to enter. The officers, disregarding his objection, forcibly entered the apartment, found marijuana inside, and charged Roger with possession. The court that heard the case held that the officers search of the apartment was illegal. The case against Roger was dismissed for lack of evidence.

This case created the general rule that a roommate who is away from the premises may not authorize police to enter and search the premises if the other roommate is on the premises and objects to the police entering and searching.

Finally, it is important to know that you give up a great deal of protection against warrantless searches of your home if your roommate is on probation or parole. A person's probation or parole is often predicated on his waiving the right to be free from unreasonable searches. This means that a police officer or probation officer can search your roommate at any time for any reason, including unannounced warrantless visits to your apartment to look for drugs. During such a search, the officer can search any area that you share in common with your roommate and any area that your roommate controls exclusively.

The officer cannot search areas that *you* exclusively control. If you live with a person on probation or parole, you are, therefore, especially well advised to keep your private items in *your own* room, rather than in the common areas shared with your roommate. That way, they remain protected from warrantless searches.

Children

Can your child consent to a search of your home? The answer to this question depends on the age of the child. In one case, the consent of an 11-year-old child was held to be ineffective on the theory that a child cannot waive the privacy rights of his or her parents. However, the older the child, the greater the chances that a court will find the child's consent valid. In addition, consent by a child is commonly ruled valid when the child was the victim or witness of a crime, and was admitting the police for that reason.

Your Home and "Exigent Circumstances"

As mentioned earlier, an officer can legally search a person's home without a warrant if "exigent circumstances" exist. The California Supreme Court has defined "exigent circumstances" as follows:

> [E]xigent circumstances means an emergency situation requiring swift action to prevent imminent danger to life or serious damage to property, or to forestall the imminent escape of a suspect or destruction of evidence.

As you can see, the definition begins quite stringently, but loosens considerably as it progresses. Because the definition of exigent circumstances features so much leeway, judges are apt to hear findings of exigent circumstances on the slightest grounds. In one case, for example, Mr. Robinson was at home when undercover police officers came to his home to try to purchase marijuana. Mr. Robinson evidently had some suspicions about his visitors, because he refused to let the undercover officers inside. However, as luck would have it, when Mr. Robinson partially opened the door to tell them to go away, one officer saw a large bag containing marijuana just inside the door. The officer blocked the door with his foot, thereby allowing the other officers to push their way into Mr. Robinson's home and arrest him. The court upheld the officer's warrantless arrest of Mr. Robinson on the grounds that immediate action was necessary to prevent the destruction of the evidence; an exigent circumstance.

Obviously, if you have items that you wish to remain private inside your home, you should be especially careful about allowing people entry. If possible, you should install a "peephole" in your door to permit you to distinguish friend from foe without even opening your door or revealing your presence. If you do not have a peephole, you should respond to any unexpected knocks by asking "Who is it?" *Do not open the door* unless you are absolutely sure it is someone you know and trust. If the day comes when the response to your question is, "Police officers," you may legally keep your door *shut* and ask them (through the door) what they want. You do not have to open your door unless they tell you they have a warrant.

In one case, officers received a call that the occupants of a specific residence were using narcotics. The officers went to the house and knocked on the door. When someone inside opened the door, the officers were engulfed by the "odor of burning marijuana emanating from within." The court held that the officers acted legally in immediately entering the home without a warrant because any delay might have resulted in the destruction of the marijuana. Therefore, the officer's warrantless entry was justified by exigent circumstances.

Exigent circumstances can also arise when someone commits a serious crime and is being chased by police officers. If the suspect is seen to enter a home, the police do not have to get an arrest warrant authorizing them to enter and arrest the suspect. The courts have held that such situations require the officers to act without delay. The exigent circumstances rule permits the officers to kick the door down and arrest the suspect without first obtaining a warrant. If they see marijuana while inside the home, they can, and will, seize it.

In a 1994 case in Virginia, officers received a telephone call from Darin Hill's next-door neighbor asking them to send an officer to check if Mr. Hill's house had been burglarized. The neighbor reported that Mr. Hill was out of town, but that his front door was open about a foot. When officers responded, they entered Mr. Hill's home to search for a possible burglar but stumbled upon a sophisticated basement growroom. The Virginia Court of Appeal upheld the lawfulness of the officers' warrantless entry of Mr. Hill's home because the report of Mr. Hill's neighbor gave them probable cause to believe that Hill's house had been unlawfully entered and that the burglar might still be on the premises. In this situation, the officers had to act quickly to be effective. They discovered the growroom in plain view during their lawful search for the burglar, and hence the incriminating evidence was lawfully seized despite the lack of a warrant. *(Hill v. Commonwealth [Va.App.1994] 441 S.E.2d 50.)*

In a similar vein, if officers reasonably believe that it is necessary to act immediately to save someone's life or to prevent serious bodily injury, they may enter a home without first obtaining a warrant. For example, John and Cindy were both unemployed and lived in a one-room apartment in a high-crime area. To support themselves, John and Cindy cultivated a yearly crop of approximately 40 *Cannabis* plants. To relieve their stress, John and Cindy engaged in weekly primal scream sessions.

One Friday evening, after John had checked the pH level of all his plants, he let loose with several blood-curdling high-intensity screams to purge himself of the week's accumulated stress. John allowed himself to collapse on the couch, enjoying a feeling of total relaxation.

Suddenly, John heard a loud knock at his door, followed by the announcement, "Police officers! Open the door!" Frozen in fear, John remained motionless, not knowing how to react. Fifteen seconds after the knock, John's front door was kicked in, and two police officers ran into his apartment with their guns drawn. Immediately upon entering, the cops saw the *Cannabis* plants and quickly placed John under arrest.

The officers' entry of John's home was legal under the exigent circumstances rule. The police officers, hearing John's scream, reasonably believed that someone in John's apartment was in need of emergency assistance and might have been the victim of a brutal crime. Therefore, the officers' warrantless entry was legal under the exigent circumstances exception to the warrant requirement. Accordingly, the plants were properly introduced in court, and John was convicted of *Cannabis* cultivation.

In contrast to the above example, if a court finds that a police officer was not reasonable in thinking that a warrantless entry was immediately required, the court will find the officer's warrantless entry illegal and exclude any evidence found. For example, in one case:

> Officer Del Rosso testified that about 9:40 p.m., on September 26, 1979, accompanied by a factory custodian, he was searching the third floor of a factory for intruders. The factory was about 40' distant (across a 32' street) from the "three-decker" apartment house in which, on the third floor, Huffman lived as a tenant. The officer's attention was attracted by lighted windows without curtains or shades. Through the windows (before he called for assistance) he observed for an appreciable time, Huffman and two other men taking a green herb from one

bag and putting it into numerous other smaller bags. Officer Del Rosso called for police assistance and then obtained binoculars . . . . He was joined by several other officers. With them, he observed Huffman and the other men through two different windows for about fifteen minutes more.

The officers went to the apartment house, found "the first door downstairs" open and the hall door unlocked. They proceeded to the third floor landing. Huffman's apartment door was partially ajar (about five or six inches), music was "blaring," and there was a strong odor [of] marijuana. Through the open door, he observed one of the men "still bagging" the green herb. The officers entered and found the three men, previously observed from the factory, sitting or standing near a table two or three feet from the windows. On a table were sixteen "baggies" containing the green herb and fifteen hand-rolled cigarettes strewn around the table. The herb on analysis proved to be marijuana. No attempt was made to obtain a search or arrest warrant. *(Commonwealth v. Huffman [Mass. 1982] 430 NE2d 1190.)*

The Supreme Court of Massachusetts held that the officers' warrantless entry of Michael Huffman's apartment was illegal because exigent circumstances did not exist. First, nothing indicated that Michael or his friends were armed or that they might attempt to escape. In fact, nothing indicated that Michael or his friends were even aware of the officers' presence. Therefore, the court reasoned, the officers had no reason to believe that immediate action was necessary to prevent Michael from destroying the marijuana. Consequently, the court reversed Michael's conviction for possessing marijuana with the intent to distribute.

CHAPTER 8

GARDENS

IN THE EYES of the legal system, all *Cannabis* gardens are not created equal. The United States Supreme Court has held that some gardens deserve more protection than others. Specifically, the constitutional protections afforded a person's *Cannabis* garden depend on whether the garden is located inside a home; outside a home, *but* inside the home's curtilage; or outside a home *and* outside the home's curtilage.

Those gardens located inside a home have the greatest constitutional protection against searches by police officers. Those gardens located outside a home, *but within* a home's curtilage, while in theory entitled to the same protection as those inside a home, in practice receive less protection. Lastly, a garden located outside a home, *and outside* the home's curtilage, receives very little, if any, protection.

Marijuana Gardens in the Home

As noted above, a *Cannabis* garden located inside the four walls and beneath the roof of a home is entitled to the same stringent constitutional protections as every other item located in the home. Therefore, the law concerning such gardens has been largely explained in the preceding chapter.

Marijuana Gardens Inside the Curtilage of a Home

As mentioned in Chapter 7, the Supreme Court has interpreted the federal constitution as providing maximum protection against police search not only of a home itself, but also of that area termed the "curtilage" of a home. Roughly speaking, a home's curtilage is the area that closely surrounds the outside of the home and for which the average person expects a high degree of privacy. If a court concludes that an area is within the curtilage of a home, the police must have a search warrant (or an exception to the warrant requirement) in order to search the area.

The Supreme Court has refused to create a "bright-line rule," which would classify an area as "curtilage" if it falls within a set distance from the home. However, the Court has formulated a test for deciding what is, and what is not, included in a home's curtilage. Under this test, the Court examines "whether the area harbors the intimate activity associated with the sanctity of a man's home and

the privacies of life." The Court has spelled out four important factors that help
to define a home's curtilage. These are:

(1) The proximity of the area to the home
(2) Whether the area is included within an enclosure surround-
    ing the home
(3) The nature of the uses to which the area is put
(4) The steps taken by the resident to protect the area from
    observation by people passing by

An example of how the Court applies these criteria when ruling on a police
officer's warrantless search is provided by the case of Mr. Dunn. DEA agents
received information that a large quantity of chemicals used to manufacture
illegal drugs had been delivered to Mr. Dunn's ranch in a truck.

The agents took aerial photographs of Mr. Dunn's ranch and saw a truck
parked outside a barn located approximately sixty yards from his home. The
agents also discovered from the photographs that Mr. Dunn's ranch was quite a
fortress. The photos revealed that the ranch was completely encircled by a fence.
In addition, there were a number of interior barbed-wire fences, one of which
encircled the home, but did not encircle the barn. The front of the barn was
blocked by an additional wooden fence with waist-high locked gates.

One evening, several DEA agents without a search warrant snuck up to
Dunn's barn–disregarding every fence in their path–to investigate the possibility
that he was manufacturing illegal drugs. They could hear a motor running in the
barn and could smell a chemical associated with illicit drug manufacturing. Based
on these observations, the agents obtained a search warrant for the barn that led
to the seizure of drug-manufacturing lab and the arrest of Mr. Dunn.

Mr. Dunn argued that the agents' initial search, which brought them onto his
property and up to the barn, was illegal because they invaded the curtilage of his
home without a warrant. The United States Supreme Court rejected Dunn's
argument, finding the barn was not inside the curtilage of Dunn's home. The
Court explained that the barn was a substantial distance from the home (60 yards),
and was not treated as an adjunct of the home. Second, the barn was not within
the fence that surrounded the home and that marked off the area that was part of
the home. Third, the agents had information prior to their entry that the barn was
not used as part of the home, but rather as an exterior drug lab. Lastly, the Court
explained that Dunn did little to protect the barn from observation by people
standing outside the property. The Court noted that the fences were all of the see-
through variety, of the type used to corral livestock, rather than the type of tall
solid fence ordinarily used to ensure privacy. Therefore, the Court concluded, the
barn was not inside the curtilage of Dunn's home and hence no warrant was
required.

Creating a Curtilage in the Eyes of a Court

Anyone desiring the increased protection given to a home's curtilage would be wise to make use of the four criteria discussed in the preceding section. If a court finds that a person's garden was within the curtilage of his home, the court will be forced to grant the garden the increased protection afforded by the Constitution. This means that the police cannot enter the garden without a warrant unless one of the exceptions to the warrant requirement applies.

In one case a sheriff observed *Cannabis* plants growing in plain view next to a man's home. The area, although not fenced off, was clearly within the curtilage of the man's home. Without getting a warrant, the sheriff walked up to the plants and pulled them up. The man was subsequently convicted of cultivating marijuana.

On appeal, however, the sheriff's warrantless seizure of the plants was declared illegal. The appellate court explained that the sheriff's plain-view *observation* of the *Cannabis* plants was entirely legal and gave the sheriff probable cause. However, because the plants were within the curtilage of the man's home, the sheriff's act of *physically entering* the curtilage without first obtaining a warrant was illegal under the Constitution. Therefore, the court of appeal reversed the man's conviction, holding that the illegally seized plants should have been excluded from evidence.

Increasing the privacy of a garden is a matter of common sense. Anything that separates a garden from the rest of humanity is a plus. To increase the chances that a court will find the garden within a home's curtilage, the cases teach that the home and garden should be surrounded by a large and impenetrable fence, one that passers-by cannot see under, through, or over. Additionally, the property should be designed to integrate, rather than separate, the garden and the home. All natural boundaries such as mounds, hedges, trees, and streams should be employed as blocking devices. A locked gate should block the driveway and all other entrances to the home. Mail should be delivered off site–for example, to a post office box. If feasible, utility meter readings should be taken by the owner to further increase privacy. "No Trespassing" signs should be liberally placed around the perimeter of the property.

In one case, a police officer peered through a knothole in a wooden fence and saw what he believed were *Cannabis* plants growing in Patrick Lovelace's backyard. He used his observations to obtain a search warrant for the residence. In court, Patrick argued that the officer's first view of his garden constituted an illegal search because the officer unreasonably invaded the privacy of his curtilage by peeking through the knothole. Patrick's attorney was able to get the officer to admit in court that he could not see over or under the fence, and was able to gain his view of the garden only by peering through a one-inch-wide knothole. The officer also testified that there were very few holes in the fence. In an attempt to counter Patrick's arguments, the prosecutor argued that the *Cannabis* garden was in plain view because the officer was on a public sidewalk, and anyone could have looked through the knothole.

The court agreed with Patrick, ruling that the officer's peeking was an unlawful warrantless search. The court based its decision on the fact that the officer originally viewed the plants by placing his face within one inch of the fence. There was no evidence that pedestrians ordinarily got within one inch of the knothole to spy into Patrick's backyard. Therefore, although the officer was legally on public property when he looked through the knothole, the judge deemed the officer's action an unreasonable and hence illegal invasion of Patrick's privacy.

The cases make clear that a person must protect his garden not only from people who may pass by at ground level, but also from possible viewing from aboveground. In many cases, a person's failure to protect his garden from the prying eyes of his neighbor's second-story window has proven fatal. For example, in one case, police officers were able to identify 77 *Cannabis* plants in the curtilage of a woman's backyard by viewing the plants from a neighbor's second-story window. The court held that although the garden was inside the curtilage of the gardener's home and could not have been viewed in any other manner, the gardener had no reasonable expectation of privacy, given that the plants could be seen in plain view from her neighbor's window.

Likewise, the United States Supreme Court has held that under certain circumstances a police officer's warrantless aerial surveillance of a person's *Cannabis* plants, even if they are within the curtilage of a home, violates no reasonable expectation of privacy and hence is not a "search" within the meaning of the Fourth Amendment.

Successfully Constructed Curtilages

Mr. Depew was a practicing nudist and lived in a remote location in Idaho so that he could enjoy his chosen lifestyle in privacy and without interference. One day, officers heard from an informant who claimed that Mr. Depew was growing *Cannabis* on his property. The officers ran Mr. Depew's name through the police computer system and discovered that he had previously been convicted of growing *Cannabis*. Based on this information (which they knew was not yet sufficient to obtain a search warrant) one of the officers in an unmarked car and wearing plain clothes drove out near Mr. Depew's house and pretended to have car trouble. He began walking up to Mr. Depew's house, but before he could get too far, Mr. Depew met him on the driveway about fifty feet from the home. The officer chatted with Mr. Depew and detected the aroma of growing *Cannabis*. The officer left without revealing his identity and obtained a search warrant based on this evidence combined with the informant's tip and Mr. Depew's police records. A search under the warrant uncovered over 1000 *Cannabis* plants.

Mr. Depew argued that the officer's entry up the driveway of his secluded house was an unlawful warrantless entry into the curtilage of his home. The Court of Appeal for the Ninth Circuit agreed with Depew and reversed his conviction.

The Ninth Circuit analyzed the previously mentioned four factors used to determine whether or not an area is within the curtilage of a home, concluding that when the officer walked up Depew's secluded and protected driveway, he entered an area that was clearly identifiable as part of Depew's home. The court explained that Mr. Depew took efforts to protect his privacy and to prevent observation of his home by outsiders. Mr. Depew's home was not visible from the road due to a long driveway and a thick row of trees. The Ninth Circuit also noted that Depew had posted "No Trespassing" signs in an effort to protect the inner areas of his land from observation. In particular, the court also noted that Mr. Depew had all his mail delivered to a post office box, so that even postal workers would not enter his property. Additionally, Depew had arranged with the utility company to make his own meter readings, thereby assuring that not even meter readers would come onto his property.

When all these factors where considered, the Ninth Circuit concluded that when the officer smelled marijuana he was standing illegally within the curtilage of Depew's home. Since the officer did not have a warrant or Mr. Depew's consent, his observations were obtained in violation of the Fourth Amendment Consequently, despite the recovery of over 1000 *Cannabis* plants, Mr. Depew's conviction was reversed. *(U.S. v. Depew [9th Cir. Nov. 1993] 8 F.3d 1424.)*

A federal district court in Florida ordered all the *Cannabis* plants seized from James Seidel's yard excluded from evidence because the police entered the curtilage of Mr. Seidel's home without first obtaining a search warrant. Police officers went to Mr. Seidel's home after flying over in a helicopter and spotting what they believed were numerous *Cannabis* plants growing in his back yard. When they arrived at his property, they found that trees and other almost impenetrable foliage surrounded Mr. Seidel's property, making it almost impossible for passersby to look into his yard. In addition, the property was surrounded by a fence on three sides, with the fourth boundary clearly marked by trees and thick foliage. "No Trespassing" signs were posted around the perimeter of the property, and the only gate onto the premises was always locked and bore a sign advising "Beep Horn and Wait."

When Mr. Seidel went to see who was beeping at his gate, he was confronted by several police cars, armed police officers, and a helicopter hovering overhead! When Mr. Seidel asked if the officers had a search warrant they told him "If you don't let us in, we're coming in anyway." Under such coercion, Mr. Seidel unlocked his gate and let the officers in. A large number of *Cannabis* plants were located in Mr. Seidel's backyard.

In a pretrial motion, Mr. Seidel argued that the officers' warrantless entry of his property violated the federal constitution's guarantee against unreasonable searches and seizures. The government countered: (1) that Mr. Seidel consented to the officers entry by opening the gate and hence no warrant was required; and

(2) that even if without Mr. Seidel's consent, the officers had a right to enter the property under the "open fields" doctrine discussed in the next section.

The court wasted no time finding that Mr. Seidel's "consent" was invalid because it was not freely and voluntarily given. The court pointed out that, faced with several police cars, a helicopter hovering overhead, and an officer who said that if Mr. Seidel didn't let them in they would come in anyway, Mr. Seidel's consent was coerced, and hence, was not valid. With respect to the government's argument that the warrantless entry was permissible because the property was not within the curtilage of Mr. Seidel's home, the court disagreed, finding that the property invaded by the officer's immediately surrounded Mr. Seidel's home, and that he had a reasonable expectation of privacy in the area. The court also emphasized that the *Cannabis* was growing very near to Mr. Seidel's residence: "The police seized some plants directly behind defendant's home, while other plants were grown in a greenhouse and outside, approximately ten to twenty yards from the back of the house."

The court also pointed out that the entire perimeter of Mr. Seidel's property was enclosed by either a fence or a natural boundary. Finally the court explained, "The third factor in defendant's favor . . . is the steps he took to protect his home from outside intrusion . . . . defendant kept his gate locked at all times. *Any* visitor would have to honk to be let in by the defendant. No one could easily see onto defendant's land and the public was intentionally excluded from access to the home and property."

Based on the above analysis, the court concluded that the plants were taken from an area within the curtilage of Mr. Seidel's home. Since the seizure was not authorized by a warrant or valid consent, all evidence had to be suppressed. *(US v. Seidel [S.D. Fla.1992] 794 F.Sup.1098.)*

Gardens Situated Outside a Home's Curtilage

The United States Supreme Court has held that any land outside of a home's curtilage maintains no reasonable expectation of privacy, despite an owner's attempt to keep the public out! This remarkable rule is known as the doctrine of "open fields." The Supreme Court has defined an open field as "any unoccupied or undeveloped area outside the curtilage. An open field need be neither 'open' nor a 'field' as those terms are used in common speech." The Supreme Court first applied the "open fields" doctrine to a marijuana case in 1984, when it examined a police officer's warrantless search of land owned by Ray Oliver.

In this case, the Supreme Court held that Ray Oliver maintained no legitimate expectation of privacy in his *Cannabis* garden, despite the fact that the garden was located on Mr. Oliver's property in a highly secluded area bounded on all sides by woods, fences, and embankments which prevented its observation from any point of public access. Additionally, Mr. Oliver had posted "No Trespassing" signs around the perimeter of his property. Similarly, in a case decided that same day, the Supreme Court held that Richard Thornton had no reasonable expectation of privacy for his *Cannabis* garden located in a secluded wooded area on his property surrounded by a chicken-wire fence and posted with "No Trespassing" signs.

The court reached these astounding decisions by reading the Constitution extremely narrowly and finding that the Fourth Amendment's protection for "persons, houses, papers, and effects" *does not extend to areas beyond the immediate surrounding of a home*. In the Court's words, "an individual may not legitimately demand privacy for activities conducted out of doors in fields, except in the area immediately surrounding the home." Even thickly wooded areas such as those hiding Mr. Oliver's and Mr. Thornton's gardens can be considered "open fields" and hence entirely unprotected by the Fourth Amendment.

In this remarkable opinion, the Supreme Court maintained that it is *impossible* for an individual to establish a legitimate expectation of privacy in an area of land outside of a home's curtilage. The Court stated:

> We reject the suggestion that steps taken to protect privacy established that expectations of privacy in an open field are legitimate. It is true, of course, that [Mr.] Oliver and [Mr.] Thornton, in order to conceal their criminal activities, planted the marijuana upon secluded land and erected fences and "No Trespassing" signs around the property. And it may be that because of such precautions, few members of the public stumbled upon the marijuana crops seized by the police. Neither of these suppositions demonstrates, however, that the expectation of privacy was legitimate in the sense required by the Fourth Amendment. The test of legitimacy is not whether the individual chooses to conceal assertively "private" activity. Rather, the correct inquiry is whether the government's intrusion infringes upon the personal and societal values protected by the Fourth Amendment. As we have explained, we find no basis for concluding that a police inspection of open fields accomplishes such an infringement. *(US v. Oliver [1984] 466 US 170.)*

In reaching its decision, the Supreme Court agreed that the officers trespassed upon Mr. Oliver's and Mr. Thornton's property in order to locate the *Cannabis* gardens. Even so, the Court held that no warrant was needed because no Fourth Amendment protections applied. In the words of one court, "the Fourth Amendment prohibits unreasonable searches and seizures, not trespasses."

An Unsuccessful Curtilage

In a 1993 case decided by a federal court in Montana, Sheriff's deputies "received information from a citizen informant who had observed what the informant believed to be marijuana growing in a green house" on John Van Damme's property. "The informant described the plants seen as three to four feet in height with long, fan-shaped groups of leaves that narrowed on the end. The informant asserted a familiarity with the appearance of marijuana plants based on public service advertisements on television and posters."

Some detectives were dispatched to determine if they could see anything unusual. Although they confirmed the location of the property, they could not see any *Cannabis* plants. The detectives continued their investigation. "On September 9, 1992, Detective Lewis caused a National Guard helicopter to fly over the Van Damme property for the purpose of photographing the premises. The helicopter conducted two separate fly-overs approximately 45 minutes apart." During these fly-overs, the helicopter, flew on the outside perimeter of Van Damme's property, never directly over his home. The detective testified that the fly-over was conducted at an altitude of over 500 feet.

"Detective Lewis observed the property through the viewfinder of a camera with a 600mm lens and took several photographs. He observed three plastic quonset-style greenhouses enclosed within a wooden perimeter fence. The greenhouse compound was not covered. The front doors of all three greenhouses were open. No other buildings were within the greenhouse compound. Through the open doors, Lewis observed marijuana growing in the greenhouses."

In the middle of night, Detective Lewis and DEA agent Williams, snuck over a barbed wire fence, and quietly entered Van Damme's' property. They then scaled a five-foot high hog wire fence, and, after walking another 100 feet, reached a 12 foot high wooden stockade fence which surrounded the greenhouses. "Williams and Lewis were able to see through the spaces between the boards in the stockade fence and observed what they recognized as marijuana growing in the greenhouses." The fence was about 200 feet from Van Damme's home.

Based upon the above evidence, the agents obtained a search warrant for Van Damme's property. When the search warrant was executed, 2,333 *Cannabis* plants were seized.

In court, Van Damme launched a series of attacks contesting the constitutionality of the agents' various actions. First, he argued that the helicopter fly-overs where unlawful warrantless searches. In support of this argument, he presented the testimony of a photogrammetry expert who testified that based on the photographs taken from the helicopter, the helicopter was flying at between 210 and 310 feet, rather than above 500 feet as Detective Lewis had claimed. Unfortunately, the expert's testimony was shot-down by the court, which held that the accuracy of the method used by the expert was unproved. As a consequence, the court accepted the truth of Detective Lewis's claim that he flew above 500 feet. This altitude, said the court, was well within the "public navigable airspace," and there was no evidence that the fly-over posed a potential hazard to persons or property below. The court also held that there was nothing unconstitutional about Detective Lewis's use of a high-powered camera.

The court then rejected Van Damme's argument that the green house was within the curtilage of his home. The court examined the four curtilage factors, particularly noting that the green houses where over 200 feet away from the home, and that the 12-foot high fence enclosed only the greenhouses, thereby making the area "a distinct portion of Van Damme's property, *quite separate* from the residence. Because of the isolation of the greenhouse compound from the rest of the property, the lack of nearby buildings or facilities, and the absence of any indica of activities commonly associated with domestic life, the investigating officers had no reason to deem the greenhouse compound as part of defendant's home."

Finally, employing preposterous standards, the court noted:

> . . . Though the stockade fence presented a significant obstacle to casual observation on the ground, Defendant did nothing to prevent observation of the interior of the compound from the air. Defendant also did nothing to prevent the viewing of the inside of the compound by someone on the outside looking through the cracks between the boards of the fence. Additionally, the doors of the greenhouses were open to exposing the plants growing inside to observation and identification from the air and the ground.

Based on the above analysis, the court held that the greenhouses were not within the curtilage of Van Damme's home.

Having found that the greenhouses were outside the curtilage and therefore subject to the "open fields" doctrine," the court held that regardless of Van Damme's attempts to shield the greenhouses from view, it was impossible to establish a reasonable expectation of privacy in an open field. In the court's words:

> Because the greenhouse compound was not within the curtilage but in the open fields, defendant had no legitimate expectation of privacy concerning the compound or that it would remain free from warrantless intrusion by government officers. Therefore, the fact that the officers entered into defendant's property, traversed open fields, climbed over fences in those open fields and stood in open fields while observing the greenhouses through the stockade fence does not constitute a violation of defendant's Fourth Amendment rights under the "open fields" doctrine. *(U.S. v. Van Damme [D. Mont. 1993] 823 F.Supp. 1552.)*

Searching Your Home Based on Seeing Your Backyard Garden

Generally speaking, if police officers discover that a person is growing *Cannabis* in his backyard, the officers can use that information for a search warrant authorizing them to search not only the person's backyard, but also the *inside* of the person's home. An actual affidavit in one such case stated:

> From the public alleyway between Deluxe Cleaners and the residence at 116 Maynell, I was able to observe the backyard of 116 Maynell .... I noted at the southwest corner of a garage and next to the fence and alleyway, several marijuana plants numbering at least four, ranging from three to five feet tall. These plants appear to have been well cared for and appear to have been specifically planted in that location as there are no other marijuana plants within the backyard. I noted that the ground around the base of the plants was moist, with the plants appearing to have been watered. I noted that these marijuana plants had the characteristics of the marijuana plant in its growing state, being medium to dark green in color and having sawtoothed-edge leaves. Being an expert on the identification of growing marijuana plants, it is my opinion that the plants observed by your affiant were, in fact, marijuana plants in their growing state.

> As an experienced narcotics officer I can also say that in the past on numerous occasions regarding the cultivation of marijuana ... I have found amounts of marijuana plants inside of a residence and outbuildings on the property being cured and manicured for the use and sale of these plants. I can further say that marijuana grown by private individuals is picked and commonly taken into residences and outbuildings to be dried and manicured. I have further found that individuals involved in the cultivation of marijuana plants keep inside of their residence and outbuildings marijuana seeds. As an expert on the identification of marijuana I can also state that marijuana is usually hung and dried out of view of the public. Marijuana is also frequently manicured and packaged for use and sale and this requires all types of implements and is also generally done out of view of the public. For those reasons I believe that there can be found inside of the residence at 116 Maynell ... marijuana and the implements used to cultivate and package marijuana for use or sale.

Presented with such an affidavit, almost every judge will find that a backyard *Cannabis* garden establishes probable cause that marijuana will also be found inside the home. Consequently, a search warrant issued on the basis of such an affidavit can legally permit the officers to search the inside of the grower's home.

However, at least one court in California has held that an officer's observation of a *single Cannabis* plant in a person's backyard may not establish probable cause that marijuana will be found inside the person's home. In this case, Officer Miller of the San Diego Police Department received information that Mitchell Pellegrin was cultivating *Cannabis* in his backyard. The officer investigated and saw in plain view a single "three-foot marijuana plant growing next to a fence at the rear of Pellegrin's residence." Based on his observations, Officer Miller obtained a search warrant and searched Pellegrin's home. Inside, he found some concentrated *Cannabis*.

The court held that the search warrant was invalid because Officer Miller's observation of a single marijuana plant in Pellegrin's backyard was insufficient to establish probable cause that marijuana could be found inside Pellegrin's house. As the court pointed out, the single plant could have been growing wild without Pellegrin's knowledge. Officer Miller failed to state in his affidavit any facts indicating that the plant was being "cultivated." The court ended its opinion by stating, "the right of the people of the United States of America to be secure in the privacy of their homes is upon too solid a foundation to be undermined by what could well be a happenstance growing of one marijuana plant in a yard." *(People v. Pellegrin [1977] 78 Cal.App.3d 913.)*

In contrast, courts have held that a *handful* of *Cannabis* plants observed growing in pots in a person's backyard *does* establish probable cause that additional evidence of marijuana use or cultivation will be found inside the residence. As one court stated, "marijuana plants do not grow in pots and planters by chance. When they are found growing in that manner, it is reasonable to infer those who controlled and occupied the premises have something to do with their planting, cultivation, or care."

Linking Remote Gardens To The Gardener

In a recent Minnesota case, state police officers discovered a booby trapped 178-plant *Cannabis* garden in a remote area. They placed the garden under surveillance and three days later observed Mark Sedzinski enter the plot and inspect the plants. The officers arrested Mr. Sedzinski and searched his home after obtaining a search warrant based on seeing him enter the garden and inspect the plants. How did the officers know that he wasn't just an innocent hiker who haphazardly wandered into the garden? In the man's home the officers found "small marijuana plants, a book entitled "Marijuana's Grower Guide," two guns, a small scale, and florescent lights. A woman who lived on the plot of land where the *Cannabis* was growing identified a second man Neil Coyle whom she said occasionally accompanied Mr. Sedzinski to the plot. The officers checked Mr. Sedzinski's telephone records and found frequent calls between the two men. When the officers searched Mr. Coyle's home they found "numerous small marijuana plants under a timed lighting system, bags of processed marijuana, marijuana residue, a digital scale, plant food, books containing information on marijuana growing, three firearms, and photographs of Coyle displaying marijuana. Inside his van they found rolling papers, a roach clip, and three pitch forks...similar to those used to 'booby trap' the marijuana plot." Not surprisingly, this was sufficient evidence to link the men together as well as to the remote garden. Consequently, both men were convicted of conspiracy to manufacture more than 100 marijuana plants in violation of federal law *(U.S. v. Coyle [8th Cir. 1993] 998 F.2d 548.)*

Evidence of an Indoor Garden Is Insufficient For A Search Warrant

Needless to say, many people enjoy the art of indoor gardening, raising roses, bonsai trees, cacti, and all sorts of plants which the government has not yet declared illegal. Recognizing the fact that indoor gardens might be entirely innocuous courts have required some evidence that the plant being raised is *Cannabis* prior to issuing a search warrant. Numerous cases teach that without some evidence that the gardener is growing *Cannabis* specifically, all the evidence in the world that the person merely has an indoor garden is insufficient grounds for a search warrant.

In one 1993 case, for example, the search warrant stated the following factors in an attempt to establish probable cause that Arthur Russell was growing *Cannabis* in a shed on his property: (1) an electric bill averaging around $150 a month, when people with houses twice as large in the same neighborhood used only about $50 of electricity per month; (2) the observation of a large vent fan on the shed wall, similar to ones the officer had previously seen to cool sheds where marijuana was growing; (3) the observation of a sprinkler on the roof of the shed, which the officer believed had the effect of further cooling the shed; (4) observation of bright light escaping through a crack in the shed wall on evenings when the officer had reason to believe that no one was in the shed; (5) Mr. Russell had arranged to read his own electric meter; and (6) he kept an aggressive dog.

An Oregon court held that the above information was *insufficient* to establish probable cause to believe that Mr. Russell was growing *Cannabis*, as opposed to some other plant, in his shed. As the court observed: "Taking the unchallenged information as a whole, a magistrate could, perhaps, conjecture that defendant was growing something in his shed. However . . . from that information alone, a reasonable magistrate could not infer that defendant was *probably* growing marijuana." *(State v. Russell [Or. App. 1993] 857 P.2d 220.)*

Police Fly-overs

Aerial surveillance by the police is becoming an increasingly common search method. For example, in recent years in California, the state has implemented a "Campaign Against Marijuana Planting," known as CAMP for short. CAMP's mode of operation is to use airplanes and helicopters to locate *Cannabis* gardens. In fact, CAMP has even used high-altitude U2 planes for detection and surveillance of marijuana crops! (A federal court approved of the use of the U2 planes, but expressed distaste for such domestic use of spy planes.) In its first two years of operation, CAMP seized hundreds of thousands of pounds of *Cannabis* plants, valued at hundreds of millions of dollars.

Currently, Federal Aviation Administration (FAA) regulations permit fixed-wing aircraft to be flown as low as 1,000 feet while over congested areas, and as low as 500 feet over uncongested areas. For helicopters, these regulations are even more lenient. The regulations permit helicopters to fly below the above altitudes if the operation is conducted without hazard to person or property on the surface. Therefore, there is no set minimum altitude for helicopters. In one case, however, a gardener was arrested for cultivating two *Cannabis* plants after a police officer in a helicopter identified the plants by hovering only 25 feet above them! The court was outraged by the officer's action, and promptly declared the search illegal.

In another case, Sheriff Jones in Florida received an anonymous tip that a Mr. Riley was growing *Cannabis* on his property. Jones drove by Riley's mobile home located on five acres of rural property. Jones could see a greenhouse about fifteen feet behind the mobile home, but was unable to tell what was growing inside it.

Jones boarded a helicopter and flew over Riley's property. When he passed over the greenhouse, which was indisputably within the curtilage of Riley's home, he observed that it was covered with corrugated roofing panels, approximately 10 percent of which were missing. Jones ordered the helicopter pilot to descend to approximately 400 feet above the greenhouse. As he hovered above the gaps in the greenhouse roof, he looked through the openings and saw some *Cannabis* plants. Jones quickly returned to the station and wrote out an affidavit of probable cause to obtain a search warrant. A judge signed the warrant and Riley's greenhouse was searched, resulting in the seizure of some *Cannabis* plants and Riley's arrest.

Riley argued all the way to the United States Supreme Court that officer Jones's fly-over was an illegal warrantless search of his greenhouse, which was located within the curtilage of his home, and that the subsequent warrant was therefore invalid. The case split the Supreme Court. The five most conservative justices rejected Riley's argument, concluding that Sheriff Jones's view from the helicopter was not an unconstitutional search. However, they disagreed as to *why* the aerial view was legal under the constitution.

Four of these justices held that the aerial view was not a even "search." In their opinion, the fact that the fly-over was permissible under the FAA regulations discussed above, was sufficient to make it constitutional. In their words:

> Riley no doubt intended and expected that his greenhouse would not be open to public inspection, and the precautions he took protected against ground-level observation. Because the sides and roof of his greenhouse were left partially open, however, what was growing in the greenhouse was subject to viewing from the air . . . Any member of the public could legally have been flying over Riley's property in a helicopter at the altitude of 400 feet and could have observed Riley's greenhouse. The police officer did no more.

They compared Riley's case to an earlier case in which police officers spotted a person's *Cannabis* garden while flying at 1,000 feet. In that case, the Supreme Court held that the fly-over was constitutional, stating:

> In an age where private and commercial flight in the public airways is routine, it is unreasonable for respondent to expect that his marijuana plants were constitutionally protected from being observed with the naked eye from an altitude of 1,000 feet. The Fourth Amendment simply does not require the police traveling in the public airways at this altitude to obtain a warrant in order to observe what is visible to the naked eye.

The fifth conservative justice, Justice O'Connor, agreed that Jones's aerial surveillance was constitutional, but expressed concern that her conservative brethren placed undue reliance on FAA regulations. In her opinion, "[t]he fact that a helicopter could conceivably observe the curtilage at virtually any altitude or angle, without violating FAA regulations, does not in itself mean that an individual has no reasonable expectation of privacy from such observation." In her opinion, the determining factor in fly-over cases is whether or not public aircraft generally travel at such altitudes in the vicinity. If such air traffic is relatively common, then a gardener surveilled by a police fly-over could not have a reasonable expectation of privacy in his garden. Under such circumstances, an officer's aerial observation would fall under the constitutional plain-view rule. However, if low-level public fly-overs were very uncommon in the garden's location, then the gardener would have a reasonable expectation of privacy. Under such circumstances, an officer's fly-over, even if within FAA guidelines, would then be an unconstitutional violation of the gardener's privacy. Having set forth her reasoning, Justice O'Connor then found that Riley failed to present any evidence that public fly-overs above his greenhouse were rare. Having no evidence that public fly-overs were uncommon, Justice O'Connor concurred with the plurality that Sheriff Jones's aerial surveillance did not offend Riley's reasonable expectation of privacy, and hence did not violate the Fourth Amendment.

Justice Brennan, along with three other justices, dissented. In the opinion of these justices, the plurality forsook the traditional "reasonable expectation of privacy" analysis in favor of total deference to FAA regulations. The dissenting justices agreed with Justice O'Connor that simply because an airborne police officer is in a place where he has a legal right to be (flying within FAA regulations), it does not necessarily follow that whatever he sees from that vantage point has been knowingly exposed to public view. In Brennan's opinion, the conservative justices were sacrificing the Fourth Amendment protections that safeguard the privacy rights of all citizens in order to facilitate fighting the War on Drugs. Justice Brennan wrote:

> It is difficult to avoid the conclusion that the plurality has allowed its analysis of Riley's expectation of privacy to be colored by its distaste for the activity in which he was engaged. It is indeed easy to forget, especially in view of current concern over drug trafficking, that the scope of the Fourth Amendment's protection does not turn on whether the activity disclosed by a search is illegal or innocuous. But we dismiss this as a "drug case" only at the peril of our own liberties . . .

> If the Constitution does not protect Riley's marijuana garden against such surveillance, it is hard to see how it will forbid the Government from aerial spying on the activities of a law-abiding citizen on her fully enclosed outdoor patio . . .

> The issue in this case is, ultimately, "how tightly the Fourth Amendment permits people to be driven back into the recesses of their lives by the risk of surveillance." The Court today approves warrantless helicopter searches from an altitude of 400 feet. . . . I find considerable cause for concern in the fact that a plurality of four justices would remove virtually all constitutional barriers to police surveillance from the vantage point of helicopters. The Fourth Amendment demands that we temper our efforts to apprehend criminals with a concern for the impact on our fundamental liberties of the methods we use. I hope it will be a matter of concern to my colleagues that the police-surveillance methods they would sanction were among those described forty years ago in George Orwell's dread vision of life in the 1980s . . . .

Justice Brennan then went on to quote Orwell's classic, *Nineteen Eighty-Four:*

> The black-mustachio'd face gazed down from every commanding corner. There was one on the house-front immediately opposite. BIG BROTHER IS WATCHING YOU, the caption said . . . In the far distance a helicopter skimmed down between roofs, hovered for an instant like a bluebottle, and darted away again with a curving flight. It was the Police Patrol, snooping into people's windows.

Brennan closed his opinion with the following comment:

> Who can read this passage without a shudder, and without the instinctive reaction that it depicts life in some country other than ours? I respectfully dissent. *(Florida v. Riley [1989] 109 S.Ct.693.)*

To sum up, as a result of this case, the law with respect to aerial surveillance by law enforcement is currently determined by the reasoning of Justice O'Connor. While FAA guidelines are an important factor, the constitutionality of a police officer's fly-over is decided by whether or not public aircraft commonly fly at such altitudes at the particular location surveilled. If a person's garden is routinely exposed to the view of passing public aircraft, a police officer's view from the same flight path does not violate the gardener's reasonable expectation of privacy, and is therefore considered constitutional. In contrast, if a person's garden is located in an area that very rarely or never has public aircraft flying overhead, a police officer's aerial surveillance of the garden, even if within FAA regulations, violates the gardener's reasonable expectation of privacy, and is therefore unconstitutional without a warrant.

It is worth stressing that this rule is currently in jeopardy because two of the four dissenting justices who agreed with O'Connor' reasoning are no longer on the Court and have been replaced by more conservative justices. Therefore, when the next fly-over case comes before the Court, it is quite likely that a police officer's fly-over will be deemed constitutional so long as it was conducted in compliance with FAA regulations whether or not public aircraft fly at such altitudes in the vicinity.

Currently, the Supreme Court of at least one state (California) has held that although the United States Constitution may not provide much protection against aerial observations of a person's curtilage, the *state* constitution *does*.

In a well-reasoned opinion, the California Supreme Court explained:

> We were not persuaded that police officers who examine a residence from the air are simply observing what is in "plain view" from a lawful public vantage point. Such reasoning

ignores the essential difference between ground and aerial surveillance. One can take reasonable steps to ensure his yard's privacy from the street, sidewalk, or neighborhood, and police on the ground may not broach such barriers to gain a view of the enclosed area. But there is no practical defense against aerial spying, and precious constitutional privacy rights would mean little if the government could defeat them so easily.

Even if members of the public may casually see into his yard when a routine flight happens over the property, we concluded, a householder does not thereby consent to focused examination of the curtilage by airborne police officers looking for evidence of crime. No law-enforcement interest justifies such intensive warrantless government intrusion into a zone of heightened constitutional privacy. *(People v. Mayoff [1986] 42 Cal.3d 1302.)*

Unfortunately, California is rather unique, in that it has a rule that only evidence obtained in violation of the *federal* constitution is excluded. Therefore, despite the California court's holding that the police performed an illegal search by spying on a curtilage garden from the air, there was, and is, *no remedy*, since the action only violated the state constitution but not the federal constitution.

The DEA's Domestic Marijuana Eradication Program

The DEA's Domestic *Cannabis* Eradication/Suppression Program, initiated about fifteen years ago, provides financial and technical assistance to state and local agencies trying to stamp out the evil weed. By the year 1990, every state was participating in the program. In 1993, the National Guard spent almost half a million flight hours looking for *Cannabis* plants.

In 1992, the program led to the eradication of over 48,000 *Cannabis* gardens and 272 million cultivated *Cannabis* plants. In 1990, the program led to the destruction of over 188 million ditchweed plants, seventy-five percent of which were found in Nebraska and Indiana. Of the total number of cultivated *Cannabis* plants eradicated, the government reports that 2 million were choice sinsemilla, seventy percent of which was eradicated in Missouri, Hawaii and Tennessee.

At first look, this program would seem to run afoul of the federal law that makes it illegal to use the Armed Forces to execute laws within the USA. This federal law, commonly known as the Posse Comitatus Act, makes it a crime (punishable by up to two years in federal prison and a $10,000 fine) to willfully use "any part of the Army or Air Force as a posse comitatus or otherwise to execute the laws."

Why doesn't the Posse Comitatus Act bar the National Guard from assisting in state marijuana eradication programs? Courts which have examined this question have pointed to a separate federal law which expressly authorizes the use of the National Guard in state run "drug interdiction and counter-drug activities." The courts have ruled that under this law, the National Guard is authorized to assist state anti-marijuana programs so long as it is not acting in "federal service."

In fact, the National Guard is not only used in general marijuana eradication programs, but it is also used in specific raids on suspected *Cannabis* cultivators. For example, in Pennsylvania a squad of National Guardsmen assisted in staking out and surveilling a farm suspected of *Cannabis* cultivation. The guardsmen took up positions in the woods all around the farm and even set up a command post in a nearby church. The court upheld the use of the National Guard for such activities on the theory that the Guard was not acting in federal service but rather was acting to assist Pennsylvania in its "local drug eradication and interdiction operations." Therefore, ruled the court, the Posse Comitatus Act was not violated. *(US v. Benish [3rd Cir. 1993] 5 F.3d 20.)*

Marijuana Gardens on Public Property

In recent years, it has become increasingly common for people to grow *Cannabis* on public lands. The legal advantage of such gardening is that it becomes more difficult for the prosecutor to link the plants to a specific person. Therefore, although the police often locate these secluded *Cannabis* gardens and destroy the plants, they often are unable to prosecute the grower. As a result, the grower loses the plants, but is only rarely subjected to an arrest or search. The other legal advantage to growing *Cannabis* on public property is that it provides some additional protection against asset forfeiture. First, the government may be unable to figure out who grew the plants and therefore unable to seize the grower's assets. Second, even if the police do catch the grower, the grower's own land is not subject to forfeiture, since it was not used to facilitate the crime. The legal disadvantage of gardening on public property is that the gardener has absolutely no right to attack a warrantless search of the garden, and any person who is convicted of cultivating marijuana on federal property is subject to a mandatory $500,000 fine, in addition to the punishment imposed under the sentencing guidelines. *(21 USC 841[5].)*

Michael Weiss and his son Jeffrey had established a 30-plant *Cannabis* garden on secluded public property in the town of Albany, Vermont. One day, unbeknownst to the Weiss', a state trooper spotted the garden during an aerial observation of the area. Ten days later the trooper and another officer went to the area on foot and verified that the plants were *Cannabis*. The officers searched the area but didn't find anyone.

About one hour later, the trooper returned to the garden with further troopers to uproot the *Cannabis* plants. When they walked into the garden area, they discovered Michael and Jeffrey Weiss tending the plants. They also found several items that had not been there an hour earlier, including two black plastic garbage bags, a plastic garbage can containing manicured marijuana, a nylon bag with shoulder straps, some pruning shears, and a loaded shotgun. The troopers arrested Jeffrey and his dad. Charges against Jeffrey were subsequently dropped, but his dad was prosecuted. Based on the items found at the garden site, the officers suspected that more evidence could be found at the Weiss home, for which the troopers sought and obtained a search warrant. Inside, the officers found additional incriminating evidence.

Michael Weiss argued that the search warrant was invalid because it failed to state facts showing probable cause that incriminating evidence would be found at his home. The Vermont Supreme Court disagreed. The court explained that the items found at the public garden site had not been there an hour earlier and that they were the sort of items commonly stored at a household. In the court's words, "the presence of the defendants at the marijuana patch with common household items created a link between the residence and the site sufficient for the court to lawfully authorize the search warrant." Therefore, the court concluded that the search warrant was valid.

High-Tech Surveillance of Government Land

Just how far the government will go to catch guerrilla *Cannabis* growers on federal land is demonstrated by a federal case from Florida. Officer John Ray of the United States Forest Service was hiking in the Ouachita National Forest in Scott County, Arkansas, when he discovered 172 cultivated *Cannabis* plants approximately ten yards off an old logging road. After discovering the plants, Officer Ray "installed a surveillance video camera that was activated by motion and body heat." When Ray checked the camera 10 days later, he found it had recorded the image of a single unidentified person. Ray continued checking the camera and after about one month he replaced it with a 35mm still camera in an attempt to obtain clearer photos. After monitoring this camera setup for a total of about two months, Ray had acquired at least 19 photographs of a man tending the *Cannabis* plants.

In March 1992, Bradley Rose was arrested on the basis of photographs and the fact that his residence was relatively close to the *Cannabis* garden. Mr. Rose was convicted of manufacturing marijuana in violation of federal law, and sentenced to sixty-three months in federal prison. *(U.S. v. Rose [8th Cir. 1993] 8 F.3d 7.)*

CHAPTER 9

MEDICINAL MARIJUANA AND THE LAW

Without question, and based on a detailed factual analyses of the available data, marijuana, in its natural form, is one of the safest therapeutically active substances known to man.

—Dr. Andrew Weil

PRIOR TO THE VILIFICATION of the *Cannabis* plant, the *Pharmacopoeia of the United States* listed *Cannabis* preparations as "approved therapeutic agents." For over half a century, extract of *Cannabis* was the most widely used analgesic in the United States.

In 1937, an absurd anti-marijuana propaganda campaign launched by the Federal Bureau of Narcotics and its director, Harry J. Anslinger, resulted in the enactment of the federal Marijuana Tax Act, the first federal prohibition against marijuana. Reminiscent of Orwell's *Nineteen Eighty-Four* in which Big Brother ordered the rewriting of all books "which might conceivably hold any kind of political significance," *Cannabis* was erased from the *Pharmacopoeia* in 1942. It has never returned. What was once medicine, is no more–at least according to the government.

Despite overwhelming evidence that marijuana continues to have a number of safe and effective medical uses, the federal government steadfastly maintains that it has "no accepted medical value in treatment." Consequently, under the federal drug control scheme, marijuana remains Schedule I (the category of drugs considered to have no medicinal value and for which legal penalties are the most severe) and hence physicians are prohibited from prescribing it.

Attempts To Reschedule Marijuana Under Federal Law

Since 1972, ongoing efforts have attempted to force the government to move marijuana from Schedule I to Schedule II so that doctors would have the option of prescribing it to ailing patients. As you can see from *Table 5*, the primary difference between Schedule I and Schedule II drugs is that Schedule II drugs have " a currently accepted medical use," and hence they available by prescription. The DEA has resisted every attempt to reschedule marijuana and, as a result, marijuana remains in Schedule I along with heroin and PCP.

Table 5. Schedule I versus Schedule II Controlled Substances

SCHEDULE I CRITERIA
(1) a high potential for abuse; and
(2) absence of any currently accepted medical use; and
(3) lack of safety even under medical supervision

SCHEDULE II CRITERIA
(1) a high potential for abuse; and
(2) a currently accepted medical use in the United States; and
(3) a potential for severe psychological or physical dependence

From summer 1986 through spring 1988, marijuana's medical efficacy was the subject of extensive public hearings held in Washington DC. Numerous experts, both doctors and patients, testified on behalf of the medicinal properties of marijuana. At the completion of the hearing, and after carefully reviewing all the evidence, Judge Francis Young, the Chief Administrative Law Judge of the Drug Enforcement Administration, issued an astounding ruling: marijuana should be rescheduled. Judge Young bravely rejected the government's argument that allowing seriously ill people to use marijuana for medicinal purposes would "send a message" that marijuana use is acceptable:

> There are those who, in all sincerity, argue that the transfer of marijuana to Schedule II will "send a signal" that marijuana is "OK" generally for recreational use. This argument is specious. It presents no valid reason for refraining from taking an action required by law in light of the evidence .... The fear of sending such a signal cannot be permitted to override the legitimate need, amply demonstrated in this record, of countless sufferers for the relief marijuana can provide when prescribed by a physician in a legitimate case.

> The evidence in this record clearly shows that marijuana has been accepted as capable of relieving the distress of great numbers of very ill people, and doing so with safety under medical supervision. It would be unreasonable, arbitrary and capricious for DEA to continue to stand between those sufferers and the benefit of this substance in light of the evidence in this record . . . .
>
> The judge recommends that the Administrator transfer marijuana from Schedule I to Schedule II." *(In the Matter of Marijuana Rescheduling Petition, September 6, 1988, Docket No. 86-22.)*

The DEA has ignored Judge Young's ruling and, to this day, refuses to reschedule marijuana even though rescheduling would permit only medical use when authorized by the prescription of a doctor and nonmedical use of marijuana would remain illegal.

Compassionate Use

From 1976 through March 10, 1992, the federal government implemented a "compassionate use" program that permitted seriously ill patients to receive government grown marijuana if it could be shown that conventional medications were inadequate. Under this program, patients applied through the Food and Drug Administration to receive free monthly shipments of government-issued joints. The application process was complex and during the 14 years of the program, the FDA approved marijuana use for only fifteen people suffering from cancer, AIDS, multiple sclerosis, spinal cord injuries, and glaucoma.

In 1991, Dr. James Mason, then director of the Public Health Service, became alarmed by the FDA's preliminary approval of approximately thirty more applications for medical marijuana. Evidently concerned that the number of approvals granted would continue to rise, Dr. Mason completely shut down the compassionate use program on March 10, 1992. Those people already granted compassionate use were permitted to continue receiving marijuana, but the door was closed to all others. Today only eight of those fifteen patients remain alive. Those eight people are the only people in the United States explicitly authorized to use marijuana for medical purposes.

In January 1994, statements issued by Assistant Health Secretary, Dr. Philip Lee rekindled hope that the compassionate use program might be resurrected under the Clinton Administration. In July 1994, however, Dr. Lee determined that legal drugs are currently available to treat all medical illness for which marijuana might be beneficial. Consequently, he concluded that patients need not resort to marijuana. As a result, the Clinton Administration quietly announced its decision to continue the federal ban on medical use of marijuana.

The Marinol Hypocrisy

Dronabinol is a synthetic preparation of THC sold by Roxane Laboratories and marketed by Unimed Pharmaceutical company under the trade name "Marinol." In July 1985, the DEA gave approval for the marketing of Dronabinol, and in April 1986, synthetic THC was quietly moved from Schedule I to Schedule II. Its use was originally indicated exclusively for the relief of chemotherapy-induced nausea, and the DEA threatened to investigate any physician caught prescribing it for other purposes. In December 1992, the FDA approved Dronabinol's use for AIDS-related wasting.

THC, the active ingredient in Marinol, is also considered to be the primary psychoactive constituent in marijuana. Given this fact, it seems absurd to place Marinol in Schedule II while leaving marijuana in Schedule I—unless one considers the enormous financial benefit to the manufacturer of maintaining this discrepancy: a single Marinol pill costs about $8, whereas a quantity of marijuana of equivalent potency would cost only pennies.

The Medical Necessity Defense

The federal government's wholesale outlawing of marijuana use leaves those who wish to use marijuana for medicinal purposes with little alternative but to become "criminals." Their only hope in the event of arrest is to present what is known as a "necessity defense" which argues that it was necessary to break the law in order to avoid a greater evil.

To present a necessity defense, a generally law abiding person caught breaking a criminal law argues that less harm was done by breaking the law than by complying with it. The classic example is breaking the speed limit in order to rush someone to the hospital. The most common application of the necessity defense has been in prison-escape cases, where a prisoner defends against a charge of escape by arguing, for example, that the prison was on fire or that another prisoner was about to kill him, and that his escape was therefore necessary to avoid a greater harm, usually death inside the prison.

The *medical* necessity defense is a particular application of the necessity defense that has been used, both successfully and unsuccessfully, by people charged with marijuana crimes. Courts in the District of Columbia, Florida, Idaho, Iowa ,and Washington have permitted use of the medical necessity defense against criminal charges of marijuana possession.

The requirements of a defense based on medical need are unclear because the case-law in this area is still developing. Considering the cases previously decided, it appears that the following elements are essential to establish the defense in a marijuana case.

(1) The defendant must have a serious illness.

(2) The illness must not be treatable with conventional medications.

(3) The defendant must believe that he or she had no other medical option but to use marijuana.

(4) The defendant's belief that marijuana would provide some relief for his illness must be objectively reasonable. (In other words, reliable medical evidence must show that marijuana helps the defendant's condition.)

(5) The amount of marijuana seized must not be so great as to raise the possibility that it may have been intended for sale or distribution.

The following conditions would also be helpful in such a case:

(1) Only small amount of marijuana were found (less than an ounce of marijuana or less than three *Cannabis* plants)

(2) The defendant has no prior convictions for drug-related crimes.

(3) There is evidence showing that defendant actually handled his or her marijuana as a medicine (he or she kept the marijuana with other medications and used marijuana only as medicine.)

(4) There is evidence that prior to being arrested the person sought, from the FDA or his or her state government, permission to use marijuana medicinally.

(5) There is no evidence of distribution.

(6) The marijuana was stored in a secure location–away from children, etc.

Denial of the Medical Necessity Defense

A recent decision by the Supreme Court of Massachusetts shows how preposterous and heartless the War on Drugs has become. In 1991, the highest court in Massachusetts upheld a lower court's refusal to permit Joseph Hutchins, a seriously ill man, from presenting a medical necessity defense to charges of marijuana possession.

Mr. Hutchins suffers from a disease known as progressive systemic sclerosis (scleroderma), a chronic disease that results in the buildup of scar tissue throughout the body. Its cause is unknown and there is no effective treatment or cure. The disease caused Mr. Hutchins to regurgitate food and stomach acid and to suffer weight loss, diarrhea, nausea, and vomiting. His esophagus continued to narrow and it became extremely difficult just to swallow. The constriction of his esophagus was treated by dilation and in 1974 became so severe that his physician advised him to have his esophagus surgically removed and replaced with a piece of his own intestine.

Because every treatment and medication proved unsuccessful, Mr. Hutchins tried smoking marijuana in 1975. He found that it made his esophagus feel better, and it alleviated his nausea. It improved his appetite and made it easier to eat, drink and swallow. Mr. Hutchins made unsuccessful attempts to obtain a legal prescription for marijuana through the Veterans Administration, the Massachusetts Legislature, and the United States Congress.

The Massachusetts Supreme Court held that even if Mr. Hutchins' medical history was proven, it still could not justify the violation of the state's anti-marijuana law:

> . . . We rule that the defendant's proffered evidence does not raise the defense of necessity. In our view, the alleviation of the defendant's medical symptoms, the importance to the defendant of which we do not underestimate, would not clearly and significantly outweigh the potential harm to the public were we to declare that the defendant's cultivation of marijuana and its use for his medical purposes may not be punishable. We cannot dismiss the reasonably possible negative impact of such a judicial declaration on the enforcement of our drug laws, including but not limited to those dealing with marijuana, nor can we ignore the government's overriding interest in regulating such substances.

The skewed thinking in Mr. Hutchins' case makes clear that the drug war has severely distorted our cultural values in a direction which no reasonable and compassionate person can condone.

Two justices, Chief Justice Liacos and Justice Nolan, dissented, arguing that the court should at least give Mr. Hutchins the opportunity to inform the jury of his medical history and his reasons for using marijuana. They charged the other judges with ignoring "the humanitarian and compassionate value in allowing an individual to seek relief from agonizing symptoms caused by a progressive and incurable illness in circumstances which risk no harm to any other individual." (*Com. v. Hutchins [Mass. 1991] 575 N.E.2d 741.*)

In the same year that *Hutchins* was decided in Massachusetts, a Minnesota court of appeal refused to allow Gordon Hanson to present a medical necessity defense after agents found over 100 *Cannabis* plants growing in his garden. In this case, it was undisputed that Mr. Hanson had suffered from epilepsy since 1956 and suffered from the side-effects of the available prescription anti-seizure medications.

The court reached its conclusion that no medical necessity defense existed in Minnesota by noting that under Minnesota law, as under federal law, marijuana is a Schedule I substance with "no currently accepted medical use in the United States." The court then explained that the Minnesota legislature had carved out a single exception by enacting the Minnesota "THC Therapeutic Research Act" (TRA). The court found that the TRA was very narrow, exempting only cancer patients undergoing chemotherapy who received marijuana under the strict controls of an approved medical research program. The court reasoned that the existence of the TRA demonstrated that the Minnesota legislature had considered the possible medical uses of marijuana and had determined that marijuana should not be available for non-cancer patients outside a medical research program. Consequently, the court of appeal ruled that an *epileptic* like Mr. Hanson had no right to present a medical necessity defense. *(State v. Hanson [Minn. App. 1991] 468 N.W.2d 77.)*

Finally, in 1993, Neal Cramer argued that he was growing *Cannabis* to relieve pain caused by an automobile accident. The Arizona Court of Appeal ruled that no medical necessity defense exists in Arizona. The court's argument centered on the fact that the Arizona legislature had refused to renew the Arizona Controlled Substances Therapeutic Act, which had expired on July 1, 1985. "The Legislature's refusal to renew the legislation in 1985," said the court, "suggests that marijuana, previously allowed for therapeutic purposes, was subsequently outlawed without exception." *(State v. Cramer [Ariz. App. Div.2 1992] 851 P.2d 147.)*

The Medical Necessity Defense Succeeds

One of the most well-publicized medical marijuana cases involved the plight of a Florida couple, Kenneth and Barbara Jenks. Kenneth Jenks inherited hemophilia from his mother and in 1980 contracted the AIDS virus from a blood transfusion. He unwittingly passed the AIDS virus to his spouse Barbara.

Mrs. Jenks' health began to decline rapidly. Because of constant vomiting, her weight dropped from 150 to 112 pounds during one three-week period. On at least six occasions she was hospitalized for two to three weeks at a time. At least six different prescription oral medications for nausea failed to provide relief. Shots for nausea left her in a stupor. Likewise, when Mr. Jenks started AZT treatment, he was not able to eat because the medication left him constantly nauseous.

While participating in an AIDS support group, a courageous member of the group told the Jenks how marijuana had helped him. Although initially reluctant, Mr. and Mrs. Jenks decided they had nothing to lose and agreed to try marijuana. To their profound relief, they found that it eased their nausea, increased their appetite and helped them stay out of the hospital. They asked their doctor if he could prescribe marijuana, but he told them he could not. Left with no legal options and preferring to avoid risks entailed by purchasing "street marijuana," Kenneth and Barbara Jenks made a decision to grow their own *Cannabis* plants.

On March 29, 1980, based on information received from an informer, 10 armed narcotics officers smashed down the Jenks' front door, held a gun to Ms. Jenks' head, and seized two small *Cannabis* plants. The Jenks were arrested and charged with felony cultivation of *Cannabis* and with possession of drug paraphernalia in violation of Florida law. (They each faced five years in state prison.) At the scene, the Jenks admitted growing the two plants and told the officers that they each had AIDS and that they used the marijuana medicinally.

At their trial, the judge ruled that Florida law did not recognize a medical necessity defense against criminal charges. Consequently, the judge determined that he had no option but to find the Jenks guilty as charged. He refused to punish them harshly, however, placing them on one year of unsupervised probation and ordering them to perform 500 hours of community service "providing care, comfort and concern for each other."

Despite the lenient punishment, the Jenks resented being made criminals for taking actions that they believed had been necessitated by their illnesses. They therefore appealed their convictions, arguing that the judge had been incorrect when he determined that Florida does not permit medical necessity defenses. The Florida Court of Appeal agreed with them. The appellate judges determined that Florida does in fact recognize medical necessity defenses and that the Jenks had established such a defense. Consequently, the court of appeal reversed their convictions.

Quoting from a treatise on criminal law, the court explained the general theory behind the necessity defense:

> The pressure of natural forces sometimes confronts a person in
> an emergency with a choice of two evils: either he may violate
> the literal terms of the criminal law and thus produce a harmful
> result, or he may comply with those terms and thus produce a
> greater or equal or lesser amount of harm. For reasons of social
> policy, if the harm which will result from compliance with the
> law is greater than that which will result from violation of it, he
> is by virtue of the defense of necessity justified in violating it.

Applying the necessity principle to the circumstances facing the Jenks, the court of appeal explained:

. . . The Jenks obviously did not intend to contract AIDS. Furthermore, the Jenks' medical expert and physician testified that no drug or treatment is available that would effectively eliminate or diminish the Jenks' nausea. Finally the Jenks established that if their nausea was not controlled, their lives were in danger. The state put on no evidence that contradicted the Jenks, and the trial court had no authority to reject the witnesses' testimony. Based upon these facts, we conclude the trial court erred in rejecting the Jenks' defense and in convicting them as charged.

In another successful case, Lynn Hastings was charged with felony possession of marijuana after police officers found ten to twelve *Cannabis* plants growing in her basement. Ms. Hastings claimed she was growing the plants because she suffered from severe rheumatoid arthritis and they were the most effective method for controlling her pain and muscle spasms. The trial judge ruled that no such defense existed under Idaho law and refused to allow her to present the defense. Ms. Hastings appealed. The court of appeal reversed the trial court's ruling, holding instead that Ms. Hastings could present her medical defense and it was for the jury to decide whether or not she established it *State v. Hastings [Idaho 1990] 801 P.2d 563.)*

CHAPTER 10

MARIJUANA, RELIGION, AND THE LAW

*Congress shall make no law respecting an establishment of
religion, or prohibiting the free exercise thereof . . . .*

—The First Amendment

IN THE OFTEN CONSTRICTED MINDS of most of our country's politicians
and judges, *Cannabis* is a vile and evil plant. Despite the fact that preparations
from the *Cannabis* plant have be used for thousands of years to facilitate religious
understanding, our country's lawmakers and judges have consistently refused to
offer any protection to religiously motivated marijuana users.

At present, all but a few trial courts in our country will refuse to allow the
presentation of a religious defense against a marijuana charge. Unless you have
a magical attorney and wind up in front of a tremendously courageous and
independently-minded judge, you very likely will be barred from presenting the
issue for consideration by the jury.

On December 22, 1965, Dr. Timothy Leary was arrested by U.S. Customs
officers after an inspector recognized him and spotted "some vegetable material
and a seed on the floor of the automobile." At his trial, Dr. Leary successfully
introduced evidence of his impressive academic background and of his member-
ship in the well-established Brahmakrishna sect of Hinduism, members of which
use marijuana in their religious rituals. Dr. Leary presented a great deal of
evidence backing up his claim of religious use, including the testimony of a Hindu
monk, an expert in psychopharmacology, and a medical doctor. Once all the
evidence was presented, Dr. Leary's attorney requested a jury instruction that
would permit the jury to acquit Dr. Leary if it found that his religious claims were
honest and made in good faith. The judge refused to give the jury the instruction,
and the jury subsequently found Dr. Leary guilty of several marijuana crimes.

Dr. Leary appealed his convictions arguing that his religious use of marijuana was protected by the Free Exercise Clause of the federal constitution, and
that the judge unfairly refused to instruct the jury regarding the religious defense.

The appellate court rejected his argument, holding that despite the clear language of the Free Exercise Clause, there was no religious defense to the anti-marijuana laws.

The published opinion of the court of appeal is an example of the manner in which judges often kowtow to the politics and hysteria of the War on Drugs. Casting marijuana as a destroyer of society, the court asserted that "the paramount interest in the enforcement of the laws relative to marijuana is the protection of society." Citing 30-year old "evidence," used to support the Marijuana Tax Act of 1937, the court asserted that marijuana users often engage in "criminal episodes of terrible character." The "evidence was voluminous and convincing," wrote the court, "that Marijuana is a serious evil to society."

With such a mind-set firmly in place, the court turned to Dr. Leary's proposal for a religious defense, and stated what continues to be the bottom line on the subject:

> Congress has demonstrated beyond doubt that it believes marihuana is an evil in American society and a serious threat to its people. It would be difficult to imagine the harm which would result if the criminal statutes against marihuana were nullified as to those who claim the right to possess and traffic in this drug for religious purposes. For all practical purposes the anti-marijuana laws would be meaningless, and enforcement impossible. The danger is too great, especially to the youth of the nation, at a time when psychedelic experience, "turn on," is the "in" thing to so many, for this court to yield to the argument that the use of marijuana for so-called religious purposes should be permitted under the Free Exercise Clause. We will not, therefore, subscribe to the dangerous doctrine that the free exercise of religion accords an unlimited freedom to violate the laws of the land relative to marijuana. *(Leary v. US [5th Cir 1967] 383 F.2d 851.)*

Anti-marijuana hysteria such as that demonstrated by this decision, is alive and well today. Courts faced with religiously motivated marijuana users have distinguished religious *belief* from religious *practice* or *action*. Applying this distinction to the Free Exercise Clause, the courts, including the United States Supreme Court, have ruled that while religious *beliefs* are fully protected by the constitution, religious *actions*, even when sincerely based on those beliefs, may be regulated or banned in order to protect a "compelling state interest."

Given the hysteria and anti-marijuana propaganda promoted by the hawks in the War on Drugs, it is no surprise that every court which has applied such an analysis to a marijuana case has found that the "compelling state interest" in enforcing the anti-marijuana laws outweighs whatever burden falls on those who claim to use marijuana for religious purposes.

The rules regarding the religious use of marijuana have not improved over time. In 1990, the United States Supreme Court decided a case involving the sacramental use of peyote by a member of the Native American Church. In a decision in which the Court ignored decades of established free-exercise jurisprudence and created new rules just for the case, the Court held that antidrug laws do not violate the Free Exercise Clause so long as they do not specifically target religious practice. In other words, the Supreme Court is prepared to uphold any general criminal law despite its impact on Free Exercise, so long as the law was not specifically crafted to impede religious practice. Obviously, under such a test, the anti-marijuana laws will never run afoul of the Free Exercise Clause.

Justice Blackmun, joined by Justices Brennan and Marshall, wrote a powerful dissenting opinion calling the majority's decision "a wholesale overturning of settled law concerning the Religion Clauses of our Constitution." Unfortunately, today, none of the three dissenting justices remain on the court.

The relatively recent addition of Ruth Bader Ginsburg to the United States Supreme Court leaves little hope that the Court will become more favorable to religiously motivated drug use any time in the near future. In 1989, Ms. Ginsburg, then a federal appeals court judge, upheld the DEA's refusal to grant a man's petition seeking a religious exemption from the federal anti-marijuana laws. In that case, Carl Olsen, a member and priest of the Ethiopian Zion Coptic Church, petitioned the DEA for a religious exemption to the federal anti-marijuana laws. The EZCC traces its origins back 6000 years and has a history of sacramental marijuana use. The DEA denied Mr. Olsen's petition, stating in part:

> In 1984, an estimated 7,800 to 9,200 tons of marijuana were illegally consumed in the United States. It has been estimated that over 20 million people in the United States use marijuana on a regular basis. Marijuana is a major public health problem in this country. Accordingly, the investigation and prosecution of marijuana traffickers, the interdiction of marijuana smuggling and the eradication of the drug at its source continue to be major concerns of drug law enforcement both domestically and internationally.

> In view of the immensity of the marijuana abuse problem in the United States and the magnitude of the criminal activity surrounding the prosecution and trafficking in this substance, the Administrator of the Drug Enforcement Administration concludes that the interest of the Ethiopian Zion Coptic Church in the ceremonial use of marijuana is outweighed by the

compelling governmental interest in controlling the use and
illegal distribution of marijuana in the United States.

Mr. Olsen did not give up. He continued the fight by filing suit against the
DEA. The case eventually ended up in the federal court where Ruth Bader
Ginsburg was a judge prior to being appointed to the United States Supreme
Court. Judge Ginsburg followed the predictable path first set out in Dr. Leary's
case, parroting another court's finding that "every federal court that has considered the matter . . . has accepted the congressional determination that marijuana
in fact poses a real threat to individual health and social welfare."

She concluded that it was simply not feasible to permit a religious exemption
for marijuana use because, under Mr. Olsen's proposal, the government would
have to supply marijuana to the church on a regular basis, and it would be nearly
impossible to monitor the church members' use of the marijuana. She noted that
between 1980 and 1987, the DEA seized over 15 million pounds of marijuana,
and expressed her concern about "the immensity of the marijuana control
problem in the United States." Judge Ginsburg concluded, "the DEA cannot
accommodate Olsen's religious use of marijuana without unduly burdening or
disrupting enforcement of the federal marijuana laws . . . [T]herefore . . . the Free
Exercise Clause does not compel the DEA to grant Olsen an exemption immuniz-
ing his church from prosecution for illegal use of marijuana." *(Olsen v. DEA [DC
Cir. 1989] 878 F.2d 1458.)*

Evidently, unless the Catholic Church makes a radical departure from its
current practice, and replaces communion wine with communion marijuana, the
courts will remain willfully blind to the spiritual importance of the *Cannabis*
plant. It's particularly aggravating to note that during Prohibition, the federal
government found it completely manageable to exempt the Roman Catholic
Church. To put it very simply, to date, *nobody* has presented a winning religious
defense to a marijuana crime. Likewise, those who have directly petitioned the
DEA for a religious exemption from the federal anti-marijuana laws have
received either denials or no response at all. *(National Prohibition Act, Title II,
Ch. 85, section 3, 41 Stat. 308 [1919].)*

The Religious Freedom Restoration Act

Faced with the Supreme Court's decision in the 1990 peyote case discussed
above, numerous religious groups banned together, lobbying Congress for a
federal law that would protect religious practice by reestablishing the compelling
state interest test in free-exercise cases. As a result of the efforts of these groups,
Congress passed The Religious Freedom Restoration Act (RFRA) which was
signed into law by President Clinton on November 16, 1993.

The express purpose of the RFRA is to restore the compelling state interest test, after "the Supreme Court virtually eliminated the requirement that the government justify burdens on religious exercise imposed by laws neutral toward religion."

The RFRA explicitly states:

(a) In General

Government shall not substantially burden a person's exercise of religion even if the burden results from a rule of general applicability, except as provided in subsection (b) of this section.

(B) Exception

Government may substantially burden a person's exercise of religion only if it demonstrates that application of the burden to the person–

(1) is in furtherance of a compelling government interest; and

(2) is the least restrictive means of furthering that compelling governmental interest. *(42 USC. sec. 2000bb - 1.)*

The RFRA reestablishes the requirement that laws burdening religious practice must pass the test of compelling state interest. It does nothing, however, to counter the effect of decades of anti-marijuana propaganda that has previously been used by courts to find that even under the compelling state interest test, permitting religious use of marijuana would excessively damage the government's interest in prohibiting drug use, and maintaining the health and welfare of individuals and society. What is needed now, therefore, is the amassing of scientific proof showing that a religious user of marijuana causes no harm to his health or to society in general. With a sufficient amount of such research, the courts may, someday, find that a person's religious use of marijuana is not harmful to the government's interest in controlling drugs, and hence, that the sacramental use of marijuana is protected under the recently enacted Religious Freedom Restoration Act.

CHAPTER 11

IF YOU'RE ARRESTED

IN GENERAL, there are only two occasions when a police officer can legally arrest a person: (1) if the officer has a warrant specifically authorizing the arrest of the person, or (2) if the officer has probable cause to believe the person committed a crime. In some states, such as California, an officer can arrest an adult for a misdemeanor only if the crime was committed in the officer's presence.

Arrest Warrants

Very few arrests for marijuana occur with an arrest warrant, so the subject of warrants will be discussed only briefly. Generally speaking, an arrest warrant is just like a search warrant. An arrest warrant is issued by a judge after a police officer presents him with an affidavit showing probable cause that a particular person committed a crime and can be found in his home. The officer then takes the warrant to the home and arrests the person.

Usually, the only circumstance under which an arrest warrant is absolutely required for an officer is when he seeks to arrest the person *inside his own home*. No warrant is needed to arrest a person outside his home in a public place, as long as the officer has probable cause to believe that the person committed a crime. Officers are well aware of these rules, and will often try to trick a person into leaving his or her house so that the person can be arrested without a warrant. For example, there are numerous cases in which police officers who have no arrest warrant go to a person's home in the hopes of arresting the person. The officers knock on the door and, when the person answers, ask him to step outside so they can talk to him. As soon as the person steps out the door, the officers can, and do, lawfully arrest him. This is another good reason why you should never open your door to a police officer who does not have either a search warrant or an arrest warrant.

If Arrested Outside, Don't Go Inside!

The United States Supreme Court has held that if a lawfully arrested person requests to enter his home before being taken to jail, the arresting officers have a legal right to accompany the person inside the residence. This rule was created by the Court after police officers arrested Carl Overdahl, a student at Washington State University. The officers arrested Carl because they observed him leave his dormitory carrying a half-gallon bottle of gin in violation of the Washington state law forbidding minors to possess alcohol. After Carl was arrested, he asked to return to his dorm room to get his identification, and the officer agreed. When Carl entered his dorm room, the officer also entered and observed in plain view what he believed were marijuana seeds as well as a seashell pipe of the type commonly used to smoke marijuana. The officer examined the seeds and confirmed that they were *Cannabis*, and also confirmed that the pipe smelled of marijuana. At this point, Carl and his roommate Neal confessed that there were three small plastic bags filled with marijuana in the apartment. After they consented to a search, the officers discovered forty grams of marijuana and some LSD.

The Supreme Court stated that once the officers had lawfully arrested Carl, they had a right to follow him into his dormitory when Carl requested to get his ID. In the Court's words:

> It is not 'unreasonable' under the Fourth Amendment for a police officer, as a matter of routine, to monitor the movements of an arrested person, as his judgment dictates, following the arrest. The officer's need to ensure his own safety—as well as the integrity of the arrest—is compelling. Such a surveillance is not an impermissible invasion of the privacy or personal liberty of an individual who has been arrested. *(Washington v. Chrisman [1982] 455 US 1.)*

The facts in Carl's case are not unusual. In fact, it is quite common for people to foolishly ask to return to their home to change into some different clothes before being taken to jail. As in Carl's case, most officers will gladly accommodate such a request, hoping that they will spot some plain-view contraband once inside the person's home.

In another case, a person was arrested on an outstanding warrant for failing to pay a traffic fine. Before going to jail, the person asked the officers to allow him to go inside to feed his dog. The officers happily agreed. When the officers accompanied the man inside, they detected a very strong aroma of marijuana and could see bright lights coming from underneath a closed door in the hallway. When they opened the door, the officers discovered forty *Cannabis* plants.

The obvious lesson to be learned from such cases is that anyone with incriminating evidence in his home should go directly to jail if arrested. There simply is no reason for returning home to change clothes, get pajamas, or feed gold fish. The jail will provide all the clothing needed, and friends can be called to take care of your pets.

No Expectation Of Privacy While In Backseat Of Police Car

A Florida court of appeal has held that police officers can surreptitiously tape conversations that occur in a police car. In this case, police officers stopped a car for speeding and tailgating. The driver and his passenger seemed nervous and gave conflicting answers when asked about their activities. Not knowing any better, the driver consented when the officers asked for permission to search his car. Before beginning their search, the officers told the two men to have a seat in the back of the police car. The search of the car uncovered 400 grams of marijuana.

While the men waited in the police car they engaged in a very incriminating conversation, believing no one was within listening range. The conversation was captured on a tape system installed in the police car. Although the men argued that the conversation was illegally taped and should be excluded from evidence, the Florida court disagreed, concluding that people have no reasonable expectation of privacy while detained in a police car and cannot, therefore, complain that their conversation was taped without their knowledge or consent. *(State v. Fedorchenko [Fl.App.2d 1993] 630 So.2d 213.)*

Searches After Arrest

A major exception to the search warrant requirement concerns searches conducted following an arrest. As you might imagine, an arrested person is not entitled to much privacy. Therefore, regardless of why the person was arrested, an officer can conduct a full search without first obtaining a search warrant. This rule excludes only strip searches and body cavity searches, which the Supreme Court considers "dehumanizing and humiliating." The courts will permit such searches only when the officer first obtains a warrant.

Besides searching the person himself, an officer who arrests a person can search the entire area within the person's reach or control. This rule was created to protect law-enforcement officers from persons who, following arrest, lunge for a weapon hidden nearby. An area search conducted incident to a person's arrest is limited to the area of lunging distance. *Any* containers within that area, whether open or closed, can be searched by the officers.

This exception to the search-warrant requirement explains why it is very rare that an officer will get a search warrant that merely authorizes the search of a person. Once an officer has probable cause to believe a person is in possession of marijuana, and the person is in a public place, the officer can simply arrest the person and then legally search him incident to that arrest.

Lastly, whenever the police arrest a person in his home, the police are entitled to search the room in which the person was arrested in order to confirm that there are no potential attackers hiding in the room. Under this rule, an arresting officer's search is limited to those areas of the room that are large enough to conceal a person (for example, closets). In addition, if the officer reasonably believes that there is someone else anywhere in the arrestee's home and has reason to believe that person poses a danger to the officer he can search the arrestee's entire home for the person. Under the plain-view rule, any marijuana the officer sees during such a search is fair game for seizure and will be admissible as evidence in court.

Booking Searches

If you are booked into jail after an arrest, the police may conduct what is known as a "booking search." The courts have held that warrantless booking searches are justified in order to safeguard people's belongings and to keep contraband and weapons out of the jail. During a booking search, an officer may search you and *anything* in your possession. The jail officers can make an item-by-item examination of everything in your pockets. They can search your wallet or purse as well as all other containers.

Every so often, the police who are booking a person into jail will suspect that an arrestee is concealing drugs or a weapon inside a body cavity. In such cases, most states permit the police to conduct a strip search or a body-cavity search. However, because such searches invade the very core of a person's privacy, most courts have held that the officer must have "reasonable suspicion" that the person is concealing contraband. Some courts go further and require probable cause. In no states can an officer perform a strip or body-cavity search merely because a person has been arrested.

Additionally, some states have further rules regulating strip and body-cavity searches. For example, in California, a search warrant is required before an officer can perform a strip or body-cavity search of a person arrested for a misdemeanor (as opposed to a felony). Additionally, the search must be conducted by someone of the same gender as the arrested person.

Miranda Rights

If you are arrested, it is quite likely that a police officer will "read you your rights" as follows:

> You have the right to remain silent. Anything you say can and will be used against you in court. You have the right to an attorney and to have the attorney present during questioning. If you cannot afford an attorney, one will be appointed for you. Do you understand and waive these rights?

The above statement, advising you of some of your constitutional rights, is commonly called your "Miranda rights," named after a defendant in a famous case. In that case, Mr. Miranda was arrested and taken to the police station for questioning. The officers questioned him in a small room without advising him of his right to an attorney or his right to remain silent. The questioning resulted in Mr. Miranda confessing to a crime.

When the Police Must Read You Your Rights

Many people believe that an officer must automatically read Miranda rights as part of performing an arrest, either immediately before or immediately after an arrest is made. This is a myth.

The truth is that the only time an officer must read a person his or her Miranda rights is when: (1) the person has been taken into custody, *and* (2) the officer is about to question the person about a crime.

Therefore, if you walk into a police station and state that you want to make a confession the officers are not required to read you your rights before taking your confession. However, in this situation, most officers will read you your rights just to be safe, or because they don't understand the law. Likewise, if an officer walks up to you as you leave your backyard garden and asks you what you are growing, he need not read you your rights before you answer. In both of these examples, *you are not in custody*; so any information you volunteer to the officer will be admissible, despite the fact that you were never read your rights.

As a final note, your Fifth Amendment right against forced self-incrimination extends only to "testimony." The courts have defined "testimony" very narrowly, as only spoken words. Therefore the Fifth Amendment does not protect you against self-incrimination based on the taking of your blood or body fluids.

Don't Waive Your Miranda Rights

It generally takes a police officer about five seconds to read your Miranda rights and ask if you agree to waive them. The decision to waive these rights, like any constitutional rights, should *not* be made hastily. Let's break down what an officer is telling you when he reads you your rights.

First, he is saying that these are your *rights*. As with all the other rights discussed in this book, you should not hesitate to exercise your Miranda rights. Your constitutional rights protect you whether you are innocent or guilty.

When an officer reads you your rights, the first right he reminds you of is your right to remain silent. This right was deemed of such importance that it was included in the Fifth Amendment to the U.S. Constitution. The Fifth Amendment is usually said to protect a person from forced self-incrimination. In practice, the Fifth Amendment permits a person to remain silent when interrogated by police officers or questioned in court. In addition, the United States Supreme Court has held that if a person exercises his or her Fifth-Amendment right and refuses to answer a police officer's questions, this fact cannot later be used against the person in court. In other words, it is improper for the prosecution to comment on the fact that a person refused to answer a police officer's questions. In fact, many cases have been reversed because of a prosecutor's comment, such as, "Ladies and gentlemen, if the defendant was really innocent, wouldn't he have answered all the questions the police asked? Wouldn't he take the opportunity to explain his innocence?" There is no reason to worry that your failure to answer the officer's questions will later be used against you. The truth is just the opposite. *Anything* you say can be used against you. Also, don't make the mistake of thinking that only *written* statements can be used against you. To repeat, *anything* you say, whether oral, written, taped, not taped, signed or not signed, will be used against you if the statement benefits the prosecutor's case.

Knowing that anything you say to a police officer can be used against you, why would you want to make a confession or answer questions? *In just about every case imaginable, a person is best off not answering any questions about his involvement in criminal activity.* The only time when it is wise to answer an officer's questions, once you're in custody, is when you are absolutely innocent of any criminal activity. In that situation, carefully answering the officer's questions may result in your quick release. However, you must be very careful not to let the officer put words in your mouth.

The second right that an officer informs you of is your right to an attorney. If you are unable to afford an attorney, the court must appoint the Public Defender or a private attorney. This is a very important right, and is based on the Fifth and Sixth Amendments. Again, you should never hesitate to exercise this right. If you request an attorney, the police officer must immediately stop questioning you and may not resume until an attorney is present.

The best way to assert your Miranda rights is to say these exact words: "I want an attorney and will remain silent until one is provided." The United States Supreme Court has held that this statement invokes protection of both the Fifth and the Sixth Amendments, and hence provides the person with the maximum protection available under the Constitution. (Alternatively, you could invoke your rights by handing the officers the cards in Appendix B.)

Generally, the last thing an officer says when he reads you your rights is, "Do you understand and agree to waive these rights?" This is actually *two* separate questions, which officers often ask in this combined form as a way of tricking people into waiving their rights. When the questions are combined in this way, many people hear only the first question–"Do you understand these rights?–and answer "yes," not fully realizing that in doing so they have just waived some of their most important constitutional rights. It is very important to know that *you can always invoke your Miranda rights even after you have waived them* (even if the waiver was in writing). You need only state that you now wish to remain silent or have a lawyer. Such a statement should bring a halt to the questioning immediately, despite the earlier waiver and despite the fact that you have already answered some questions.

Police Interrogation Techniques

The Miranda case is important for two reasons. First, as described above, it established the rule that whenever a person is questioned while in custody, he or she must be advised of the right to remain silent and the right to have an attorney. Second, this case became an opportunity for the Supreme Court to document some of the interrogation techniques taught to police officers. While the opinion was written in 1966, the Court did *not* outlaw these techniques, many of which are therefore still in use today. The following quote from the Court's opinion provides some insight into these police interrogation techniques:

> An understanding of the nature and setting of this in-custody interrogation is essential to our decisions today. The difficulty in depicting what transpires at such interrogations stems from the fact that in this country they have largely taken place incommunicado. From extensive factual studies undertaken in the early 1930s, including the famous Wickersham Report to Congress by a Presidential Commission, it is clear that police violence and the "third degree" flourished at that time. In a series of cases decided by this Court long after these studies, the police resorted to physical brutality—beatings, hanging, whipping—and to sustained and protracted questioning incommunicado in order to extort confessions. The Commission on Civil Rights in 1961 found much evidence to indicate that "some policemen still resort to physical force to obtain confessions." The use of physical brutality and violence is not, unfortunately, relegated to the past or to any part of the country. Only recently in Kings County, New York, the police brutally beat, kicked, and placed lighted cigarette butts on the back of a potential witness under interrogation for the purpose of securing a statement incriminating a third party.
>
> Interrogation still takes place in privacy. Privacy results in secrecy and this in turn results in a gap in our knowledge as to what in fact goes on in the interrogation rooms. A valuable source of information about present police practices, however, may be found in various police manuals and texts that document procedures employed with success in the past, and that recommend various other effective tactics. These texts are used by law-enforcement agencies themselves as guides. It should be noted that these texts professedly present the most enlightened and effective means presently used to obtain statements through custodial interrogation. By considering these texts and other data, it is possible to describe procedures observed and noted around the country.

The officers are told by the manuals that the "principal psychological factor contributing to a successful interrogation is privacy—being alone with the person under interrogation." The efficacy of this tactic has been explained as follows:

> "If at all practicable, the interrogation should take place in the investigator's office or at least in a room of his own choice. The subject should be deprived of every psychological advantage. In his own home he may be confident, indignant, or recalcitrant. He is more keenly aware of his rights and more reluctant to tell of his indiscretions or criminal behavior within the walls of his home. Moreover his family and other friends are nearby, their presence lending moral support. In his office, the investigator possesses all the advantages. The atmosphere suggests the invincibility of the forces of the law."

To highlight the isolation and unfamiliar surroundings, the manuals instruct the police to display an air of confidence in the suspect's guilt and from outward appearance to maintain only an interest in confirming certain details. The guilt of the subject is to be posited as a fact. The interrogator should direct his comments toward the reasons why the subject committed the act, rather than court failure by asking the subject whether he did it. Like other men, perhaps the subject has had a bad family life, had an unhappy childhood, had too much to drink, had an unrequited desire for women. The officers are instructed to minimize the moral seriousness of the offense, to cast blame on the victim or on society. These tactics are designed to put the subject in a psychological state where his story is but an elaboration of what the police purport to know already—that he is guilty. Explanations to the contrary are dismissed and discouraged.

The texts thus stress that the major qualities an interrogator should possess are patience and perseverance. One writer describes the efficacy of these characteristics in this manner:

> "In the preceding paragraphs emphasis has been placed on kindness and stratagems. The investigator will, however, encounter many situations where the sheer weight of his personality will be the deciding factor. Where emotional appeals and tricks

are employed to no avail, he must rely on an
oppressive atmosphere of dogged persistence. He
must interrogate steadily and without relent, leaving the subject no prospect of surcease. He must
dominate his subject and overwhelm him with his
inexorable will to obtain the truth. He should interrogate for a spell of several hours pausing only for
the subject's necessities in acknowledgment of the
need to avoid a charge of duress that can be technically substantiated. In a serious case, the interrogation may continue for days, with the required inter-
vals for food and sleep, but with no respite from the
atmosphere of domination. It is possible in this way
to induce the subject to talk without resorting to
duress or coercion. The method should be used only
when the guilt of the subject appears highly probable."

The manuals suggest that the suspect be offered legal excuses
for his actions in order to obtain an initial admission of guilt.
Where there is a suspected revenge-killing, for example, the
interrogator may say:

"Joe, you probably didn't go out looking for this
fellow with the purpose of shooting him. My guess
is, however, that you expected something from him
and that's why you carried a gun—for your own
protection. You know him for what he was, no
good. Then when you met him he probably started
using foul, abusive language and he gave some
indication that he was about to pull a gun on you,
and that's when you had to act to save your own life.
That's about it, isn't it, Joe?"

Having then obtained the admission of shooting, the interrogator is advised to refer to circumstantial evidence that negates
the self-defense explanation. This should enable him to secure
the entire story. One text notes that "Even if he fails to do so,
the inconsistency between the subject's original denial of the
shooting and his present admission of at least doing the
shooting will serve to deprive him of a self-defense 'out' at the
time of trial."

When the techniques described above prove unavailing, the
texts recommend they be alternated with a show of some

hostility. One ploy often used has been termed the "friendly-unfriendly" or the "Mutt and Jeff" act:

> ". . . . In this technique, two agents are employed. Mutt, the relentless investigator, who knows the subject is guilty and is not going to waste any time. He's sent a dozen men away for this crime and he's going to send the subject away for the full term. Jeff, on the other hand, is obviously a kindhearted man. He has a family himself. He has a brother who was involved in a little scrape like this. He disapproves of Mutt and his tactics and will arrange to get him off the case if the subject will cooperate. He can't hold Mutt off for very long. The subject would be wise to make a quick decision. The technique is applied by having both investigators present while Mutt acts out his role. Jeff may stand by quietly and demur at some of Mutt's tactics. When Jeff makes his plea for cooperation, Mutt is not present in the room."

The interrogators sometimes are instructed to induce a confession out of trickery. The technique here is quite effective in crimes which require identification or which run in series. In the identification situation, the interrogator may take a break in his questioning to place the subject among a group of men in a lineup. "The witness or complainant (previously coached, if necessary) studies the lineup and confidently points out the subject as the guilty party." Then the questioning resumes "as though there were no doubt about the guilt of the subject." A variation on this technique is called the "reverse lineup":

> "The accused is placed in a lineup, but this time he is identified by several fictitious witnesses or victims who associated him with different offenses. It is expected that the subject will become desperate and confess to the offense under investigation in order to escape from the false accusations."

The manuals also contain instructions for police on how to handle the individual who refuses to discuss the matter entirely, or who asks for an attorney or relatives. The examiner is to concede him the right to remain silent. "This usually has a very undermining effect. First of all, he is disappointed in his expectation of an unfavorable reaction on the part of the interrogator. Secondly, a concession of this right to remain silent impresses the subject with the apparent fairness of his interrogator." After this psychological conditioning, however, the officer is told to point out the incriminating significance of the suspect's refusal to talk:

> "Joe, you have a right to remain silent. That's your privilege and I'm the last person in the world who'll try to take it away from you. If that's the way you want to leave this, O.K. But let me ask you this. Suppose you were in my shoes and I were in yours and you called me in to ask me about this and I told you, 'I don't want to answer any of your questions.' You'd think I had something to hide, and you'd probably be right in thinking that. That's exactly what I'll have to think about you, and so will everybody else. So let's sit here and talk this whole thing over."

> Few will persist in their initial refusal to talk, it is said, if this monologue is employed correctly. (*Miranda v. Arizona [1966] 384 US 436*.)

The point here is that once you have been arrested, police officers are *not* your friends. Don't believe anything they say and do not try and explain anything to them. They are trying to get incriminating statements out of you and often don't put any other statements in their reports. All defense attorneys agree: if you are ever arrested assert your Fifth Amendment right to remain silent.

The Right to Counsel

It should be clear from the information in this book that our criminal-justice system is adversarial. If you are suspected of committing a crime, the resources of the state and/or federal government are marshaled against you. The police will do their best to arrest you and get your confession. Detectives will do their best to gather evidence against you, both physical and testimonial. Forensic scientists employed by the prosecutor will work to examine the evidence and relate it to your guilt. At trial, the government is represented by a prosecutor whose goal is to prove, beyond a reasonable doubt, that you are guilty of the crime charged.

Fortunately, the Sixth Amendment to the United States Constitution states "in all criminal prosecutions, the accused shall enjoy the right to have the assistance of counsel for his defense." The boundaries of the right to counsel have shifted over time. Currently, the Supreme Court has held that, despite the clear language of the Sixth Amendment, the right to counsel does *not* apply in *all* criminal prosecutions. Rather, the Court has ruled that the right to counsel only extends to cases in which the defendant can actually be sentenced to jail. Theoretically then, you can be criminally prosecuted and denied the right to counsel so long as the actual punishment you receive is "only" a fine and you receive no jail time. Consequently, in most states, if you are charged with "petty offenses," such as traffic citations, or a marijuana crime that is punishable only by a fine, you may not be entitled to an attorney at the state's expense. Practically speaking, however, most marijuana crimes do carry the potential penalty of imprisonment; hence, if you cannot afford an attorney one will be provided.

Public Defenders and Court Appointed Attorneys

Most people who are charged with crimes cannot afford an attorney. In such cases, if the defendant could receive imprisonment as a punishment, the government will provide the defendant with a public defender or a court-appointed attorney.

Public defenders often get a bad rap. Many people believe they are untrained pawns of the government who get paid for walking the defendant through the system to a quick conviction. This viewpoint is inaccurate. First, despite the widespread belief to the contrary, public defenders *are attorneys*. They have been to law school and have passed a rigorous exam just like all other attorneys. Additionally, because public defenders who handle misdemeanor cases are often young attorneys just out of law school, they are usually well versed on the latest legal trends and are up-to-date on the rules of law and evidence. Similarly, also because they are often young, many public defenders are enthusiastic about their job and see themselves as legal warriors fighting for the rights of the poor and underprivileged. Such a public defender is often a strong advocate. Lastly, because public defenders handle a large case load of nothing but criminal cases, they are usually very familiar with the local judges and district attorneys, as well as with the standard punishments for particular crimes.

Of course, there are some disadvantages to having a public defender. They are usually very overworked, often carrying three or four times as many cases as a private attorney. A public defender can therefore rarely spend as much time on your case as a private attorney. Similarly, if your case is extremely complex, requiring lots of investigation and expert testimony, the public defender may have difficulty getting an approval to spend the money necessary to do the job properly.

All in all, however, representation by a public defender is usually better than most people think. Your biggest problem will be getting your public defender to focus on *your* case. Do whatever you can to keep your name and case in the public defender's mind. Don't be afraid to politely, but regularly, check in to get an update on the case. Also, ask him or her what you can do to assist in your defense (for example, locating witnesses, taking photographs, etc.). The old saying about "the squeaky wheel getting the oil" is definitely appropriate when it comes to public defenders and their heavy caseloads.

In some situations, rather than receive a public defender, you may be provided with a private attorney whose fees are paid by the government. There are two ways this can occur. First, in some counties there is no public-defender organization. Rather, the county maintains a list of private attorneys who are appointed by the court to represent indigent defendants. Therefore, if your county has no public-defender office, you will receive a private court-appointed attorney. The second way to receive a private attorney at little or no cost to you is if your case involves other defendants in addition to yourself. Often in cases with multiple defendants, the court will require *each* defendant to have his or her *own* attorney. The public defender can represent one such defendant, but then private attorneys will be appointed to represent the remaining defendants.

As with public defenders, there are advantages and disadvantages to receiving a court-appointed attorney. On the positive side, most court-appointed attorneys will have more time to spend on your case than a typical public defender, because unlike a public defender, a private court-appointed attorney can turn down cases when he feels he is becoming overburdened. On the negative side, many attorneys who are appointed by the court to handle misdemeanor cases are extremely inexperienced at handling criminal matters. In fact, many counties allow *any* attorney to receive misdemeanor appointments. Many young attorneys who are just starting out in practice apply to receive misdemeanor appointments. This means that an attorney who has just passed the bar exam, and who has never even been inside a courtroom before, *could* be appointed to handle your misdemeanor case. Fortunately, if you are charged with a felony, most counties will require your appointed attorney to have proven experience in criminal matters. In fact, if you are charged with a felony and given a court-appointed attorney, you may very well get an expensive attorney whom others would pay thousands of dollars to retain.

Choosing a Private Attorney

For people who can afford to hire their own attorney, the selection process can be confusing. If you are charged with a marijuana or other drug crime, you need a trial attorney that handles only criminal cases and preferably one who specializes in drug cases. You don't want an attorney that handles business matters, divorces, and wills. Such attorneys spend almost all their time drafting legal documents, spend little time in court, and generally have little trial experience. Additionally, although twenty years ago a lawyer could be a general practitioner and remain competent to handle criminal matters, today the criminal laws are so complex and ever-changing that a "jack-of-all-trades" lawyer cannot possibly represent you as well as a focused criminal lawyer can.

Again, what you need if charged with a marijuana crime is an attorney who handles *nothing but* criminal cases. If you know a judge, a court bailiff, or a court reporter, ask them to recommend a good criminal attorney in your area. Think twice about using an "attorney referral service." Many such services are filled with brand-new attorneys or unsuccessful attorneys scraping to make a living. If you use such a referral service, ask the service what qualifications an attorney must have to be a member of the service. Reject any service whose attorneys are not experienced at handling criminal cases.

For most marijuana cases, it is usually best to retain an attorney who has a solo practice or is a member of a law firm with no more than 5 lawyers. With a sole practitioner you know who is handling your case and hence whom to contact with any new information, or to get an update. Often larger law firms have several attorneys work on a file. In theory there should not be a problem with this practice. Some people like the idea of having several attorneys working together on their case. Such representation may be valuable if each attorney is interested in your case and effectively communicates his thoughts to the other attorneys working your case. In practice, however, problems often arise because no single person is fully involved, and therefore fully prepared, in all aspects of the case. Likewise, large law firms often employ paralegals and law clerks to conduct legal research and to prepare many of the legal motions and memoranda filed in court. Why pay a big firm to handle your case when a paralegal is doing much of the work?

Criminal defense attorneys can be located by thumbing through the yellow pages, or by asking around among your friends. When looking through the yellow pages, you will see many criminal defense attorneys who advertise that they began their careers by working for a prosecuting agency before going out on their own. These attorneys are often very experienced. However, I would not recommend such attorneys, simply because their employment history indicates a fundamental ideological problem: they used to earn their paychecks by convicting people who smoke or grow marijuana! Rather than hire such an attorney, look for one who presents himself or herself as ideologically opposed to the government's prosecution of people for marijuana crimes. You want an attorney that really believes in the case he or she is fighting for. Such an attorney is more enthusiastic, a harder worker, and often more effective. Therefore, look for someone that has never worked for the government as a prosecutor. Prior experience as a public defender may be advantageous, suggesting that the lawyer cares about defending people.

Once you have selected several attorneys you think might be good, call them and arrange a free consultation. Almost all criminal attorneys will meet with you for free to hear about your case and quote you a fee. Set up several such interviews on a single day and choose the attorney that most impresses you and whose fee you can afford. You should retain the attorney who is most enthusiastic about defending you, intelligent, and very well-versed on defending marijuana cases.

Attorney Fees

Today, most criminal defense attorneys charge a flat retainer fee rather than billing by the hour. It is very important to clearly understand what services are covered by the retainer. For example, you should make sure you understand (and that the retainer agreement clearly spells out) whether or not the following services are covered by the retainer: copy charges, computer research charges, pretrial motions, and most importantly, trial fees and appeal fees. You might also want to make sure that the attorney you are meeting with will be the actual attorney handling the case and appearing in court on your behalf. Unless it's spelled out that a particular attorney will be handling the case and making all appearances, some law firms might use an experienced attorney to obtain your retainer, but send inexperienced attorneys to handle your court appearances.

Private Investigators

An important part of your attorney's job is to coordinate the investigation of your side of the case. In contrast to murder or other complex cases which might involve numerous eyewitnesses, and dozens of pieces of evidence, the typical marijuana case usually doesn't require a lot of investigation. In some marijuana cases however, your attorney might want to retain the services of a private investigator. As mentioned earlier, you should make clear to your attorney that *you* have the final say as to whether or not a private investigator will be retained. That way prior to spending lots of money on an investigator, your attorney will have to come to you, explain why he thinks an investigator is necessary, and get your approval before incurring investigator expenses.

Working With Your Attorney

Fighting a marijuana charge is a collaborative effort. Your attorney knows the law, but depends on you to tell him or her the facts. Defense attorneys take the attorney client privilege very seriously, and you should feel perfectly safe discussing your case with your attorney.

All private conversations about your case between yourself and your attorney are privileged. This means that no one, not the police, not the prosecutor, not your parents or spouse, and not the court, can find out what the two of you discussed. The privilege applies to all private communications with your attorney, whether in person, over the phone, or in writing.

Whenever you meet with your attorney, you should listen very carefully and answer the questions he or she asks you. It is to your advantage to answer the questions as truthfully and as accurately as possible. Your head holds the greatest advantage you have over the prosecutor. Both the prosecutor and your attorney have the police reports, but only your attorney is privy to you. Most attorneys handling marijuana cases prefer to know everything—all the facts—whether good or bad. (There is a small group of attorneys who just want to know certain information. For technical reasons pertaining to attorneys' ethical duties, these attorneys will ask you very specific questions directed at getting the information they want to know while avoiding learning something that they don't want to know.)

Your attorney might give you a copy of the police report and ask you to carefully review it and point out any inaccuracies or omissions. Many attorneys will ask you to go home and type out an honest and complete account of the pertinent information surrounding your arrest. Such information will allow your attorney to capitalize on sloppy or corrupt police work. Equally importantly, by knowing the negative or incriminating information ahead of time, your attorney can carefully avoid dangerous subject areas in court and be prepared to minimize and counter the impact of such information if it comes out in court. Your private written statement also helps your attorney by making available your account of the facts while working on your case before it gets to trial. As discussed above, there is no way that your statement can get into the wrong hands, so don't be afraid to write down everything your attorney requests. You do not want your attorney to be caught by surprise during the trial.

Not only should you answer all your attorney's questions, but you should also follow his or her advice. If you're convinced that your attorney is giving you bad advice, fire him or her and get another attorney. The worst thing to do is stay with an attorney without following his or her legal advice. It is extremely important that you understand the advice that your attorney is giving you. If you have a good attorney, you should feel completely comfortable asking every single question you have. Failure to fully understand the advice will result in failure to follow the advice, which can lead to disaster. Remember, you are paying your attorney for legal advice; you *must* understand it or it is less than worthless.

Once your attorney has a good grasp of the facts in your case, the two of you will discuss your general strategy. Case strategy varies depending upon the strengths and weaknesses of the facts, as well as the client's wishes.

You have a right to a trial even if the facts in your case are quite incriminating. As discussed earlier, the prosecutor in a criminal case has the burden of proving your guilt. You do not need to prove your innocence. Defense attorneys go to trial on many cases in which the facts are incriminating and by cross-examining the witnesses against their client, try to raise a reasonable doubt in the minds of the jurors. (As discussed in Chapter 2, you can be convicted only if the jury finds you guilty *beyond a reasonable doubt*.)

Your attorney can advise you of your chances of winning if you take your case to trial. If he is a private attorney he will also tell you how much he will charge to try your case. You are the one who must make the final decision as to whether or not to go to trial based on your chances of winning, the punishment if you lose versus the punishment if you strike a plea bargain, and the cost of paying your attorney's fees.

Plea Bargains vs. Going To Trial

The vast majority of marijuana cases do not go to trial. Instead, the case is resolved by a plea bargain. Why would you want to plead guilty rather than have a trial? Often the decision to plead guilty is made because the facts in the case make it practically impossible to win at trial. Perhaps the defendant made incriminating statements or admissions, or for innumerable other reasons the government's case against the defendant is extremely strong. In such situations, you might be well-advised to strike the best bargain possible rather than proceed to trial.

In other cases, a defendant might accept a plea bargain if the terms of the bargain bar the forfeiture of his property. Similarly the prosecutor sometimes mistakenly fails to charge the defendant with certain crimes that could have been charged. If those crimes are serious, you might choose to accept a plea to the charged crime in order to close the case and prevent the prosecutor from realizing his or her mistake.

Plea-bargaining is an art. Your attorney and the prosecutor meet, sometimes in the presence of a judge, and argue about the strengths and weaknesses of the case. In addition, they will discuss your prior record and your life in general. Often, if the case against you is very strong, your attorney will concentrate on convincing the prosecutor that your crime was nonviolent and not particularly sophisticated. Your attorney will also point out that you are a productive member of society, currently employed or in school. Most importantly, your attorney will argue (if this is indeed the case) that you have no serious prior convictions. The prosecutor, on the other hand, will try and highlight facts about your case that make it more serious than the run-of-the-mill marijuana case.

Based on a discussion of this sort, your attorney and the prosecutor will try and agree on an appropriate punishment, hopefully much less severe than what you could get if you went to trial and lost. Once such an agreement has been reached, your attorney will communicate it to you and give you his or her advice as to whether or not you should accept it. The decision to accept or reject a plea bargain is yours and yours alone.

Obviously, if you are innocent of the crime, you should reject any plea bargain and proceed to trial. Also, some marijuana users who are activists choose to proceed to trial for the purpose of generating publicity and making a political point.

Should You Testify?

In any criminal trial, the defendant has an absolute right to testify. In the majority of criminal cases, however, the defendant does not testify for several reasons. In most states, a defendant who testifies can be impeached by the prosecutor by evidence of the defendant's prior felony convictions. Therefore, if you have previously been convicted of a felony, many defense attorneys will want to keep you off the stand to prevent the jury from hearing about your unsavory past.

(Except for unusual circumstances, a defendant's prior convictions can only be mentioned if the defendant testifies.) A defense attorney will also want to keep you off the stand if you made unfavorable statements to the police, which could also be used to impeach your testimony.

There are innumerable other reasons why your attorney might advise you not to testify. You are well-advised to follow such counsel. If, for some reason, you are determined to testify but your attorney advises against it, you should get another attorney who will prepare your defense with consideration of your testimony. Whatever you do, don't demand to testify in the middle of a trial when your attorney has advised against it and has not prepared for it.

Tips On Testifying

When a defendant takes the stand and testifies, this event is usually the highlight of the trial. The jury will be extremely interested in what you have to say for yourself. Consequently, if you do testify, you should be aware that you probably hold your fate in your hands. The jury will scrutinize *everything* about you.

You should continually keep in mind that the jurors are judging you and behave accordingly. When testifying you should *very carefully* listen to your attorney's questions and answer them narrowly. Answer the exact question asked and elaborate only at your attorney's request. If you do not understand a particular question, make sure you ask for clarification before answering. If you do not know the answer to a question, say so.

When the prosecutor cross-examines you, be aware that he or she is trying to sabotage your answers, and also trying to aggravate you so the jury sees your "mean" side. Whenever the prosecutor is asking you questions, you should allow a few second pause before you answer. This gives your attorney a chance to object if necessary, and also gives you a chance to collect your thoughts. If your attorney makes an objection, listen carefully, as such objections often contain hidden advice to you in regards to how you should respond and proceed. If your attorney objects, you should think about what the prosecutor is trying to get you to say, and do your best not to fall into the prosecutor's trap.

Monitoring Jail-House Conversations

If you are arrested on a marijuana charge and taken to jail, there are several things you need to know. First, while jail can be a very scary and intimidating environment, it is not the place to seek support or legal advice from other inmates. The "doctrine of misplaced trust," discussed earlier, is often applied to jail-house conversations in which one inmate confesses his crimes to another inmate. In such cases, it is not uncommon for the prosecutor to force inmate number two to testify at the trial of inmate number one and tell the jury all about inmate number one's jail house confession. Needless to say, this is not a good thing if you are inmate number one.

A person in jail whether before, during, or after trial, is not entitled to much privacy. You should assume that every phone call you make from jail is recorded and monitored by the jail staff. You should also assume that the visiting booths used to visit your family and friends are electronically monitored. Even the letters which you send out and those which you receive will be opened and, in some detention facilities, read. In all of the above instances, anything you say or write can and will be used against you.

About the only circumstances in which you can feel safe speaking about your case while you are in jail is when you are speaking to your attorney in a special room set aside for attorney-client visits. It is illegal for the government to monitor conversations with your attorney which occur in these booths. Also, if you write any letters to your attorney while in jail, you should clearly mark the outside of the envelope "Confidential Attorney Correspondence." Such communications are covered by the attorney-client privilege and remain private. Your attorney should mark all his letters to you with the same notice. Be sure and inform him if you think that his letters are being opened by the jail staff.

Release Pending Trial

In the vast majority of marijuana arrests, the defendant is taken to the police station, booked, and immediately released with a promise to appear in court on a given date. However, if you are arrested for a possessing, cultivating, or transporting a large amount of marijuana, or if weapons or other signs of violence are linked to your marijuana crime, you might be held in custody following your arrest. In order to get released pending your trial, your attorney will have to convince the judge that you should be released on your own recognizance (*OR release*) or that your bail should be set low enough for you to afford.

The issue of *OR release* or bail reduction is usually raised during your first appearance before the judge. Whether you will be OR'd depends entirely on the facts of your crime and on your criminal history. You should be OR'd if yours is a small-time marijuana crime and you have never been convicted of a crime before. However, if your marijuana crime involves a high degree of sophistication, a large amount of marijuana, if your record is not perfect, or if there is any reason to fear that you might flee, the judge will most likely set bail.

To administer the bail system, most counties have established bail schedules. These schedules list various crimes and attach a suggested bail amount to each crime. The judge will start with the guideline amount and then increase or decrease your bail based on arguments presented by the prosecutor and your attorney. The judge will be trying to determine if you are likely to flee the area if you make bail, and whether or not you are a threat to a particular person or to the community at large. Your attorney will need to argue that you are not going to run or hurt anyone by showing that your crime was victimless and did not involve weapons, threats, or violence of any kind (if this is, in fact, the case). To argue that you are not likely to flee the area, your attorney will try to demonstrate that you have strong ties to the community by showing that:

> You're employed or attend school in the area.
> You rent an apartment or, better yet, own a home, in the local area.
> You have resided in the area a long time.
> You are married and your spouse lives and works in the area.
> You have children in school in the area.

If your record is supportive, your attorney will also argue that you have never been in trouble before, or, if you have been, that you have always appeared in court as directed. Your attorney can also argue (and in fact the prosecutor may try and demand) that your release on bail contain a condition that you stay away from certain areas and not associate with certain people, or stay employed or in school. Sometimes, agreeing to such release conditions will convince a judge to set bail at a reasonable amount.

It is legal for a judge to deny bail in certain circumstances. However, this is very rare in marijuana cases, and will only occur if a cache of weapons is found, or there is clear evidence that you are a danger to someone if released. Although a judge rarely denies bail in a marijuana case, it is quite common for the judge to set bail at an amount too high for the defendant to financially post.

For example, in one case, Mike was arrested for cultivating over 70 *Cannabis* plants in his basement. When he was taken to jail, he felt intimidated by the other inmates, and wanted to show them he was tough. Mike waited in line to use the phone and when it was his turn, he picked up the phone, acted like he was dialing, and then said to the imaginary person on the other end, "I know why I was arrested. Joey talked. I want you to hurt him real bad." Unfortunately, Mike was overheard not only by his fellow inmates, but also by a deputy police officer standing nearby. This officer quickly wrote down a report of the conversation and it was used against Mike during his bail hearing. Because of these statements by Mike, the judge set bail at $250,000, when the bail schedule was only $5,000 for the cultivation offense. Because of Mike's ploy, his attorney was unable to get the bail reduced, Mike could not make bail, and he was forced to stay in jail for two months pending his trial.

How Bail Is Paid

In the vast majority of cases, bail is paid in one of two ways. The best way, if you are lucky enough to have the money, is to post cash bail. For example, if your bail is set at $5,000, you simply pay the jail cashier $5,000 and you're out. As long as you make all your court appearances, the full $5,000 will be returned to you once your case concludes.

Since most people don't have thousands of dollars lying around, the most common method of making bail is to contact a bail bondsman. In most jurisdictions, you pay the bondsman about ten percent of the bail amount, and he posts a bond with the court for the full amount of the bail. For example, if your bail is set at $5,000, you can pay a bondsman $500 and he will post a $5,000 bond with the court. He will also require collateral equal to or greater than the bond amount. The bondsman keeps your $500 no matter what happens. It's gone forever. If you make all your court appearances, the court releases the $5,000 bond back to the bondsman who then comes out $500 ahead. If you skip bail (leave the area or fail to go to your court appearances) the court will take the bondsman's $5,000 bond and whatever you used as collateral will become his. In addition, the court will issue a no-bail warrant for your arrest. This means that if you are ever stopped by a police officer and he runs a warrant check, you will be arrested and taken back to jail. If that happens, you will not only be facing the original marijuana charges, but also the additional charge (usually a felony) of jumping bail. To make matters worse, the judge will probably deny you bail, so you'll end up spending several months in jail while you await your trial date.

Tips On Going To Court

Before the actual trial, there will be several court dates where preliminary matters will be hashed out. In some jurisdictions, your attorney can appear at these proceedings without you. However, in other jurisdictions, you will be required to appear personally at every court date. One of the worst things you can do is fail to appear for a scheduled court date. In most cases, the judge will issue a warrant for your arrest and, unless you have a great excuse, the judge will thereafter treat you like an untrustworthy deadbeat. Obviously, it's best not to upset the judge.

The second worst thing you can do is show up late to a court date. Make it a point to arrive at the court house at least 20 minutes early. Parking around courthouses is always difficult, and it's often a confusing mayhem inside, as defendants are transferred from one courtroom to another.

As soon as you walk into the courtroom, even if there are many other people there, you and anyone who is with you should be on best behavior. The basic rule is to behave respectfully toward everyone. Little things can make a difference. Listen to what the bailiff tells you, and follow his orders promptly and politely. When the judge speaks to you, you should look him or her in the eye, and end your sentences with ". . . your honor." Also, dressing up makes a positive visual impression on the judge and indicates that you take the charges seriously and have respect for the court. Remember, many judges have very big egos, and fully expect to be treated like royalty. It therefore behooves you to treat the judge with utmost respect.

The real theater starts when your trial begins. By then your attorney will have settled on the general theory of the defense to be presented. As soon as the jury is brought into the room you'll want to give the impression that you are a kind, gentle and decent person. Remember, even if you never take the stand to testify, your actions are continually being judged by the jurors. Jurors will look to see how you react to certain testimony and evidence. They'll look to see how you relate to your attorney. They'll look to see how you relate to your family and friends and whether they look like "decent" people. They'll also look to see how you relate to the bailiff, the court clerk, and the court reporter.

During trial, stand up and face the jurors whenever they enter or leave the courtroom. Try to make nonthreatening eye contact and look like the innocent and decent person you are. Don't talk to jurors in or out of the courtroom. Watch what you do and say even in the hallways of the courthouse, because it is very possible that a juror will be watching.

Cleaning Up a Marijuana Conviction Record

Supposing the worst has happened, and you've been convicted of a marijuana offense. Is there anything you can do to make it all better? Well, in some states, for certain marijuana convictions, the answer is "yes."

For example, in California, if, *after* December 31, 1975, you were arrested or convicted of either (1) possession of any amount of marijuana (but not for sale), or (2) offering to transport, transporting, offering to give away, or giving away less than one ounce of marijuana, then your record will automatically be destroyed two years after your arrest or conviction. This happens *only* if you successfully complete all the terms of your sentence.

If your marijuana arrest or conviction occurred *prior* to January 1, 1976, you can still get your records destroyed, but it is slightly more difficult, and will cost you a few dollars. Here's the rule: If, prior to January 1, 1976, you were arrested or convicted of either (1) possession of any amount of marijuana (but not for sale), or (2) possession of paraphernalia used to smoke marijuana, or (3)visiting or being present in a place where marijuana was being used, or (4)being under the influence of marijuana, you can get your records destroyed by submitting a simple form to the Department of Justice (DOJ).

The form is very simple to fill out, and can be obtained from any police or sheriff's station, or by writing or calling the California Department of Justice. Tell them you want the form titled "Application to Destroy Arrest/Conviction Records" and that this is pursuant to Health and Safety code section 11361.5(b).

Once you get the form, simply fill in the boxes, write a check for $37.50 (the cost as of this writing), and send it off as the form instructs. Occasionally, the DOJ has problems finding a person's records, and in such cases requests a copy of your fingerprints within fifteen days. Most defense attorneys advise their clients to go ahead and submit their prints. Others are less trustful, and advise their clients to drop the whole thing if the DOJ makes such a request. The decision in such a case is yours.

Assuming everything goes well, the DOJ will soon notify you by mail that all records held by the DOJ, the FBI, the local police agency that arrested you, the probation department, and the DMV concerning your arrest/conviction have been destroyed.

Once your records have been destroyed, either automatically or by sending in the form and receiving a confirmation by the DOJ, you can legally answer that you have never been arrested or convicted for those crimes. Likewise, no public agency like a real-estate licensing board or medical board can deny you a professional license because of your arrest/conviction.

CHAPTER 12

DRUG TESTING

IN THE LAST FEW YEARS, drug testing has spread like a virus. A few years ago, it was possible for a general criminal defense attorney to stay abreast of most issues related to drug testing, today, however, the field has expanded into its own specialty. At both the federal and state levels, there are numerous laws and regulations controlling drug testing and an increasing number of court decisions interpreting those laws and regulations. It is, therefore, simply impossible to give a complete rundown of all drug testing laws and regulations within the space of this book. Therefore, this chapter will cover only the most important drug testing issues affecting marijuana users. Readers interested in learning more about drug testing are encouraged to read Kevin Zeese's "Drug Testing Legal Manual," an up-to-date and reliable source for information about the legal aspects of drug testing. Also don't miss Ronin Press' *Drug Testing at Work*, by Beverly Potter and Sebastian Orfali.

Urine Tests

Of the methods currently used to test for drugs, the most widely used is urine testing. It's not only easy, cheap, and quick, but (with the exception of hair testing) provides the farthest look backward in time. These factors also account for why 95% of pre-employment drug testing is via urine tests.

Urine tests do not show whether or not a person has *marijuana* in their urine. Instead, a urine test can only determine whether or not a sample of urine contains marijuana *metabolites*. Marijuana metabolites are what remain after the body physiologically processes marijuana.

Metabolites do not appear in urine immediately after marijuana is smoked. It takes time for the body to metabolize marijuana. As a result, cannabinoids (one kind of marijuana metabolite) can occur in urine at any time from 3 days to 27 days after marijuana is ingested. Since metabolites do not appear immediately, urine tests are unable to indicate whether a person was impaired or high when the sample was taken. Indeed, because the metabolites aren't yet in the urine it is possible for an irregular marijuana smoker to pass a urine test while high. A regular smoker, on the other hand, could test positive for the presence of metabolites even though he has not smoked for several weeks. Also, since the rate of metabolism is not constant among all people, two people who smoke an identical amount of marijuana at the very same time are likely to produce marijuana metabolites at different rates, and hence test differently.

The concentration of marijuana metabolites in a person's urine varies even over the course of a single day. For this reason, most urine tests seek a sample from the first urination of the day—the time when the maximum amount of metabolites is likely to be present. Scientific studies have shown that because the concentration of marijuana metabolites can change on an hourly basis, it is possible for a person who smokes on Sunday night to test positive in his first urination on Monday morning, negative in another urination at midday on Monday, and then positive on Monday night once the metabolites have had a chance to build up again.

In addition to the variations caused by differing metabolic rates, urine tests can be unreliable for a number of other reasons. Legal substances can cross-react to cause false positives. Human error, including improper handling of the urine sample, can contaminate the sample and cause incorrect results. In one study, the Center for Disease Control secretly sent a drug-laced urine sample as well as a clean control sample to thirteen different urine testing companies. Errors ranged from five percent in some labs to one hundred percent in others! The researchers at CDC concluded that only one of the thirteen companies was competent.

The American Medical Association's Council on Scientific Affairs has estimated that cannabinoids are detectable in urine up to 3 days after a single use of marijuana, up to 10 days after a daily marijuana user quits smoking, and up to 27 days after a "chronic" marijuana user quits smoking. Another scientific test found that a drug-free male who eats a single marijuana brownie will excrete marijuana metabolites in his urine for up to fourteen days.

Creating False Negatives

For our purposes, a "false negative" drug test is one which indicates mistakenly that a person has not used marijuana when in fact the person has. In other words, a false negative test pronounces a "guilty" person "innocent." Rumors abound on how to cause false negatives in urine tests. Many companies are making money from teas and other drinks that they claim can defeat a urine test.

The scientific literature, however, indicates that the simplest way to create a false negative is to avoid giving a sample of the first urination of the day, and instead give a sample from an afternoon urination. Studies have shown that when this technique is combined with drinking lots of fluids, the concentration of marijuana metabolites in urine can be reduced to below the test's cutoff point, thereby causing a negative reading. Some people have followed a routine of voiding their bladders on the morning of the test, and then drinking a large volume of various liquids in the intervening hours before giving their urine sample. Drinking a wide variety of liquids, such as coffee, tea, juice, and plain water, is preferable to simply drinking straight water because the various fluids add some color to the urine. Clear urine is an indication of "water-loading." Other people, who prefer to drink straight water, take a B-complex vitamin to add some color to their urine.

Some people advocate the adding of adulterants to the urine sample. Tests have shown that adding such common substances as Visine, vinegar, or table salt to a urine sample can cause a false negative. Adulterating a urine sample is risky business, however, because the risk of detection is high. Similarly, all urine tests employ tactics for preventing or detecting attempts by people to dilute their urine. Most well-conducted urine tests place bluing agents in the toilet tanks to prevent dilution of urine samples. Exclusion from the testing area of all other water sources is also common. Well-conducted tests will take the temperature of a urine sample within four minutes of its collection and will reject a sample that is not within an established temperature range. In addition, many tests require the person to remove any unnecessary outer garments that could conceal substances used to adulterate or dilute a sample. Likewise, purses and brief cases are generally excluded from the collection area. Even if one succeeds at adulterating or diluting a sample, most of today's urine tests will uncover the adulteration. In some states, such as Florida and Texas, it is a crime to attempt to defraud a drug test.

False Positives

In contrast to false negatives, a false positive occurs when a drug test pronounces an "innocent" person "guilty." Prior to 1986, false positives often occurred because the standard urine test commonly mistook ibuprofen for a marijuana metabolite. However, this problem was, for all practical purposes, solved in 1986 when most urine tests switched to using a different enzyme.

Although it probably won't do any good under the new tests, it is always important to list on the pretest form any ibuprofen, fenoprofen, or naproxen drugs you may be taking. Those drugs are found in such brand name products as Advil, Motrin, and Nuprin.

Finally, while it is technically not a "false positive," it is possible for urine to test positive when a nonsmoker has been in the room while others smoked marijuana. While secondhand smoke generally only reaches subthreshold levels, there are cases where it has caused false positives.

Blood Testing

Your blood transports the psychoactive constituents of marijuana to your brain. If you feel high, you can be sure that a blood test will be positive. Within twenty-four hours after smoking, it is unlikely that a standard blood test would reveal marijuana metabolites. A blood test is the best test to take if you haven't smoked for at least 24 hours. It's the worst test to take if you're high.

Hair Testing

While currently one of the least-used drug testing methods, the use of hair testing seems to be on the rise. One advantage of hair testing is that drug metabolites in the hair are very "stable", which means that they remain in the hair in their original molecular form for a very long time. As an executive from one of the hair testing companies put it, "we literally have little tape recorders coming out of our heads." In fact, marijuana metabolites remain in the hair for as long as the hair exists! Recently, in fact, anthropologists used hair testing on 500 year old corpses to determine what, if any, drugs the people ingested while alive.

There are, however, several problems that make hair testing currently extremely unreliable. A sloppily-cleaned hair sample, for example, can be contaminated with airborne drugs. Since most marijuana is smoked, it is not unusual for a non-marijuana user to test positive simply because he was in the room while others smoked. For this reason and others, the FDA has called hair testing for drugs "an unproved procedure unsupported by the scientific literature," and the National Institute on Drug Abuse has refused to certify any hair-testing labs for drug testing of federal employees.

"Possession" Of Marijuana Based On A Positive Drug Test

As the use of drug testing has expanded, the question has arisen as to whether or not a person can be convicted of the crime of possession of marijuana based solely on positive drug test results. Obviously, if courts begin upholding possession convictions based solely on positive drug tests, possession convictions would skyrocket overnight. Since this has only recently become an issue, few courts have had to deal with it. To date, however, courts in Indiana, Minnesota and Kansas, have reached the sensible conclusion that *without more evidence*, a positive drug test is *not* enough to prove, beyond a reasonable doubt, that the person was in possession of marijuana. The courts have reached this conclusion based on different rationales.

A Kansas case held that the presence of a drug in a person's blood is circumstantial evidence that the person possessed the drug previously, but it is insufficient to establish the crime of possession because the test does not prove the knowledge element (see Chapter 1) of the crime. In contrast, a Minnesota court reasoned that the positive test did not establish the "dominion and control" element of a possession offense, explaining, "[t]he usual and ordinary meaning of the term 'possession' does not include substances injected into the body and assimilated into the system. After a controlled substance is within a person's system the power to exercise dominion and control necessary to establish possession no longer exists . . . ." (*State v. Lewis [1986] Minn.App. 1986) 394 N.W.2d 212.*) Another argument for rejecting a positive drug test as sufficient evidence for a possession conviction is that the laws prohibit possession of "marijuana," and, as mentioned above, the substances found in drug tests are *not* marijuana, but rather the metabolites of marijuana. The primary metabolite, 9-carboxy-THC, is inert, meaning that it is *not* psychoactive.

Some states consider a positive drug test circumstantial evidence of prior drug use, and will consider it in conjunction with other evidence of possession. For example, a possession conviction was upheld in Maryland based on a positive drug test *and* statements by the defendant that he used drugs. New Mexico also considers a drug test in conjunction with other evidence sufficient for a possession conviction.

Drug Tests While on Probation Or Parole

As a condition of parole or probation, all states as well as the federal government require that the parolee or probationer "obey all laws," including, of course, the anti-marijuana laws. The primary means of enforcing this condition is drug testing. Such tests are generally scheduled in advance. However, in many states the testing can be conducted without notice whenever the probation or parole officer so chooses.

Because the standard of proof at probation and parole revocation hearings is much lower than the "beyond a reasonable doubt" standard required for criminal conviction, most states will permit the revocation of parole or probation based on nothing more than a positive test for marijuana.

Employment Drug Testing

As part and parcel of the "War on Drugs," many public and private employers are beginning to test their employees, and potential employees, for use of marijuana and other drugs. At the time of this writing, more than 20 million people are subject to drug testing, including most police officers, military personnel, defense contractors, transportation workers, and nearly half the employees who work for Fortune 500 companies.

Your rights with regard to drug testing at work depend primarily upon whether you're employed by the government (or in an industry or profession that's heavily regulated by the government) or privately employed.

Government Employees

In a relatively recent case, the United States Supreme Court established a scheme for deciding the constitutionality of mandatory drug testing of government employees. The Court held that this issue must be decided by applying a balancing test in which a court must weigh the government's interest or purpose in requiring the drug tests against the employees' reasonable expectation of privacy. The drug test will be legal if the Court concludes that the government's interest outweighed the employees'. When the Court wrote its opinion, it was clear from the outset that employees have a very reasonable expectation privacy regarding their own bodily fluids. Given this clear and strong expectation of privacy, the Court concluded that drug tests of government employees are only constitutional, and hence legal, if the government can show a truly *compelling* interest in requiring an employee to submit to a drug test.

The case itself involved a federal regulation requiring mandatory blood and urine tests of *privately* employed railroad employees who were involved in train accidents. The federal government argued that the railroads are private organizations and that therefore their actions are not regulated by the Constitution. In opposition, the employees argued that the railroad industry was so heavily regulated by the government that the companies, in effect, act as the agents of the government. The Court agreed with the employees, finding that the private railroad companies have to follow so many government regulations that they practically function as an arm of the government. Accordingly, the Court held that the railroad employees are subject to the Fourth Amendment, and hence any mandatory drug testing must to comply with the Constitution.

The Court then explained, however, that the government has a compelling interest in promoting the safety of rail travel that permits the government to prohibit railroad employees from using drugs while on duty. Therefore, the Court concluded, the mandatory drug tests are necessary to ensure that railroad employees abide by the no-drugs rule. The Court also explained that no search warrants are required to conduct the tests because such a procedure would hinder the program's effectiveness.

After finding that the testing passed muster under the Fourth Amendment, the Court next addressed the issue of whether some indication that an employee is using drugs should be required before an employee can be forced to submit to a drug test. To resolve this question, the Court again resorted to a balancing test. The Court weighed the railroad employees' expectation of privacy against the government's interest in maintaining safe rail travel. The Court concluded that safe rail travel was extremely important and that the industry has always been subject to extreme regulation. Therefore, the Court concluded, an employee can be forced to take a drug test even without any indication that the employee uses drugs.

Subsequent federal cases have upheld random drug testing of probation officers, law-enforcement personnel, military personnel, air-traffic controllers, pilots, aircraft mechanics and attendants, school-bus drivers, nuclear-power-plant workers, and racehorse jockeys. Fortunately, many state courts have interpreted their own state constitutions as giving employees greater protection than that offered by the federal constitution. In many such states, a state employee cannot be drug tested without at least a reasonable suspicion that he is using drugs on the job.

Drug Testing of Private Employees

As explained in earlier chapters, the United States Constitution provides you with protections only against actions by the government or its agents; so a private company is rarely restrained by constitutional protections against unusual searches and seizures. However, many states are now enacting legislation controlling drug testing at work and some states give private employees fairly extensive protection. For example, a Connecticut law, similar to those of many other states, holds that an employee can be forced to take a drug test only if there is reasonable suspicion that the employee is under the influence of drugs at work and that the suspected drug use is adversely affecting his job performance. In addition, in order for the company to take a personnel action against the employee, a positive test must be confirmed by two additional tests. Moreover, persons applying for work in Connecticut can be subjected to drug testing as part of the application process only if they are given prior written notification of the test and are provided a copy of any positive results. Most importantly, in Connecticut, any positive test results are considered confidential and *cannot* be used in a criminal proceeding.

The Drug-Free Workplace Act of 1988

In 1988, Congress passed what is commonly known as "The Drug-Free Workplace Act." This law applies to private companies that receive federal contracts worth $25,000 or more. The Act requires these companies to create and publicize an "antidrug" policy and to create a "drug-free awareness program." In addition, employees of such companies must be notified that they must report any workplace drug offenses that result in their conviction.

What to Expect If You're Urine-Tested at Work

The exact procedures used in employee drug testing will depend on your state, your occupation, and your employer. Usually you can expect roughly the following procedure.

Often drug tests are performed not by the company itself but by an independent company hired for this purpose. Accordingly, the people conducting the test have never met the employees and hence will require that you provide proof of your identity. This is to prevent employees from secretly sending other drug-free people to take the test in their place. Therefore, the testing company will require some form of photo identification.

Once sufficient evidence of your identity has been presented, the tester will give you a questionnaire form asking if you have taken any legal drugs (over-the-counter or prescription) within the last thirty days. (If you answer that you have taken a prescription drug, the tester will usually require that you to present them with the prescription or the bottle itself.) The tester asks this question because, as mentioned earlier, some of the older testing commonly returned false positive results for marijuana cannabinoids when the person had recently taken Ibuprofen.

It is also possible for other legal drugs to cause false positives, so be sure and list any and all medications you may be taking.

Once the questionnaire has been completed, the next step is obtaining the sample. Almost all employee drug testing is performed by way of a urine sample. Usually you are allowed to urinate in private, without the tester observing the actual act of urination. However, in some states and with some employers, your urine sample will be produced under the watchful eye of an observer. Beware that if you're permitted to urinate in private, the testers will usually place a blue-coloring agent in the toilet to prevent you from diluting your urine sample with fresh water from the toilet.

Once you have filled your container, you will probably be asked to sign a small label to be placed on the container and then to hand it to the tester. The tester will first look at the sample for any obvious indication that you have attempted to dilute it. Next, the tester will take your sample's temperature to make sure it's within the temperature range of liquids that have recently emerged from a human body. If everything looks legitimate, your sample will then be taken to the laboratory for the actual drug analysis. Usually you will learn of the results within two weeks.

EPILOGUE

As A PRACTICING criminal-defense attorney, I have become convinced that the constitutional rights created to protect us against runaway government are being sacrificed in the "War on Drugs." The *Cannabis* plant is not evil; arbitrary government is. It is time to change our way of thinking about drugs. Long after the hysteria has subsided, we will be left not with a drug-free society, but rather with a less-free society. Constitutional rights are not second-class rights. Rather, as Justice Jackson wrote:

> [Constitutional rights] belong in the catalog of indispensable freedoms. Among deprivations of rights, none is so effective in cowing a population, crushing the spirit of the individual and putting terror in every heart. Uncontrolled search and seizure is one of the first and most effective weapons in the arsenal of every arbitrary government.

If "We the People" are ignorant of our constitutional rights, or unwilling to assert them, they are of no worth. We, not the government, will be to blame for the resulting society, in which few individual freedoms will remain. George Orwell predicted that 1984 would be the year by which the government would have become superior to the individual. Unless we rethink our current policy with regard to marijuana and other drugs, Orwell's prediction may turn out to be only slightly premature.

> It was always at night—the arrests invariably happened at night. The sudden jerk out of sleep, the rough hand shaking your shoulder, the lights glaring in your eyes, the ring of hard faces round the bed. In the vast majority of cases there was no trial, no report of the arrest. People simply disappeared, always during the night. Your name was removed from the registers, every record of everything you had ever done was wiped out, your onetime existence was denied and forgotten. You were abolished, annihilated: vaporized was the usual word. *(George Orwell, Nineteen Eighty Four)*

APPENDIX A
Bill of Rights

The First Amendment

Congress shall make no law respecting an establishment of religion, or prohibiting the free exercise thereof; or abridging the freedom of speech, or of the press; or the right of the people peaceably to assemble, and to petition the Government for a redress of grievances.

The Second Amendment

A well-regulated Militia being necessary to the security of a free State, the right of the people to keep and bear Arms shall not be infringed.

The Third Amendment

No Soldier shall in time of peace be quartered in any house without consent of the Owner, nor in time of war, but in a manner to be described by law.

The Fourth Amendment

The right of the people to be secure in their persons, houses, papers, and effects, against unreasonable searches and seizures, shall not be violated, and no Warrants shall issue, but upon probable cause, supported by Oath or affirmation, and particularly describing the place to be searched, and the persons or things to be seized.

The Fifth Amendment

No person shall be held to answer for a capital or otherwise infamous crime, unless on a presentment or indictment of a Grand Jury, except in cases arising in the land or naval forces, or in the Militia, when in actual service in time of War or public danger; nor shall any person be subject for the same offense to be twice put in jeopardy of life or limb; nor shall be compelled in any criminal case to be a witness against himself, nor be deprived of life, liberty, or property, without due process of law; nor shall private property be taken for public use, without just compensation.

The Sixth Amendment

In all criminal prosecutions, the accused shall enjoy the right to a speedy and public trial, by an impartial jury of the State and district wherein the crime shall have been committed, which district shall have been previously ascertained by law, and to be informed of the nature and cause of the accusation; to be confronted with the witnesses against him; to have compulsory process for obtaining witnesses in his favor, and to have the Assistance of Counsel for his defense.

The Seventh Amendment

In Suits at common law, where the value in controversy shall exceed twenty dollars, the right of trial by jury shall be preserved, and no fact tried by a jury shall be otherwise reexamined in any Court of the United States, than according to the rules of the common law.

The Eighth Amendment

Excessive bail shall not be required, nor excessive fines imposed, nor cruel and unusual punishments inflicted.

The Ninth Amendment

The enumeration in the Constitution of certain rights shall not be construed to deny or disparage others retained by the people.

The Tenth Amendment

The powers not delegated to the United States by the Constitution, nor prohibited by it to the States, are reserved to the States respectively, or to the people.

APPENDIX B
Wallet Cards

Clip cards. Laminate. Keep in wallet or purse. Give 4th Amendment card to officer who asks you to consent to a search. Give 5th/6th Amendment card to officer who reads you your Miranda rights.

NONWAIVER OF FOURTH AMENDMENT

I have been advised never to waive a constitutional right protecting my liberty. In respect for the wisdom of our founding fathers who knew well the dangerous of dictatorial government, I hereby invoke my rights as guaranteed by the Fourth and Fourteenth Amendments to the United States Constitution.

I do not consent to a search of my person, my belongings, my automobile, my home, or any other item. I also do not consent to any further detention of my person, my belongings, my automobile, or any other item.

If you search me or detain me without the requisite justification under the law, you are hereby advised that I will take all possible legal actions against you personally as well as against your employer.

_____
Signature

NONWAIVER OF 5TH/ 6TH AMENDMENTS

I have been advised never to waive a constitutional right protecting my liberty. In respect for the wisdom of our founding fathers who knew well the dangerous of dictatorial government, I hereby invoke my rights as guaranteed by the Fifth, Sixth, and Fourteenth Amendments to the United States Constitution.

I hereby invoke my Sixth Amendment right to an attorney as well as my Fifth Amendment right to remain silent. I will remain silent until an attorney is provided.

If you question or interrogate me in the absence of my attorney, you are hereby advised that I will take all possible legal actions against you personally as well as against your employer.

_____
Signature

APPENDIX C
State-By-State Punishment for Marijuana Crimes

Alabama

Possession:
>   ≤1 kg for personal consumption: 0-1; $2,000
>   ≤1 kg otherwise: 1-10; $2,000

Possession of paraphernalia; $2,000

Cultivation/delivery/sale:
>   >2.2 lb: 3 M; $25,000; possible 10-99
>   >100 lb: 5 M; $50,000
>   >500 lb: 15 M, $200,000
>   >1,000 lb: life without parole M

Sale to minors: 2-20; $10,000

Sale within 3 miles of a school or public housing project: 5

Drug trafficking enterprise:
>   1st offense: 25-life; $50,000-$1,000,000
>   2nd offense: life M, no parole

Driver's license suspension: 6 months

Alaska

Possession:
>   ≤8 oz: up to 90 days; $1,000
>   >8 oz: up to 1; $5,000
>   >1 lb: up to 5; $50,000

Possession of over 1 oz with intent to distribute: up to 5; $50,000

Sale within 500 ft of a school: 1; $50,000

Manufacture/delivery: >1 oz: 0-5; $50,000

>   (Manufacture means growing or producing with the intent to give to someone else.)

Maintaining a structure/dwelling for purpose of manufacturing/delivery: 0-5; up to $50,000

Suspended imposition of a sentence available for 1st offense if not a felony: 2-3 probation

Note: if the referendum of 1990 is overturned and the *Ravin* decision reinstated, up to 4 oz will be legal for personal possession

Arizona

Possession or use:
>   <2 lb: 0.5-1.5; $750-$150,000
>   ≥2 lb: 9 months-2; $750-$150,000
>   >4 lb: 1.5-3; $750-$150,000

Production/cultivation:
>   <2 lb: 9 months-2; $750-$150,000
>   ≥2 lb: 1.5-3; $750-$150,000
>   >4 lb: 2.5-7; $750-$150,000

Sale/possession for sale:
>   <2 lb: 9 months-2; $750-$150,000
>   ≥2 lb: 2.5-7 M; $750-$150,000
>   >4 lb: 4-10; $750-$150,000

Sale within 1,000 ft of a school: 1; $2,000

Delivery or transport for sale:
>   <2 lb: 2.5-7; $750-$150,000
>   ≥2 lb: 4-10; $150,000

Offenders placed on probation or early release generally are required to perform 24 to 360 hours of community service.

Arkansas (C)

Possession:
>   ≤1 oz: up to 1; $1,000

Cultivation/delivery/sale:
>   ≥1 oz: 4-10; $25,000
>   ≥10 lb: 5-20; $15,000-$50,000
>   ≥100 lb: 6-30; $15,000-$100,000

Sale to Minor: 5-20; $15,000

Sale within 1,000 ft of a school, public park, community/recreation center, skating rink, or video arcade: 5-20; $15,000

Driver's license suspension: 6 months

California (D)

Possession:
>   ≤28.5 g: $100; no booking if you can show officer I.D. and promise to appear in court
>   >18.5 g: 0-6 months; $500

Possession of no more than 28.5 g on grounds of school when school is open:
>   1st offense: $250
>   2nd offense: 10 days; $500

Cultivation:

For personal use only: suspended sentence, drug education, charges dropped

For non-personal use: up to 16 months, 2-3 probation available. No plant number or weight breakdown

Selling/giving away/importing/transporting into California: 2-4

Colorado (D)

Possession:
>   ≤1 oz: $100
>   >1 oz: 0-2; $500-$5,000
>   >8 oz: 1-3; $1,000-$100,000
>   Generally, one prior conviction over 1 oz doubles penalties

Possession of paraphernalia: $100

Cultivation/delivery/sale:
>   ≤100 lb: 2-6; $5,000-$500,000
>   >100 lb: 24 M; $5,000-$1,000,000

Sale of paraphernalia: 0-1; $250-$1,000

Sale to minor: 2-8; $2,000-$5,000

Two prior violations involving marijuana: 2 M

Connecticut

Possession:
>   ≤4 oz: 0-1; $1,000
>   >4 oz: 0-5; $2,000

Possession of paraphernalia: 90 days; $500

Cultivation/delivery/sale:
>   <1 kg: 0-7; $25,000
>   ≥1 kg: 5-20 M

Professional licenses suspension

Delaware (C)

Possession (any amount): up to 6 months; $1,150

Paraphernalia:
>   Possession: 1; $2,300
>   Manufacture/delivery: up to 2
>   Delivery to a minor: up to 5

Cultivation: up to 5; $10,000

Trafficking:
>   ≥5 lb: 3 M; $25,000
>   ≥100 lb: 5 M; $50,000
>   ≥500 lb: 15 M; $100,000

Any delivery: 5; $10,000
Maintaining a dwelling or vehicle (including smoking in your car): up to 3;
court's discretion on fine
Delivery to minor: up to 5
        if minor is under 16, 6 months M
        if minor is under 14, 1 M
Sale within 1,000 ft of school: 15; $250,000
Suspended sentences for marijuana offenses except for trafficking

District of Columbia (C)

Possession (any amount): 0-180 days; $1,000
Cultivation/delivery/sale (any amount): 90-1; $10,000
Sale to minor: penalty doubles
First time possession offenders are eligible for probation followed by dismissal
Driver's license suspension: 6 months

Florida

Possession:
        ≤20 g: 0-1; $1,000
        >20 g: up to 5; $5,000
Possession of paraphernalia: 0-1; $1,000
Sale (any amount): up to 5; $5,000
Sale to minor: 15; $10,000
Sale within 1,000 ft of school, public housing project, or public park: 15; $10,000
Trafficking: ≥100 ≤2,000 lb: $25,000
Possession of over 20 grams is assumed to indicate intent to distribute
Driver's license suspension: 6 months
Professional licenses suspension
A vehicle can be confiscated for any felony amount

Georgia

Sale or possession:
        <1 oz: 0-1; $1,000
        (For <1 oz, if arrested in a municipality you can choose to appear in city
court instead of state court: maximum 60 days; $500)
        ≥1 oz: 1-10; $1,000
        >5 lb: 3 M; $25,000
        >100 lb: 5 M; $50,000
        >500 lb: 15 M; $100,000
Possession of paraphernalia: 0-1; $1,000
Cultivation: up to 10; $100,000
Trafficking: see sale or possession

Use of a communications facility (including mail or telephone) in committing drug felony may add 1-4; $30,000
Sale within 1,000 ft of school, public park, public housing project: up to 20; $20,000
Driver's license suspension: 6 months (reinstatement only with treatment)
Professional licenses suspension
Second drug felony is punishable by life in prison

Hawaii (C)

Possession:
>   <1 oz: 0-30 days; $1,000
>   >1 oz: up to 1; $2,000
>   >2.2 lb: up to 5; $10,000
>   >40 lb: up to 10; $25,000

Cultivation:
>   25+ plants: up to 5; $10,000
>   100 or more plants: up to 10; $25,000

Sale:
>   <2 oz: 1; $2,000
>   ≥2 oz: 5, $10,000
>   > 2.2 lb: 10; $25,000

Sale within 750 ft of a school: 5
Presence of marijuana in a vehicle constitutes possession for all passengers, unless found on the person of an occupant
Distribution to minors: 10; $25,000

Idaho (C)

Possession:
>   <3 oz: 0-1; $1,000
>   >3 oz: up to 5; $10,000
>   by a prisoner: 1-5; $1,000
>   by a minor (misdemeanor amounts): 30 days detention; $300

Possession of paraphernalia: 0-1; $1,000
Cultivation/delivery/sale:
>   <1 lb: up to 5; $15,000
>   ≥1 lb (or 25-49 plants): 1 M; $5,000
>   ≥5 lb (or 50-99 plants): 3 M; $10,000
>   ≥25 lb (or 100+ plants):: 5 M; $15,000
>   Possible maximum: 15; $50,000

Manufacture/sale of paraphernalia: 9; $30,000
Sale to minor: doubled prison time
Sale on school grounds: penalty doubles

A person's presence in a place where, with his/her knowledge, illegal drug activity is taking place is punishable by up to 3 months; $300

Required evaluation of all drug convictions; court can order treatment

Illinois (C)

Possession:
        <2.5 g: 0-30 days; $500
        ≥2.5 g: up to 6 months; $500
        ≥10 g: up to 1; $1,000
        ≥30 g: 1-3; $10,000
        ≥500 g: 2-5; $10,000

Cultivation:
        1-5 plants: 0-1; $1,000
        5-20 plants: 1-3; $10,000
        20-50 plants: 2-5; $10,000
        >50 plants: 3-7; $100,000

Sale/delivery:
        <2.5 g: up to 6 months; $500
        >2.5 g: up to 1; $1,000
        >10 g: 1-3; $10,000
        >30 g: 2-5; $50,000
        >500 g: 3-7; $100,000
        >2500 g is considered trafficking: 6-14 M; $100,000

Sale to minor: penalty doubles

Sale within 1,000 ft of school: 3-7; $200,000

Calculated criminal conspiracy: 2-5; $200,000

Indiana (C)

Possession:
        ≤30 g: 0-1; $5,000
conditional discharge possible

2nd possession of any amount or 1st possession >30 g: 6 months-3; $10,000

Possession of paraphernalia: $5,000

"Reckless possession of paraphernalia": 0-1; $5,000

Cultivation/delivery/sale:
        ≤30 g: 0-1; $5,000
        >30 g: 6 months-3; $10,000
        ≥10 lb: 2-8; $10,000

Manufacture/sale of paraphernalia: 0-3; up to $10,000

Sale to minor: 1.5; $10,000

Sale within 1,000 ft of school: 2-8; $10,000

Driver's license suspension: 6 months-2

Knowingly visiting a place where drugs are used in punishable by up to 180 days; $1,000

Iowa (C)

Possession/sale:
>   <50 kg: up to 5; $1,000-$5,000
>   ≥50 kg: up to 10; $1,000-$50,000
>   ≥100 kg: up to 25; $5,000-$100,000
>   >1000 kg: up to 50; $1,000,000

Sale to minor within 1,000 ft of school or public park: 10-25 M
Driver's license suspension: 6 months

Kansas (C)

Possession of marijuana (any amount), paraphernalia, or delivery of paraphernalia: up to 1; $2,500
Possession with intent to sell, cultivate:
>   1st offense: up to 1; $2,500
>   2nd & subsequent: 23-26 months

Possession, attempt to buy or sell up to 500 g, or 25 plants: optional non-prison available if appropriate treatment likely to be more effective and will serve community safety
Sale to minor: 1-10
Sale within 1,000 ft of school: 60-68 months

Kentucky (C)

Possession/sale:
>   ≤8 oz: up to 1; $500
>   >8 oz: 1-5; $10,000
>   >5 lb: 5-10; $10,000

Cultivation:
>   <5 plants: up to 1; $500 (1st offense)
>   1-5; $3,000-$5,000 (subsequent offenses)
>   ≥5 plants: 1-5; $3,000-$5,000 (1st offense)
>   5-10 (subsequent offenses)

Sale to minor: 1-5; $10,000
Sale within 1,000 ft of school: 1-5; $3,000-$5,000
Possession of more than 8 oz is considered prima facie evidence of intent to sell
Driver's license suspension for minors only: 1-2

Louisiana (C)

Possession (no quantity specified; usually under 2 oz in one container):

0-6 months; $500 (1st offense)
0-5 hard labor; up to $2,000 (2nd offense)
0-20 hard labor (3rd offense)
Possession with intent to distribute, cultivate, or sale:
    <60 lb: 5-30 hard labor; up to $50,000
    ≥60 lb: 5-30 hard labor; $25,000-$50,000; no probation or parole
    ≥2000 lb: 10-40 hard labor; $50,000-$200,000; no probation or parole
    ≥10,000 lb: 25-40 hard labor; $200,000-$500,000; no probation or
parole
Sale to minor: penalty doubles
Sale within 1,000 ft of school: at least half of maximum term for offense served
without parole or suspension
Driver's license suspension: 90 days-1

Maine (D)

Possession:
    <1.25 oz: $400
    >1.25 oz is considered evidence of intent to furnish marijuana; see
penalties for sale
Possession of paraphernalia: 0-6 months; $200
Cultivation:
    100-500 plants: 1-5 M; $5,000
    500+ plants: 2-10 M; $20,000
Delivery/sale:
    <1.25 oz: 0-1; $1,000
    ≥1.25 oz: 0-1; $2,000
    ≥2 lb: 1-5 M; $5,000
    ≥20 lb: 2-10 M; $20,000
Sale to minor: $5,000
Possible suspension of professional license
Court can override minimums if it finds it will be a substantial injustice to
defendant and won't hurt public, and no prior criminal history

Maryland

Use/possession (any amount): 0-1; $1,000
Possession of paraphernalia: $500
Cultivation/delivery/sale:
    <50 lb: 0-5; $15,000
    ≥50 lb: 5 M

Smuggling into state: ≥100 lb: 0-25; up to $50,000
Using a minor: 0-20; $20,000

Massachusetts (C)

Possession (any amount): 0-6 months; $500 (possible probation)
Cultivation/delivery/sale:

        <50 lb: 0-2; $5,000
        ≥50 lb: 2.5-15; $10,000; 1 M
        ≥100 lb: 3-15 M; $25,000
        ≥10,000 lb: 10-15; $200,000

Sale to minor: 2.5-15; $1,000-$25,000
Sale within 1,000 ft of school: 2.5-15; $1,000-$10,000
Manufacture/sale of paraphernalia: 1-2; $500-$5,000
Sale of paraphernalia to minor: 3-5; $1,000-$5,000
First time possession offenders are placed on probation
Driver's license suspension: 6 months
Distribution: license suspension for 2
Distribution over 50 lb: license suspension for 5

Michigan (C)

Use: 0-90 days; $100
Possession (any amount): 0-1; $1,000
Cultivation/delivery/sale (any amount): 0 4; $2,000
Sale to minor: penalty doubles
Sale within 500 ft of school: penalty doubles
Manufacture/sale of paraphernalia: 3 months; $5,000

Minnesota (C, D)

Possession:

        "small amount" (≤42.5 g): $200 & drug education
        <10 kg: up to 5; $10,000
        ≥10 kg: up to 20; $250,000
        ≥50 kg: up to 25; $500,000
        >100 kg: up to 30; $1,000,000

Sale/delivery:

        ≥2 kg: up to 5; $10,000
        ≥5 kg: up to 20; $250,000
        ≥25 kg: up to 25; $500,000
        >50 kg: up to 30; $1,000,000

Sale to minor: up to 20; $250,000
Sale within 300 ft or 1 city block of school, public park, or public housing: 15-30; $100,000-$1,000,000
Driver's license suspension: 30 days

Possession of more than 1.4 g in a motor vehicle is punishable by up to 1 in prison & $1,000

Mississippi (D)

Possession:

>   ≤1 oz: $100-$250
>   \>1 oz: 0-1; $1,000
>   ≥ 1 kg: up to 20; $1,000-$1,000,000

Possession of paraphernalia: up to 6 months; $500

Sale/delivery:

>   <1 oz: up to 3; $3,000
>   ≥1 oz: up to 20: $30,000
>   ≥1 kg: up to 30; $100,000-$1,000,000
>   \>10 lb: life without parole

Sale to person under 21: penalty doubles

Sale within 1,500 feet of school: penalty doubles

Additional penalties for possession in a motor vehicle (trunk excepted)

Driver's license suspension: 6 months

Missouri (C)

Possession:

>   ≤35 g: 0-1; $1,000
>   \>35 g: 0-7; $5,000
>   \>30 kg: 5-15
>   \>100 kg: 10-life

Possession of paraphernalia: 0-1; $1,000

Sale:

>   <5 g: 0-7; up to $5,000
>   \>5 g: 5-15
>   \>30 kg: 10-life
>   \>100 kg: life without parole

Sale to minor: 5-15

Sale within 1,000 ft of school or public housing project: 10-30

Sale of paraphernalia: 0-5; $5,000

Additional penalties for sale near government-assisted or public housing

Cultivation (any amount): 5-15

Montana

Possession:

>   ≤60 g: 0-6 months; $100-$500
>   \>60 g: 0-20; $50,000

Possession of paraphernalia: up to 6 months; $500

Cultivation/delivery/sale:
>   ≤1 lb: 1-life; $50,000
>   >1 lb (or >30 plants): 2-life; $50,000

Sale to minor: 4-life; $50,000
Sale within 1,000 ft of school: 3-life; $50,000
Continuing criminal enterprise: additional penalty 2-3 times that of underlying offense
A minimum of 1 kg is required to trigger intent to sell

Nebraska (D)

Use: 0-3 months; $500
Possession/sale:
>   <1 oz: $100
>   >1 oz 1 lb: 0-7 days; $500
>   ≥1 lb: 0-5; $10,000

Sale to minor moves penalty for offense to next highest classification
Sale of paraphernalia to minor: 0-1; $1,000

Nevada (C)

Use/possession (any amount):
>   1-6; $5,000 (1st offense)
>   1-10 (2nd offense)
>   1 20 (3rd offense)

Cultivation/delivery/sale (<100 lb):
>   1-20 (1st offense)
>   5-20; no parole or probation (2nd offense)
>   15-life; no parole or probation (3rd offense)

Cultivation/delivery/sale (≥100 lb):
>   3-20; no parole or probation (1st offense)
>   5-20; no parole or probation (2nd offense)
>   15-life; no parole or probation (3rd offense)

Possession of paraphernalia: up to 6 months; $1,000
Sale to minor:
>   1-20 (1st offense)
>   Life (2nd offense)

Sale within 1,000 ft of school, video arcade, public pool, youth center: penalty doubles

New Hampshire (C)

Possession (any amount): 0-1; $1,000
Cultivation/delivery/sale:
>   <1 oz: 0-3; $25,000

≥1 oz: 0-7; $100,000
≥5 lb: 0-20; $300,000
Sale within 1,000 ft of school: penalty doubles
Sale of paraphernalia: up to 1; $1,000
Drug enterprise: 25-life; $500,000 M
Driver's license revocation is authorized for convictions with intent to sell. Any license may be revoked for 60 days-2 for possession while operating a motor vehicle

New Jersey

Under the influence/possession:
<50 g: 0-6 months; $1,000
>50 g: 18 months; $7,500
Sale to minor: penalty doubles
Sale within 1,000 ft of school:
<1 oz: 1-5 M
>1 oz: 3 M
Manufacture/distribution:
<1 oz: 0-18 months; $7,500
>1 oz: 0-5; $15,000
>5 lb: 5-10; $100,000
Driver's license suspension: 6 months-2

New Mexico (C)

Possession:
≤1 oz: 0-15 days; $100 (1st offense)
0-1; $1,000 (subsequent offenses)
>1 oz: 0-1; $1,000
>8 oz: 0-2; $6,667 (1st offense)
0-4; $6,667 (subsequent offenses)
Possession of paraphernalia: 0-1; $50,000
Distribution/cultivation:
Small amounts, no remuneration: same as possession
≤100 lb: 0-2; $6,667 (1st offense)
0-4; $6,667 (subsequent offenses)
>100 lb: 0-3; $5,000
Sale to minor: 0-3
Sale within 1,000 ft of school: 0-3
Any part of penalty can be suspended
All first offenders eligible for probation, no time, and expungement of conviction

New York (C, D)

Possession:

  ≤25 g: $100
  >25 g: 0-3 months; $500
  >2 oz: 0-1; $1,000
  >8 oz: 0-4; $5,000
  >1 lb: 0-7; $5,000
  >10 lb: 0-15; $5,000

Delivery/cultivation:

  ≤2 g for no consideration: 0-3 months; $500
  <25 g: 0-1; $1,000
  ≥25 g: 0-4; $5,000
  >4 oz: 0-7; $5,000
  >1 lb: 0-15; $5,000

Sale to minor: 0-7; $5,000
Driver's license suspension: 6 months

North Carolina (C, D)

Possession:

  <.5 oz: 0-30 days; $100; time sentence must be suspended
  ≥.5 oz: 1-120 days, community service or intermediate/active program
  >1.5 oz: 8-13 months
  >50 lb: 25-30 months; $5,000
  >100 lb: 35-42 months M; $25,000
  >2,000 lb: 70-84 months; $50,000
  ≥10,000 lb: 175-219 months M; minimum fine $200,000

Manufacture/cultivation/sale: 2-5
Paraphernalia:

  Possession: up to 1; $500
  Manufacture/delivery: up to 2; $1,000

Sale to/employing a minor:

  18-21 years old: felony, 1 class higher than normal penalty
  21 or older: 2 classes higher

North Dakota (C)

Possession/sale/delivery/cultivation:

  <.5 oz: 30 days; $500
  ≥.5 oz: 1; $1,000
  ≥1 oz: 8 months+; $5,000
  >100 lb: 1+; $10,000

Sale to minor: 4 M

Sale within 1,000 ft of school: 4; $1,000
Possession under .5 oz while operating a motor vehicle: 1; $1,000

Ohio (C, D)

Possession:
>   <200 g: $100
>   ≥200 g: .5-5; $2,500
>   >600 g: 2-10; $5,000
Possession of paraphernalia: 0-30 days; $250
"Corrupting another with drugs": 0-3 months; $2,500
Sale/cultivation/delivery:
>   <200 g: 1.5-5; $2,500
>   >200 g: 2-10; $500
>   >600 g: 2-10; $5,000
Sale to minor: 1; $1,000
Sale within 1,000 ft of school: 1 M
Sale of paraphernalia to minor: 6 months; $1,000
Driver's license suspension: 6 months-5
Professional licenses suspension

Oklahoma (C)

Possession (any amount):
>   0-1; $500 (1st offense)
>   2-10; $5,000 (2nd offense)
Cultivation: 2-life; $20,000
Possession of paraphernalia: 1; $1,000
Delivery/sale:
>   <25 lb: 4-life; $20,000
>   ≥25 lb: 5-life; $25,000-$100,000
>   ≥1,000 lb: 5-life; $100,000-$500,000
Sale to minor: penalty doubles
Sale within 1,000 ft of school: penalty doubles
Driver's license suspension

Oregon (C)

Possession:
>   <1 oz: $500-$1,000
>   >1 oz: $0-10; $200,000
Manufacture: up to 20
Possession of paraphernalia:
>   up to 1; $5,000 plus civil fine of $2,000-$5,000
Delivery:
>   <5 g: $500-$1,000
>   >5 g: up to 1; $5,000

>1 oz: 0-10; $200,000
Sale (any amount): 0-10; $200,000
Sale to minor: 0-20; $300,000
Sale within 1,000 ft of school: 0-20; $300,000

Pennsylvania (C)

Possession:
>   ≤30 g: 0-30 days; $500
>   >30 g: 0-1; $5,000
Cultivation/delivery/sale:
>   (any amount): 0-15; $250,000
>   ≥2 lb or ≥10 live plants: 1 M; $5,000
>   ≥10 lb or ≥21 live plants: 3 M; $15,000
>   ≥50 lb or ≥51 live plants: 5 M; $50,000
Sale to minor: penalty doubles
Sale within 1,000 ft of school or college: 1-2 M
Possession of paraphernalia: 0-1; $5,000
Sale of paraphernalia to minor: 2; $5,000
Driver's license suspension: 6 months

Rhode Island

Possession:
>   <1 kg: up to 1; $200-$500
>   ≥1 kg: 10-50; $10,000-$500,000
>   >5 kg: 20-life; $25,000-$1,000,000
Manufacture/possession with intent to deliver: (no amount specified): 0-30;
$3,000-$100,000
Sale to minor: 1; $10,000
Sale/possession within 1,000 ft of school: enhanced penalties
Driver's license suspension for offenses involving use of motor vehicle

South Carolina

Possession: <1 oz: 0-30 days; $100-$200
Possession of paraphernalia: $500
Cultivation:
>   100-1,000 plants: 25+ M; $25,000
>   >1,000 plants: 25+ M; $50,000
>   >10,000 plants: 25+ M; $200,000
Sale/delivery:
>   10 lb-100 lb: 1-10 M; $10,000
>   100 lb-2,000 lb: 25+ M; $25,000
>   2,000-10,000 lb: 25+ M; $50,000

>10,000 lb: 25+ M; $200,000
License suspension: 6 months
Possession of more than 1 oz is deemed to be possession with intent to distribute

South Dakota

Possession:
>   <1/2 lb: 0-1; $1,000
>   ≥1/2 lb: 0-2; $2,000
>   ≥1 lb: 0-5; $5,000
>   >10 lb: 0-10; $10,000

Additional civil penalty of up to $10,000 for any possession offense
Possession of paraphernalia: 0-30 days; $200
Cultivation/delivery/sale:
>   ≤1 oz: 15 days-1; $1,000
>   >1 oz: 30 days-2; $2,000
>   ≥.5 lb: 30 days-5; $5,000
>   ≥1 lb: 30 days-10; $10,000

Mandatory minimum of 30 days for sale of any amount
Sale to minor: 5 M; $10,000
Sale within 500 ft of school, youth center, public pool, video arcade: 5 M
Driver's license suspension: 90 days

Tennessee

Possession: ≤.5 oz: up to 1; $2,500
Possession of paraphernalia: up to 1; $2,500
Cultivation/delivery/sale:
>   >.5 oz: 1-5; $5,000
>   ≥10 lb: 4-10; $10,000
>   ≥70 lb: 8-12; $200,000

Sale to minor under 12: penalty classification moves one level higher
Sale of paraphernalia: 1-6; $3,000

Texas

Possession:
>   ≤2 oz: up to 180 days: $2,000
>   >2 oz: up to 1; $4,000
>   >4 oz: 180 days-2; $10,000
>   >5 lb: 2-10; $10,000
>   >50 lb: 2-20; $10,000
>   >2,000 lb: 5-99; $50,000

Possession of paraphernalia: $500
Sale/delivery:

<.25 oz for no remuneration: up to 180 days; $1,500
<.25 oz for remuneration: up to 1; $3,000
≥.25 oz: 180 days-2; $10,000
≥5 lb: 2-20; $10,000
≥50 lb: 5-99; $10,000
≥2,000 lb: 10-99; $100,000
Sale to minor: 2-20; $10,000

Sale within 1,000 ft of school or 300 ft of youth center, public pool, video arcade: penalty doubles
Sale of paraphernalia: up to 1; $3,000
Spending funds derived from the sale of more than 50 lb is in itself an offense punishable by 5-life or 99 and a fine of $40,000-$1,000,000
Driver's license suspension: 6 months

Utah

Possession:
<1 oz: 0-6 months; $1,000
≥1 oz: 0-1; $2,500
≥16 oz: 0-5; $5,000
>100 lb: 1-15; $10,000

Possession of paraphernalia: 6 months; $1,000
Sale: 0-5; $10,000
Sale of paraphernalia: 1; $2,500
Sale of paraphernalia to minor: 0-5; $5,000
Sale within 1,000 ft of school, public park, amusement park, recreation center, church, synagogue, shopping mall, sports facility, theater, or public parking lot increases level of offense by 1 degree
Any drug offense with minor present: 5 M

Vermont

Possession:
<2 oz: 0-6 months; $500
≥2 oz: 0-3; $10,000
≥1 lb: 0-5; $100,000
>10 lb: 0-15; $500,000

Cultivation:
4-10 plants: 0-3; $10,000
11-25 plants: 0-5; $100,000
>25 plants: 0-15; $500,000

Delivery/sale:
≥.5 oz: 0-5; $100,000
≥1 lb: 0-15; $500,000

Penalties enhanced by sale/delivery to minors

Virginia (C)

Possession:
>   <5 lb: 0-30 days; up to $500 (1st offense)
>   0-1; up to $2,500 (2nd offense)
>   ≥5 lb: 1-10; $1,000

Cultivation (any amount): 5-30; $10,000
Delivery/sale:
>   ≤.5 oz: 0-1; $2,500
>   >.5 oz: 1-10; $2,500
>   ≥5 lb: 5-40; $500,000

Sale to minor: 10-50 (1 M); $100,000
Sale within 1,000 ft of school: 1-5 M; $2,500-$100,000
Sale of paraphernalia: 1; $2,500
Sale of paraphernalia to minor: 1-5; $2,500
Driver's license suspension: 6 months

Washington

Possession:
>   <40 g: 0-90 days; $1,000; 24 hours in jail M
>   ≥40 g: 0-5; $10,000

Possession of paraphernalia: 0-90 days; $1,000
Cultivation/delivery/sale (any amount): 0-5; $10,000
Sale to minor: penalty doubles
Conspiracy to cultivate/deliver/sell: 0-12 months
Cultivation/delivery/sale within 1,000 ft of a school can increase time of sentence by 24 months if armed with a deadly weapon
Driver's license suspension: 90 days for those under 21

West Virginia (C)

Possession:
>   <15 g: automatic conditional discharge; $1,000
>   >15 g: 1-5; $15,000

Cultivation/delivery/sale (any amount): 1-15; $25,000
Sale to minor: 2 M
Sale within 1,000 ft of school: 2 M
First-time possession offenders may be placed on probation without further penalties

Wisconsin (C)

Possession (any amount): 0-6 months; $1,000 (for 1st offense; 2nd offense doubles penalty)
Possession of paraphernalia: 0-30 days; $500
Cultivation:
>   ≤10 plants: up to 3; $500-$25,000
>   11-50 plants: 3 months-5; $1,000-$5,000
>   >50 plants: 1-10; $1,000-$100,000
Delivery/sale:
>   ≤500 g: up to 3; $500-$25,000
>   >500 g: 3 months-5; $1,000-$50,000
>   ≥2500 g: 1-10; $1,000-$100,000
Delivery to prisoner: penalty doubles
Sale to minor: penalty doubles
Sale within 1,000 ft of school, public park, public pool, youth center, community center, school bus: 1 M (up to 24 g or 4 plants over that amount: 3 M) (5 can be added to regular penalty)
Possession near the above: 100 community service M
Delivery of paraphernalia and/or possession with intent to distribute: up to 9 months; $10,000
Sale of paraphernalia to minor: 0-90 days; $1,000
Sale of marijuana or paraphernalia to a minor: seller must be 3 years older for increased penalties to apply
Mandatory doubling of sentences for 2nd and subsequent offenses
Courts can undercut a sentence if it is in the best interest of the community and public won't be harmed
Driver's license suspension: 6 months-5

Wyoming (C)

Use: 0-90 days; $100
Possession (any amount): 0-6 months; $750
Cultivation (any amount): 0-6 months; $1,000
Delivery/sale (any amount): 0-10; $10,000
Sale to minor: penalty doubles
Sale within 500 ft of school: 2; $1,000 M

NOTES:

The penalties listed apply to first-offense convictions only. Most states have increased penalties for subsequent offenses.
Many states have additional or enhance penalties for certain offenses, such as sale within a specified distance of a school. These offenses and all applicable penalties have been noted, when possible. However, it should not be assumed that such penalties do not apply just because they have not been listed for a particular state.

Any amount listed for "possession" generally implies that it is intended for personal consumption. Possession of large amounts of marijuana will, in most cases, lead to charges of "possession with intent to distribute" (same as "sale"). Units of weight vary from state to state. For comparative purposes:

One ounce (oz) = 28.35 grams (g)

One pound (lb) = 16 oz = 453.39 g

One kilogram (kg) = 1,000 g = 2.2 lb

Except where otherwise noted, sentences are in years. They usually indicate the maximum possible prison sentence, however, a multitude of other factors are involved in determining the sentence duration.

The listing of a penalty, immediately followed by the letter "M," indicates a "mandatory" minimum prison sentence. This means that the judge must sentence an individual convicted of the said offense to a prison sentence at least the duration of that listed. The offender is not eligible for parole and must serve the full term of the sentence.

Except where otherwise indicated, the stated fine indicates the maximum possible fine for the offense.

KEYS

D = The state has "decriminalized" marijuana to some degree. In general, this means that there is no possible prison time or criminal record for first-time possession of a specified amount for personal consumption. Instead, it is treated like a minor traffic violation.

C = State allows for the conditional release or alternative/diversion sentencing of first-time possession offenders. In general, this means that an individual can be put on probation instead of on trial. Upon successful completion of the program, the individual is spared any of the stated penalties and accompanying criminal record.

Compiled by the National Organization for the Reform of Marijuana Laws (NORML), 1001 Connecticut Avenue NW, Ste. 1010, Washington, DC, 20036; phone: 202-483-5500, fax 202-483-0057, email natlnorml@aol.com.

APPENDIX D
The 13 Federal Circuits

CIRCUIT	COMPOSITION
District of Columbia	District of Columbia
First	Maine, Massachusetts, New Hampshire, Puerto Rico, Rhode Island
Second	Connecticut, New York, Vermont
Third	Delaware, New Jersey, Pennsylvania, Virgin Islands
Fourth	Maryland, North Carolina, South Carolina, Virginia, West Virginia
Fifth	District of the Canal Zone, Louisiana, Mississippi, Texas
Sixth	Kentucky, Michigan, Ohio, Tennessee
Seventh	Illinois, Indiana, Wisconsin
Eighth	Arkansas, Iowa, Minnesota, Missouri, Nebraska, North Dakota, South Dakota
Ninth	Alaska, Arizona, California, Idaho, Montana, Nevada, Oregon, Washington, Guam, Hawaii
Tenth	Colorado, Kansas, New Mexico, Oklahoma, Utah, Wyoming
Eleventh	Alabama, Florida, Georgia
Federal	All Federal Judicial Districts

Index

(Includes Subject, Cases, Codes, Titles, and Persons)

Numbers

18 USC 3607[a]. 40
1995 Guideline's Revision
  equivalency provision 42–44
  "plant" defined 45
  terms defined 20–21
  Sec. 2D1.1 Application Note 1 46
  *Sec. 2D1.1 Application Note
    22* 45
  *Sec. 2D1.1 Revised Background
    Commentary* 43
  Sec. 2D1.1 [c] n. 42
  wet vs. dry marijuana 46
21 CFR 1316.91 27
21 USC 841[5]. 180
21 USC 841[e]. 34
21 USC sec. 802[16]. 18
21 USC sec. 844. 40
21 USC sec. 860. 37
21 USC sec. 863. 29
42 USC. sec. 2000bb - 1. 197
9-carboxy-THC 227

A

Abandoning
  "dropsy cases" 109–110
  and the exclusionary rule 109
  by denying ownership 110
  by throwing from vehicle 134–
    135
Abate v. United States [1959] 60
Abuse, "high potential for" 38, 184
Aerial surveillance. *See* fly-overs,
    police
Affidavits, invalid 146
Agnello v. United States [1925] 143
Aiding & abetting a marijuana
    crime 33

Air fresheners
  establishing probable cause 127–
    128
Alaska referendum 25
AMA (American Medical Association)
  Council on Scientific Affairs 224
Anslinger, Harry J. 183
Anti-drug "education programs" 74
Anti-marijuana hysteria 194
Anti-marijuana propaganda 183
  and the Marijuana Tax Act 183
  current 104
  going against 197
Aroma, marijuana 111–114
  and dog sniffs 112–113
  and probable cause 129
Arrest 98–100
  allowing vehicle search 134
  conditions of legality 100
  defined 98
  inside household 99
  probable cause for 99
  search warrant for 99
  warrants 98, 199
    similarity to search war-
      rants 199
Arrest/conviction records, application
    to destroy 220
Asset forfeiture
  and federal arrests 50
  and public property 180
  and the Double Jeopardy
    Clause 48
  and the Eighth Amendment 48
  by default 48
  California statistics of 46
  Donald Scott case 47
  Justice Dept. bulletin support-
    ing 47

proceedings
  civil charges   47
  civil vs. criminal   48
  file time   48
  police motivation to conduct   46
Assets subject to forfeiture
  linked to crime   49
  linked to marijuana trafficking   49
Attorney
  court-appointed   211
  fees   212
  following advice of your   214
  private   211–212
    criminal defense   212
    how to choose   211
    "jack -of-all-trades"   211
    privileged correspondence
      with   213, 217
    public defender   210–211
    working with your   213–214
Austin v. U.S. [1993]   48

B

Bail
  and demonstration of community
    ties   218
  cash payment of   218
  denial of   218
  payment through bondsman   219
  reduction   217
  schedules   217
Bill of Rights   233
Binoculars, police use of   152–154
  and the Fourth Amendment   152–
    154
  without a warrant   154
Blood money certificates   67
Blood testing. See Drug testing:
    blood tests
Body cavity searches   114–115
Bogus marijuana, selling   28
Boobytrap, defined   33–34
Boobytrapped gardens   33–34
Booking searches   202
Border searches   114–115
  at airports   114
  mail contents, opening of   114
  officer jurisdiction at   114

reasonable suspicion, involv-
    ing   114
  routine   114
  strip searches   114–115
Brave New World Revisited   65
"bright-line rule"   163
Burden of proof   61
Bureau of Intergovernmental Drug
    Enforcement   76

C

California Highway Patrol
    (CHP)   141
California v. Greenwood [1988] 486
    US 35.   78
CALJIC (California Jury Instruction
    Code) 2.90   61
Camera, high-powered
    police use of   171
Campaign Against Marijuana Planting
    (CAMP)   175
Cannabinoids, in urine sample   223
Cannabis
  indica vs. sativa   18
  ruderalis   18
Cannabis plant, federal definition   44
  based on root formation   44
  under 1995 guidelines revision   45
Carroll, Lewis   17
Children as informers   73
Citizen informer   65–70, 170
  anonymous   66–67
  defined   65
Clone pagers, police use of   121
Com. v. Hutchins [Mass. 1991]   189
Commission on Civil Rights   205
Commonwealth v. Huffman [Mass.
    1982]   162
"Compassionate use" of mari-
    juana   185
"Compelling state interest"   194
Confession inducing tactic, po-
    lice   208
Confidential informant   67–69
  and outrageous government
    conduct   68
  not presumed reliable   68
  vs. citizen informer   68

Consent to search 102–104
  example of refusing 104
  home 154–157
    and children 159
    and landlords & hotel employ-
      ees 158
    and roommates &
      spouses 158–159
    involving curtilage 168
    refusing 156
    voluntary requirement to 156
  no obligation to 103
  nothing gained by 104
  right not to 102
  unintentional, validity of 155
  vehicle 138
  withdrawing 138
Constructive possession
  example scenario 23
  theory of 23
Contact 87–88
  defined 87
Containers, defined 134
"Controlled buys" 70
Conviction record, cleaning up 220
Court, tips on going to 219–220
Craig v. State [Ark. 1993] 32
Curtilage
  unsuccessfully constructed 170–
    171
  and the front door 144
  legal creation of 165–168
  legal factors defining 164
  maximum protection under 144
  of home, defined 163
  requiring search warrant 165
  successfully constructed 166–
    168

D

DARE (Drug Abuse Resistance
  Education 66, 74
DEA 76
  NADDIS Database 84–85
Deception tactics
  "fellow criminal deception" 71
  "loyal friend" deception 71
  "mundane or ordinary visitor" 71

"obtaining consent to enter by
  deception" 71
stranded motorist ploy 72
Delosreyes v. State [1st Dist.
  1993] 145
Demanding to See Your Identification 92–93
Denying ownership 110
  as abandonment 110
Dept. Of Revenue of Montana v.
  Kurth Ranch et al. 36
Detainment
  of belongings 91–92
    and reasonable suspicion 91
  of visitors to home being
    searched 149
Detention 88–98
  and reasonable suspicion 89
  as seizure, defined 88
  exceptions to reasonable suspi-
    cion 95
  factors determining 89–90
  Fourth Amendment 88
  purpose of 91
  unlawful example of 92
  "youthful appearance" factor 98
"Ditchweed" 18
Dog sniffs 91–100
  canvassing 113–114
  constitutionality of 112
  defined as a search 113
  probable cause, leading to 113
Domestic Marijuana Eradication
  Program 179–180
Double Jeopardy Clause 36, 60
Driver performance study 141
Driver's license suspension 34
Driving under the influ-
  ence 33, 139–141, 141
Dronabinol 186
"Dropsy" cases 109
Drug Equivalency Table (DET) 41
"Drug package profile"
  factors determining 123
Drug Quantity Table 40
Drug testing 223–230
  at work 227–230
  blood tests 141, 225

constitutional rights concern-
    ing 227
during probation or parole 227
for government employees 227–
    228
    requiring compelling inter-
        est 228
for private employees 228
hair tests 225
mandatory 227–228
possession charge for posi-
    tive 226
urine tests 223–225, 229–
    230. *See also* urine testing
Drug traffickers, database of sus-
    pected 85
Drug use by agents
    immunity clause
        governing 73. *See also*
    undercover agents
Drug-carrying devices, distinct
    defined 106
    examples 107
    plastic garbage bags 107
    warrantless searches of 106
Drug-courier profile 95–98
    and reasonable suspicion 95
    four secondary characteristics 96
    local characteristics 97
    seven primary characteristics 96
Drug-Free Workplace Act of
    1988 229
Due process 69
    and sting operations 69
    violation of 68, 117

E

Eighth Amendment 48, 234
Electric bill
    and probable cause 79
    as evidence 79–80
Equivalency provision 42
    and "plant as 100 grams" 43
Ethiopian Zion Coptic Church 195
Evasiveness 91
    as consciousness of guilt 92
Evidence, destruction of
    measures against 147

Excessive force, bar against 117
Exclusionary rule 54–59, 101
    "good faith exception" to 55–56
    purpose of 54
Exigent circumstances
    involving destruction of evi-
        dence 160
    involving police pursuit 160, 115–
        118
    and nighttime searches 147
    and the home 159–162
    defined 115, 159
    fire as example of 116
    involving emergency assis-
        tance 161
    judicial requirements for 160
    "on slightest grounds" 160–161
    swallowing evidence 117
Expectation of privacy, reason-
    able 53
    and aboveground viewing 166
    and fly-overs 176
        violation from 178
    and gardens outside curti-
        lage 169
    and searches 104
    as crucial concept in
        searches 101
    at front door 145
    for marijuana thrown from ve-
        hicle 134
    in backseat of police car 201
    in excrement 110
    of common areas in home 158
    of pen registers 120
    of trap & trace devices 120
    violation of 54
    when arrested 200

F

FAA regulations 175
False negatives
    creating 224–225
    defined 224
False positives 225
FBI Law Enforcement Bulle-
    tin 71, 89
Federal Aviation Administration 175

Federal Bureau of Narcotics 183
Federal circuit courts 257
Federal marijuana crimes, schedule
    I 38
Federal sentencing
    based on weight 19
    for simple possession 40
    guidelines 19
Fifth Amendment 203, 233
    and double jeopardy 36–
        37, 38, 48, 60–61
    and Miranda rights 203, 235
    and the right to remain silent 209
First Amendment 25, 29, 193, 233
First offender
    probation eligibility 40
    punishment for 40
Flat retainer fee 213
Florida v. Riley [1989] 178
Florida v. Royer [1982] 88
Florida v. Wells [1990] 495 US 1. 135
Fly-overs, police 175–179
    determining factor for privacy 176
    helicopter 176
    state protection against 178
Forfeiture, of currency &
        property 51. *See also* asset
        forfeiture
Forward looking infrared scopes
        (FLIR's) 80-84
    and "heat waste" 81
    and searches 80
    dog sniff analogy, rejection of 84
    garbage search analogy 81
Fourth Amendment 228, 233
    and aerial surveillance 166, 167–
        168, 176
    and dog sniffs 112
    and drug testing 228
    and excessive force 117
    and exclusionary rule 54–55
    and expectation of privacy 53–55
    and fly-overs 177
    and garden outside curtilage 169
    and high-tech surveillance 81–
        82, 120–121
    phone taps 119–120
    and home searches 143–145
    and mail 121–122

    and "misplaced trust" doctrine 70
    and monitoring arrestee's move-
        ments 200
    and police contact 87–88
    and police use of binoculars 152–
        153
    and school searches 118
    and searches by private per-
        sons 57
    and transportation of suspect 90
    and vehicle searches 133
        inventory 135
    and waiving rights by consent to
        search 158
        refusing 156
    and warrantless
        searches 78, 101–102
        of excrement 110
Free Exercise Clause 195
Free-exercise jurisprudence 195
Frisk (or "pat-search") 93–95
    defined 93
    illegal use of 93
    of visitors to home being
        searched 149
    soft vs. hard objects 94
"Fruit of the poisonous tree," doctrine
    of 54
Fully Informed Jury Association 63
Furtive movement, defined 137

G

Garbage
    as evidence 77–79
    searches
        and expectation of privacy 78
        and probable cause 79
        federal vs. state rights 78
Gardens 163–181
    backyard 172–173
    constitutional protection for 163
    increasing privacy of 165
    indoor
        and search warrants 174
    inside home's curtilage 163–164
    on public property 180–181
    remote 173–174
"Good faith exception". *See* Exclu-
    sionary rule

Government-issued joints 185
*Grimes v. Superior Court [1981] 120
    Cal.App.3d 582.* 146
Growing marijuana. *See* Manufactur-
    ing marijuana

H

Hashish, defined
  under revised federal guide-
      lines 20
Hashish oil
  defined 20
    under revised federal guide-
        lines 21
  psychoactive effect 20
  THC percentage 20
*Health and Safety code section
    11361.5(b)* 220
"Heat waste"
  and expectation of privacy 81
"Herbal bliss" 51
High Times magazine 74, 75, 76
Hill v. Lawson [Tenn.App. 1992] 50
*Hill v. Commonwealth
    [Va.App.1994]* 161
*Holliman v. State [Tex.App.
    1985]* 28
Home
  consenting to search of 154
  entering
    knock-notice rule require-
        ment 148
    search warrant require-
        ment 143
  highest degree of privacy admit-
      ted 143
  possession of marijuana in-
      side 151
  search
    example of legal 146
    nighttime 147–148
    resulting from backyard gar-
        dens 172–173
  search, warrantless
    for roommates on proba-
        tion 159
    involving voluntary con-
        sent 156

Hotel maid example of search 57–
    58
Howard v. Com. [Va.App. 1993] 18
Huxley, Aldous 65
Hyatt v. State [GA.App. 1993] 59

I

Illegal entry, warrantless
  police example of 161
Illegal searches and seizures
  police motivation 54. *See also*
      searches; seizures; asset
      forfeiture
Illinois v. Gates [1983] 99
Intent to sell
  based on weight 27
  elements establishing 27
  evidence of 27
Intrusiveness, degree of
  as determining factor 114
Inventory searches
  strategies against 136

J

Jackson, Justice 231
Jail-house conversations, monitor-
      ing 216–217
  and the doctrine of misplaced
      trust 216
Jo, Vanessa Grimm 85
Judge the law
  citizens' rights to 63
  jury's power to 62–63
Judge Young ruling 185
Jury duties 62
Juvenile truants and curfew violators,
      detention of 98

K

Knock-notice rule 148–149
Kurth Ranch decision 36

L

Leary, Dr. Timothy 193–194
Leary v. US [5th Cir 1967] 194

M

Mail 121–124
and private carriers 58–59
no protection from 122
arrest statistics involving 121
covers 122
first-class, protection of 121
orders
as evidence 74–76
UPS shipping records, use
of 76
search warrant requirements 121
Mandatory minimums
safety valve 39–40
table 39
under federal law 39
Manufacturing marijuana
"attempted" 32
conviction, prior to planting 32
defined 31
Marijuana
defined
separating seeds and
stems 18
under federal law 17
vs. hashish, hashish oil 19
Marijuana crimes
state defined
based on weight 19
Marijuana Paraphernalia Crimes 29
Marijuana plant, multiple-
stemmed 45. *See also*
Cannabis plant
Marijuana Policy Project 35, 42
Marijuana possession
elements of, defined 21. *See
also* Possession, marijuana
Marijuana Tax Act 183, 194
Marinol 186
*McElroy v. State [Ala.Crim.App.
1992]* 18
Medical efficacy hearings, marijuana 184
Medical use, marijuana
legal. *See also* Necessity defense,
medical
for AIDS patients 190–191
for chemotherapy patients 189

for rheumatoid arthritis patients 191
no currently accepted 183
Medicinal marijuana and the
law 183–191
Metabolites 227
*Michigan v. Long [1983] 463 US
1032.* 127
Miranda rights 202–204
and the Fifth Amendment 203
conditions requiring reading 203
invoking after waiving 204
*Miranda v. Arizona [1966] 384 US
436.* 209
Misplaced trust, doctrine of 70, 216
no Fourth-Amendment protection 70
"Momentary possession" defense 25
"Monopoly" analogy 17
Moore v. State [Ga.App. 1993] 52

N

NADDIS (Narcotic and Dangerous
Drug Information System 84
and probable cause 85
"Narcs" 70
National guard 180
National Prohibition Act 196
Native American Church 195
Necessity defense, medical 186–
191
conditions establishing 187
denial of 187–189
successful cases 189–191
theory behind 190
"Net worth" analysis 49
*New Jersey v. T.L.O. [1985] 469 US
325.* 118
New York v. Belton [1981] 134
*Nineteen Eighty-
Four* 73, 178, 183, 231
Ninth Amendment 234
"No knowledge" defense
for marijuana found in mail 123–
124

O

Olsen v. DEA [DC Cir. 1989]   196
"Open fields" doctrine
    defined   168
"Open fields" doctrine   168, 171
Oral consent   103
Orwell, George   73, 178, 183, 231
Own Recognizance (OR) re-
    lease   217

P

Paraphernalia
    drug, defined   29
        examples   29
    marijuana
        as proof of sales   26
        court instructions concern-
            ing   30
        exception to ban   30
        federal statute concerning   31
        sales as tobacco products   30
    plain-view   106
Pat-search. See frisk
Pen registers   120
Penalties, marijuana
    possession   34. See also
        Appendix C
People v. Daugherty [Ill. App.2d
    1987]   156
People v. Gregg [1974]   132, 133
People v. Henry [1992]   57
People v. Hilber [1978] 269 NW2d
    159.   129
People v. Jones [1989]
    209.Cal.App.3d 725.   117
People v. Mayoff [1986]   179
People v. Pellegrin [1977]   173
People v. Ravin [1975]   25
People v. Rubacalba [1993]   24
Petition to reschedule marijuana   185
Peyote, sacramental use of   195
Pharmacopoeia of the United
    States   183
    erasure of Cannabis from   183
Pipes as paraphernalia   31. See
    also Paraphernalia
Plain-view rule   104–114, 202

and search warrants   149
and the home   152–154
    automobile exception to   105
    inside the home   105
    legal documents   106
    legal requirements for officer
        concerning   152
    limit to   105
    outside the home   105
    regarding common sense   105
Plea bargains, versus going to
    trial   214–215
Police encounters
    categories of   87
Police interrogation tech-
    niques   205–209
    court opinion on   205
    importance of privacy in   206
    legal excuses tactic   207
    line of questioning   206
    manipulating refusal to talk   209
    "Mutt and Jeff" act   208
    "reverse lineup" tactic   208
    trickery used in   208
Police over-intrusiveness   57
Posse Comitatus Act   179
    and the National Guard   180
"Possession for sale"   26
Possession laws
    challenges to constitutionality
        of   25
Possession, marijuana
    based on positive drug test   226–
        227, 21
    actual   22
    and the home   151
    constructive   22
    defined   21
    elements of   22
    knowledge of
        actual vs. circumstantial   23
        jury requirements   23
    legal   25
    requirements inside home   151
    vehicle passenger   139
Posters N Things, Ltd. v. US [1994]
    114 S.Ct. 1747.   31
Privacy. See Expectation of privacy,
    reasonable

Private investigators 213
Private mail
no reasonable expectation of
privacy 58
Probable cause 150
and entering the home 143
and hand-rolled cigarettes 130
and indoor gardens 174
and vehicle trunks 132
as arrest requirement 201
circumstances surrounding 99
determination of, by judge 146
establishing from "experience and
training" 99
for passenger compartment vs.
trunk 132
forfeiture proceedings 49
from aroma, defenses
against 111
from furtive movements 138
legal definition 99
lest, gestalt nature of 99
to arrest example 99
to search, based on aroma 111
Prosecution, state and federal for
same crime 38. See also
double jeopardy; Separate
sovereigns, doctrine of
"Protective sweep" 156
no legal justification for 157
Public Health Service 185
Punishment. See Sentencing
for selling or manufacturing 37–
38
by state 237–256
federal
based on weight of "mix-
ture" 19
for public gardens 180–181
for possession, intent to distribute 37

R

Ramey v. State [Ark.App. 1993] 147
Reasonable doubt 61
Reasonable suspicion
factors determining 90
and vehicles 125
for body or strip searches 202

series of facts determining 91
vs. probable cause 90
Refusal to talk
police manipulation of 209
Relation back, doctrine of 51
Release pending trial 217–
219. See also bail
Religious Freedom Restoration
Act 196–197
Religious use of marijuana
and the Ethiopian Zion Coptic
Church 195
no winning cases for 196
Timothy Leary case 193–194
Rescheduling petition, for Schedule II
marijuana 185
Reward statutes 67
RFRA (Religious Freedom Restora-
tion Act)
and the test of compelling state
interest 197
Rice v. Com. [Va.App.1993] 28
Right of jury to "nullify" a law 63
Right to counsel 204, 209–212
exceptions to 210
Right to remain silent 203
Roadblocks 125–126
Roommate, consent to search
from 158–159

S

"Safe" containers 109
Sale or distribution, marijuana 26–
29
intention requirement 26
of bogus marijuana 28–29
offering to sell as crime 29
prosecution requirements 26–29
Schedule I 38, 183
criteria 38, 184
Schedule II 185
criteria 184
Scientific Affairs, AMA's Council
on 224
Search warrant 145–152
and deception tactics 72
and general search authorization 149

and indoor gardens   174
and police evasion   61–62
and public gardens   181
and surveillance
   aerial   175
   high-tech   80–84
and the plain-view rule   149
and visitors to home   149
based on anonymous tips   66
based on children as informants   74
based on "controlled buys"   70
based on "drug package profile"   123
based on electric bill   79
based on finding remote gardens   173
based on mail-order records   75
based on seeing backyard garden   172
exception
   due to consent   104
   following arrest   201, 202
   for containers in vehicles   137
   for distinct drug-carrying
      devices   107
   for dog sniffs   112
   for drug testing   228
   for exigent circumstances   115
   for garbage   77–79
   for marijuana aroma   111
   for pen registers & trap/trace
      devices   120–121
   for unintentional consent   155
   regarding taped message   150
   to exclusionary rule ("good
      faith")   55
   to home search require-
      ment   144
   for private persons   57
invalidation
   failing to state probable
      cause   67
   from outrageous police con-
      duct   56
officers' threat to obtain   157
requirement
   concerning privacy, expectation
      of   101

daylight   147, 148
for arrest, example of   99
for first-class mail   121
for home search   143–144
for home's curtilage   163–
   165, 170
for opening luggage   91
for police use of binocu-
   lars   152–154
for telephone conversa-
   tions   118
neutral magistrate   146
unauthorized nighttime execution
   of   147
Searches
after arrest
   warrant requirements   201–202
and police use of binoculars   152
at public school   118
by private mail-carriers   58
by private persons   57
conditions defining   53
daytime, exceptions to   147
exceptions to the warrant requirement   101
garbage
   any   77
   state protections for   78
hotel maid example   57
illegal
   based on aroma   129
   based on peeking   166
   of vehicle trunks   131
invalidation of, from police conduct   56
of students
   and reasonable suspicion   118
strip and body-cavity
   rules regulating   202
two-part test   53
under citizen-government alli-
   ance   57
unreasonable   53, 167
   illegality of   101
vehicle. See vehicle searches
vehicle inventory   135–136
warrantless   101
   after arrest   201
   and exigent circumstances   115

and probable cause   152
by abandonment   110
deception tactics, via   72
impounded vehicles   136
legal instances of   102
of cordless phones   119
of vehicle   126
Second Amendment   233
Seed, sterilized   19
Seizures
and loss of assets. *See* asset
forfeiture
defined   53
illegal
hand-rolled cigarettes   130
Sentencing. *See also* Punishment
federal
based on equivalency provision   43–44
based on sex of plants   45
for first offense   40
for possession, factors determining   34
for previously convicted   40
guidelines   41
Separate sovereigns, doctrine of   60
double prosecution under   60
theory   38
Seventh Amendment   234
Sex of marijuana plant, policy
regarding   45–46
Sixth Amendment   15, 234
and invoking Miranda
rights   204, 235
and the right to counsel   200, 210
Smith v. Maryland [1979]   120
Smoke A Joint, Lose Your License   34
Sniff, human
at garage door   145. *See also*
Dog sniffs
Sobriety tests   140
State constitutions
guaranteeing greater liberties   60
vs. federal constitution   59
State Driver's License Suspension
Provisions table   35
State Taxes On Marijuana—Double
Jeopardy   36

State v. Ball [N.H. 1983]   130
State v. Bethel [1978]   19
State v. Blacker [Or.App. 1981]   153
State v. Daly [1979] 274 NW2d 557.
129
State v. Citta [N.J. Super.L.
1990]   154
State v. Cramer [Ariz. App. Div.2
1992]   189
State v. Diamond [Me. 1993]   76
State v. Fedorchenko [Fl.App.2d
1993]   201
State v. Garza [Mo.App.S.D.
1993]   128
State v. Hanson [Minn. App.
1991]   189
State v. Hastings [Idaho 1990]   191
State v. Holstine [Mont. 1993]   72
State v. Horsely [1979]   31
State v. Hyzer [Mo.App. 1991]   19
State v. Josophoon [Idaho
1993]   67, 79
State v. LaMaster [Mo.App.
1991]   32
State v. Lewis [1986]   226
State v. Lynch [1978, Az.App.] 587
P.2d 770.   129
State v. Mcintyre [Or. App.
1993]   144
State v. Meister [Mo.App.W.D.
1993]   52
State v. Mosley [Mont. 1993]   80
State v. Russell [Or. App.
1993]   79, 174
State v. Shoendaller [1978] 578 P.2d
730.   129
State v. T.T. [Fla.App. 5 Dist.
1992]   111
State v. Taylor [Mo. App. S.D.
1993]   116
State v. Tucker [1993]   28
State v. Wallace [N.C.App.
1993]   157
State v. Weiss [VT 1990]   148
State v. Wilson [Wash. 1981]   33
State v. Young [WA 1994]   84
Sting operations   69
Superior Growers Supply, Inc.   75
Surveillance, high-tech   181. *See*

also Thermal imaging device;
Forward looking infrared scope.
Suspected drug traffickers, database
of   84
Swallowing evidence   116–124
Synthetic equivalents   21

T

Telephone conversations
and expectation of privacy
with   118
and warrantless searches of   119
tapping of   118
Tenth Amendment   234
Testifying   215–216
and the jury   216
and the prosecutor   216
reasons to abstain from   215–216
right to testify   215
tips on   216
Testing. *See* Drug testing; Urine
testing
Tetrahydrocannabinols
human-made   21
THC content
hash oil   20
THC Therapeutic Research Act   189
Thermal imaging device (TID)   80–84
constitutional rights concerning   80
constitutional violations concerning   81
heat waste analogy, rejection
of   83
"private affairs," violation of   83
unconstitutional use of   82
Third Amendment   233
Thomas v. Superior Court
[1972]   100
Through The Looking Glass   17
Throwing from moving vehicle   134–
135
TID. *See* Thermal imaging device
Transportation of marijuana   33
Trap & trace devices   120
Truancy violation   98
"Turn In Pushers" (TIP) program   66

U

Undercover agents   73
and "misplaced trust" doctrine   70–72
Urine testing
adding adulterants to   225
AMA study on   224
and creating false negatives   224–
225
and false positives   225
and first urination   224
and water-loading   224
as most widely used   223
cannabinoids in   223
marijuana metabolites in   223
*US DOJ, Asset Forfeiture, Informants
et al.*   122
*US DOJ, Asset Forfeiture, Public
Record et al.*   47, 77
*US v. $405,089.23 U.S. Currency [9th
Cir. 1994]*   48
US v. Benish [3rd Cir. 1993]   80, 180
US v. Burke [1st Cir. 1993]   44, 66
US v. Coyle [8th Cir. 1993]   174
US v. Deaner [3rd Cir. 1993]   76, 79
*US v. Depew [9th Cir. Nov.
1993]*   167
US v. Diaz [6th Cir. 1994]   113
US v. Gallant[1st Cir. 1994]   45
US v. Garcia [C.A.7 Ind. 1991]   46
US v. Gravelle [S.D. Fla. 1993]   20
US v. Jacobsen [1984]   59
US v. Leake [CA 6 KY 1993]   67
US v. Ludwig [10th Cir. 1993]   114
US v. Lumba [D.Colo. 1993]   92
US v. McKeever [5th Cir. 1993]   76
US v. Mendenhall [1980]   89
US v. Moylan [4th cir. 1969]   63
US v. Oliver [1984]   169
*US v. Ornelas-Ledesma [7th Cir.
1994]*   85
*US v. Penny-Feeney [D. HW
1991]*   81
*US v. Pinedo-Montoya [C.A.10 N.M.
1992]*   46
US v. Pinson [8th Cir. 1994]   76, 81
US v. Place [1982] 462 US 696.   112

US v. Ramos-Saenz [9th Cir. 1994] 115
US v. Robinson [9th Cir.1994] 45
US v. Rose [8th Cir. 1993] 181
US v. Ross [1982] 127
US v. Seidel [S.D. Fla.1992] 794 F.Sup.1098. 168
US v. Schults [S.D. Ohio 1992] 20
US v. Thomas [9th Cir. 1994] 69
US v. Van Damme [D. Mont. 1993] 171
US v. Vincent [6th Cir. 1994] 19
US v. White [1970] 71
US v. Wright [8th Cir. 1981] 71
Usable amount 24
  as any amount 24
  requirement 24
  state defined 24

V

Vehicle
  "driving," defined 140
  inventory search, defined 135
  marijuana hidden in 139
  "operating," defined 140
  ordering driver out of 126
  reasonable suspicion to stop 125
Vehicle searches
  and the "protective search" 127
  based on probable cause 127
  consent to 128
  containers in cars 136–137
  for "officer safety" 126–127
  incident to arrest 133–135
  of passenger compartment 131
  of passenger compartment accessibility 127
  of trunk
    without probable cause 132
  warrantless 126

W

Wallet cards asserting rights 235
War on Drugs 34
  and drug testing 227
Warrantless searches. *See* Searches: warrantless

Washington v. Chrisman [1982] 455 200
Weapons searches 93
Weight, marijuana 18–19
  dry vs. wet 46
  personal use, quantity 27
  under *1995 Guidelines* 46
Weight of a controlled substance
  defined 19
Weil, Dr. Andrew 183
Wormsway Garden Supply 75

Z

"Zero tolerance" rule 50